ENGLISH

with **Chapter-wise**
Previous 10 Year
(2013 - 2022) Questions

DISHA Publication Inc.

45, 2nd Floor, Maharishi Dayanand Marg,
Corner Market, Malviya Nagar, new Delhi -110017
Tel: 49842349/ 49842350

Typeset By

DISHA DTP Team

Preface

We are pleased to launch the 4th edition of **Olympiad Champs English Class 4** which is the first of its kind book on Olympiad in many ways.

The Unique Selling Proposition of this new edition is the inclusion of past year questions till 2022 of different Olympiad exams held in schools.

The book is aimed at achieving not only success but deep rooted learning in children. It is prepared on content based on National Curriculum Framework prescribed by NCERT. All the text books, syllabi and teaching practices within the education programme in India must follow NCF. Hence, Olympiad Champs become an ideal book not only for the Olympiad Exams but also for strengthening the concepts for Class 4.

There is an exhaustive range of thought provoking questions in MCQ format to test the student's knowledge thoroughly. The questions are designed so as to test the knowledge, comprehension, evaluation, analytical and application skills. Solutions and explanations are provided for all questions. The questions are divided into two levels-Level 1 and Level 2. The first level, Level 1, is the beginner's level which comprises of questions like fillers, analogy and odd one out. When the child covers Level 1, it means his basic knowledge about the subject is clear and now it is ready for Level 2. The second level is the advanced level. Level 2 comprises of techniques like matching, chronological sequencing, picture, passage and feature based, statement correct/ incorrect, integer based, puzzle, grid based, crossword, venn diagram, table/ chart based and much more.

The first concern which each parent faces is how to make their children read a book especially when it is based on academics. Keeping this in mind interesting facts, real life examples, historical preview, short cut to problem solving, charts, diagrams, illustrations and poems are added. In addition to this, we have introduced comic strip which increases the readability quotient and make the reading experience for the children more exciting.

With the vision to remove all the misconception a child may have pertaining to the subject, to relate his knowledge to the real world and to develop a deeper understanding of the subject this book will cater all the requirements of the students who are going to appear in Olympiads.

While preparing this book, some errors might have crept in. We request our readers to identify those errors and send it across on **feedback_disha@aiets.co.in.**

We wish you all the best for your Olympiads and happy reading.......

Team Disha

For feedback : feedback_disha@aiets.co.in.

CONTENTS

10 Principles to CRACK ANY EXAM

1. Chase consistency, not intensity.

Doing intensive study makes your day. But it also exhausts you in the long run, leading to lesser output and added pressure. Toppers always focus on doing consistent work daily, for consistency is far more valuable than intensity.
Remember consistent study of 4 hours every day is more important and powerful than studying 12 hours a day and then not studying at all for next 2 days.

2. Go beyond the surface.

Most students only see a few reasons (teacher, coaching, books, etc) behind Toppers' success, which is only the tip of the iceberg. What they donot see is Toppers Mindset, self belief, habits and discipline and that is where the real problem is.

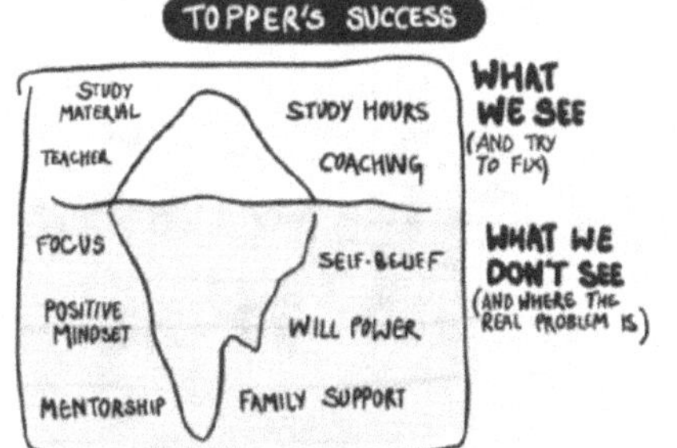

3. Focus on giving your best, not chasing the best.

We want the best coaching, the best teacher, best batch and the best books but we are not ready to give our BEST. Success comes only when we are ready to give our best. We must focus on giving our best than chasing excuses to cover up our failures.

4. Clarity of concept is the key

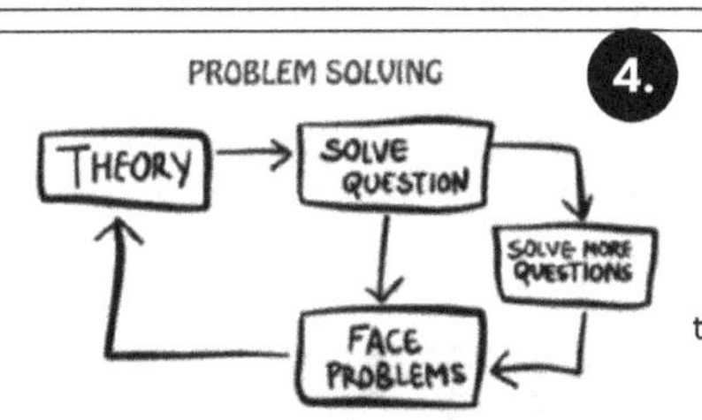

Concept clarity is critical. If you cannot solve a question, you must go back to the theory and thoroughly examine the concept instead of referring to the solutions. Remember question is one of the chehra(face) of the concept. When toppers get stuck in a problem, they go back and refer the theory(read the concept again and again on which the question is based)

5. Every failure should be a lesson learned.

Most students do not learn from their failures and repeat their mistakes. Toppers also face failures, but they learn from mistakes and elevate themselves. Making mistakes and learning from them is the key to success.

6 Choosing the quality of resources is more important than quantity.

More than 90% of the questions in most books are the same as their substitutes. Instead of practicing from four books and failing to complete them, it is best to prepare from two books and complete them with thorough revisions.

7

Difficult things become easy by taking it one day at a time.

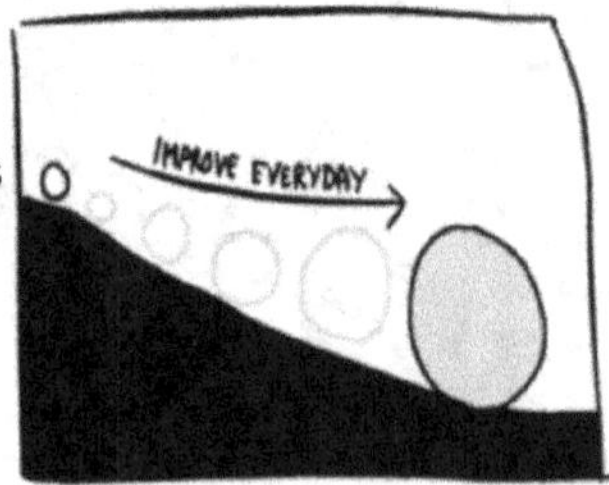

The best way to take any preparation forward is by taking it one day at a time. It makes the impossible possible by taking small steps every day.

Starting a difficult subject. No worries. Keep on working session by session, day by day and week by week and one day you will become unstoppable force.

8. Everything is easy

Before starting everything looks difficult. Once you take a first step, it slowly starts looking easy and over a period of time you become master in the activity. This is toppers secret to become master in any subject.

9. Nobody is gifted

We think toppers are god gifted. We think toppers have high IQ. We think toppers are special/lucky. But the truth is every topper was once an average student(no body is born topper). What makes them different is their consistent and focused efforts

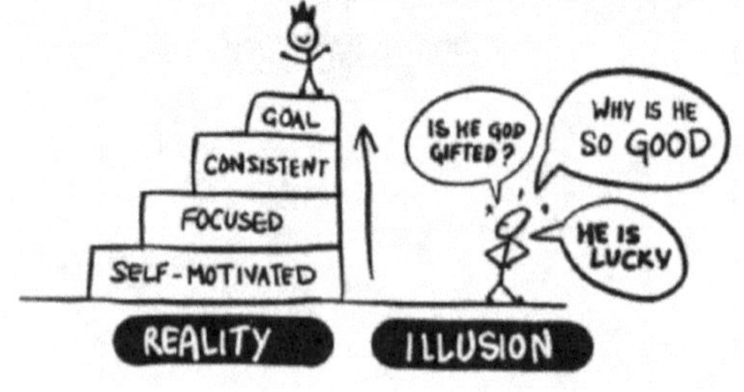

10. Believe in your journey and success will come to you.

There is never a straight path to success; hard work & patience is required for the results to show up. Keep on working hard without thinking too much about the results and success will come to you eventually.

1 CHAPTER FOREWORD

Hey there! After having learnt what a sentence is would it not be interesting to learn their types?

Let's learn about the types of sentences in this chapter.

I. Directions: Identify the following different types of sentences as assertive, interrogative or exclamatory.

1. Where is the party arranged? ______________________.
2. The Sun rises in the East. ______________________.
3. What a boring day! ______________________.
4. Where do they belong to? ______________________.
5. How did you do it? ______________________.
6. Where were you going yesterday? ______________________.
7. Kapil is a rude boy. ______________________.
8. You did a fabulous job! ______________________.
9. What a big house! ______________________.
10. Susan is playing with a doll. ______________________.

1 Chapter
Types of Sentences

LEARNING OBJECTIVES

This lesson will help you to:—

- Understand the various types of sentences
- Analyse different types of sentences and their distinguishing factors
- Identify the sentences and its types.

QUICK CONCEPT REVIEW

A sentence is a group of words arranged in a specific order which makes complete sense. There are different kinds of sentences.

- Assertive or declarataive sentences
- Interrogative sentences
- Imperative sentences
- Exclamatory sentences
- Optative sentences

Assertive sentences : Sentences that make a statement are called assertive or declarative sentences. These sentences end with a full stop.

For example :

- I like reading books.
- It is raining.
- She lives in Mumbai.

Interrogative sentences : Sentences which ask questions are called interrogative sentences. These use a question mark at the end.

For example :

- What is her name?
- Who lives here?
- Can you solve this puzzle?

Imperative sentences : Sentences which express orders, command, requests, advice, proposals or suggestions are called imperative sentences. These sentences use a full stop to punctuate, but may sometimes use an exclamation mark too.

For example :

- Leave this place at once!
- Please help me.
- Let's go for a movie.

Exclamatory sentences : Sentences which express strong feelings or emotions such as joy, sorrow, regret, surprise, wonder etc. are called exclamatory sentences. They use an exclamation mark to punctuate.

For example:

- How beautiful the flower is!
- Hurrah! We have won.
- Alas! She is no more.

Optative sentences : Sentences which express an ardent wish, prayer, curse etc. are called optative sentences. They end with an exclamatory mark.

For example:

- May you live long!
- May God help you!

Multiple Choice Questions

LEVEL-1

Directions (Qs. 1 to 10) : Read the sentences and identify the type by choosing the correct option.

1. Wow! He jumped so high.

   (a) imperative (b) declarative (c) exclamatory (d) optative

2. Go to your room.

   (a) declarative (b) imperative (c) interrogative (d) exclamatory

3. Don't hurt anyone's feelings on purpose.

   (a) imperative (b) declarative (c) interrogative (d) exclamatory

4. It is too late to convince Jane not to go.

   (a) imperative (b) declarative (c) interrogative (d) exclamatory

5. That was so exciting!

   (a) exclamatory (b) declarative (c) interrogative (d) optative

6. Do you know how to play chess?
   (a) declarative (b) interrogative (c) optative (d) none
7. May his soul rest in peace!
   (a) optative (b) exclamatory (c) declarative (d) interrogative
8. How many marbles were there in the bag?
   (a) interrogative (b) declarative (c) optative (d) imperative
9. Some volcanoes are dormant or extinct, while others are still active.
   (a) imperative (b) declarative (c) exclamatory (d) interrogative
10. May you pass your examination with flying colours!
   (a) imperative (b) optative (c) exclamatory (d) declarative

Directions (Qs. 11 to 15) : Which of the following has the correct punctuation? Choose the correct option.

11. (a) May you be happy in life. (b) May you be happy in life?
    (c) May you be happy in life! (d) may you be happy in life:
12. (a) I have been playing? (b) I have been playing.
    (c) I have been playing! (d) I have been playing;
13. (a) Sumit has killed the bird. (b) Sumit has killed the bird?
    (c) Sumit has killed the bird! (d) Sumit has killed the bird:
14. (a) Has the milkman come today? (b) Has the milkman come today!
    (c) Has the milkman come today: (d) Has the milkman come today.!
15. (a) Wow! This party is awesome. (b) Wow, this party is awesome;
    (c) Wow, this party is awesome? (d) Wow, this party is awesome.

Identify the kind of sentence :

16. Don't make noise in the class. **[2018]**
   (a) Assertive (b) Interrogative (c) Imperative (d) Exclamatory
17. Can you solve this problem? **[2018]**
   (a) Assertive (b) Interrogative (c) Imperative (d) Exclamatory
18. I asked him some questions. **[2019]**
   (a) Assertive (b) Interrogative (c) Imperative (d) Exclamatory
19. She lives in Delhi. **[2019]**
   (a) Assertive (b) interrogative (c) imperative (d) exclamatory

20. Identify the kind of tense.

Nowadays, computer has become a significant part of our life. **(2022)**

(a) Simple present

(b) Present continuous

(c) Present perfect

(d) Present perfect continuous

LEVEL-2

Directions (Qs. 1 to 5) : Read the sentences and choose the correct option.

1. Ice-cream parlours have so many flavours to offer.
   (a) statement (b) desire (c) question (d) exclamation
2. My mother will not let me go.
   (a) desire (b) question (c) exclamation (d) statement
3. Where are you going?
   (a) optative mood (b) command (c) answer (d) question
4. Walking is a great way to stay fit and healthy.
   (a) declaration (b) statement (c) question (d) desire
5. What ingredients are used to make a cake?
   (a) exclamation (b) statement (c) wish (d) question

Directions (Qs. 6 to 10) : Read the passage and answer the questions that follow.

FIGS FOR THE EMIR

Hassan was generously rewarded when he gifted the Emir some pomegranates. A few months later, he got a bumper crop of turnips and decided to present a sackful to the Emir. When his neighbour got to know this, he said to Hassan, "How could you even think of presenting such a lowly vegetable to the Emir?" he yelled. "They'll drive you away! Take some figs instead. Your figs are the sweetest I've ever tasted!!"

Unfortunately for him, the day he brought the figs to the royal court, the Emir was in a foul mood. When he was told that a farmer had brought figs he was so annoyed that he ordered his guards to pelt the farmer with the figs and drive him away.

Hassan was bewildered when the guards began pelting him with the figs. He tried to protect his face with his hands, all the while shouting, "Thank you, Qadir! Thank you, Qadir!" This aroused the Emir's curiosity.

"Who is this Qadir, and why are you thanking him?"

"Qadir is my neighbour", explained the farmer. "I was bringing turnips and he advised me to take figs instead. My head would have broken by now if I had brought turnips."

The Emir was so amused that he apologized to Hassan and compensated him handsomely.

6. Hassan was rewarded because he presented to the Emir ....

(a) turnips (b) pomegranates (c) figs (d) vegetabes

7. Hassan initially decided to present turnips to the Emir because ....

(a) the turnips were very sweet (b) the Emir liked turnips

(c) he had a bumper crop of turnips (d) he did not have any sweet figs

8. Hassan was beaten by the guards because ....

(a) he had brought figs for the Emir (b) he had not brought pomegranates

(c) the Emir was in a bad mood (d) the figs were not sweet

9. The Emir was amused because ....

(a) Hassan had brought figs (b) Hassan proved intelligent and witty

(c) Hassan was beaten (d) Hassan was laughing

10. The word 'bewildered' (Paragraph 3) means ....

(a) sad (b) angry (c) pleased (d) confused

Directions (Qs. 11 to 15) : Based on the above passage, answer the following questions by choosing the correct option.

11. Does the passage have any optative sentence?

(a) yes (b) no

(c) can't say (d) none of the these

12. "Your figs are the sweetest I've ever tasted!!" is an example of

(a) statement (b) desire (c) wish (d) exclamation

13. "Who is this Qadir, and why are you thanking him?" The sentence expresses

(a) exclamation (b) question (c) desire (d) anger

14. The Emir was so amused that he apologized to Hassan and compensated him handsomely. It expresses

(a) statement (b) question (c) exclamation (d) desire

15. Is there any incomplete sentence in the passage?

(a) Yes (b) No

(c) Can't say (d) None of the these

RESPONSE GRID

LEVEL 1

1. a b c d	2. a b c d	3. a b c d	4. a b c d	5. a b c d
6. a b c d	7. a b c d	8. a b c d	9. a b c d	10. a b c d
11. a b c d	12. a b c d	13. a b c d	14. a b c d	15. a b c d
16. a b c d	17. a b c d	18. a b c d	19. a b c d	20. a b c d

LEVEL 2

1. a b c d	2. a b c d	3. a b c d	4. a b c d	5. a b c d
6. a b c d	7. a b c d	8. a b c d	9. a b c d	10. a b c d
11. a b c d	12. a b c d	13. a b c d	14. a b c d	15. a b c d

Solutions with Explanation

LEVEL-1

1.	(c)	2.	(b)	3.	(a)	4.	(b)	5.	(a)
6.	(b)	7.	(a)	8.	(a)	9.	(b)	10.	(b)
11.	(c)	12.	(b)	13.	(a)	14.	(a)	15.	(a)
16.	(c)	17.	(b)	18.	(a)	19.	(a)	20.	(c)

LEVEL-2

1.	(a)	2.	(d)	3.	(d)	4.	(b)	5.	(d)
6.	(b)	7.	(c)	8.	(c)	9.	(b)	10.	(d)
11.	(b)	12.	(d)	13.	(a)	14.	(a)	15.	(b)

2 CHAPTER FOREWORD

Jumbled sentences are those in which the words are not arranged in right order and they make no sense.

Let us unjumble the sentences.

Directions : Unscramble the following words to make meaningful sentences.

1. Dubai/ with/ shopping/ she/ go/ in/ her/ friends/ to/ when/ Johnsons/ Mrs./ likes/ is

2. baby/ gave/ apple/ her/ the/ mother/ a/ red

3. what/ do/ me/ see/ you/ you/ at/ to/ the/ airport?/ off

4. place/ our lines/ music/ important/ has/ in/ an.

5. the/ weekend/ I/ can/ love/ down/ be/ I/ myself/ because/ and/ dress.

6. some/ believe/ in/ do/ not/ unfortunately/ god.

7. most/ bats/ to/ people/ are/ harmless.

8. cooks/ broth/ the/ spoil/ many/ too.

Chapter 2 Jumbled Sentences

LEARNING OBJECTIVES

This lesson will help you to:—

- make the students aware of importance of arranging the words properly.
- make the pupil able to arrange the letters in proper order to form words.
- make the pupil able to form a proper sentence.
- make the pupil able to use the language correctly.

QUICK CONCEPT REVIEW

As we all know that there are 26 letters in English alphabet. The letters form the words and the words together form a sentence. To make a right word the letters are arranged in a proper order. Similarly to make a right sense the words are also put in proper sequence to make a sentence. In this exercise you will learn to arrange the letters to make a meaningful word. If you know which letters are used in a word but you do not know the proper sequence, then it is of no use. For example if we know that a certain word contains--- - t,i,n,a,r,u,c but do not know the order these are to be used then it is of no use. When we arrange the letters and form the word "curtain" then it is meaningful.

Jumbled sentences are a sort of language proficiency test question. Here is an example:

Which is the correct word order for the following words to make a meaningful sentence?

(a) eating (b) cookies

(c) his mother's (d) under the tree

(e) sat (f) a young fellow

(g) fresh-baked

Proper sentences are divided into phrases. These phrases are jumbled. The student is expected to look at the jumbled phrases, comprehend the meaning implied, and put the sentence in order.

Amazing Facts

- You might not realize it, but your brain is a code-cracking machine.

  For emaxlpe, it deson't mttaer in waht oredr the ltteers in a wrod aepapr, the olny iprmoatnt tihng is taht the frist and lsat ltteer are in the rghit pcale. The rset can be a toatl mses and you can sitll raed it wouthit pobelrm.
- S1M1L4RLY, YOUR M1ND 15 R34D1NG 7H15 4U70M471C4LLY W17H0U7 3V3N 7H1NK1NG 4B0U7 17.

Shortcut to Problem Solving

It's always a good idea to read the answer options to figure out the most correct sentence, rather than to try solving the jumbled sentence yourself. First identify the jumbled sentence then try and solve the predicate. After this find the tense and then the verb.

Multiple Choice Questions

LEVEL-1

Directions (Qs. 1 to 10): Form a meaningful sentence from the following jumbled words.

1. **Twice/day/brush/teeth/a/your**
   (a) Brush your teeth twice a day
   (b) Twice a day your teeth brush
   (c) A day twice brush teeth your
   (d) Your teeth twice a day brush
2. **Sky/in/are/blue/birds/flying** **[2015]**
   (a) Sky blue in birds are flying
   (b) flying sky in blue are birds
   (c) Birds are flying in blue sky
   (d) None of these
3. **A/ story/I/be/narrating/will/tomorrow**
   (a) I story will be a narrating tomorrow
   (b) I will be narrating a story tomorrow
   (c) A story will be narrating I tomorrow
   (d) Will tomorrow be a story I narrating
4. **God/pray/to/daily/we/should** **[2016]**
   (a) To daily we should pray God
   (b) Pray we God should to daily
   (c) We daily to should pray God
   (d) None of these
5. **Doctor/apple/an/keeps/a/the/away/day** **[2014]**
   (a) A doctor an day keeps the apple away
   (b) An apple a day keeps the doctor away.
   (c) A doctor an apple keeps the day away
   (d) away an apple keeps the doctor a day
6. **Dog/hungry/meat/a/the/stole/shop/a/from/piece/of**
   (a) The hungry dog stole a piece of meat from a shop.
   (b) A dog stole a hungry piece of meat from the shop.
   (c) The meat stole a piece hungry a dog shop of from.
   (d) None of these.
7. **Went /I/ Shimla/to**
   (a) Shimla went to I.
   (b) I went to Shimla.
   (c) To Shimla I went.
   (d) Went Shimla to I.
8. **Father/my/me/trusts** **[2015]**
   (a) Trusts me my father.
   (b) Father my me trusts.
   (c) Trusts father me my.
   (d) My father trusts me.

9. Delhi /fort/in/is/red

(a) Red fort is in Delhi.
(b) Delhi is in red fort.
(c) In Delhi red fort is.
(d) Is in red Delhi fort.

10. The/ball/is/with/Rohan/playing

(a) Rohan is playing with the ball.
(b) Is playing with Rohan ball with?
(c) Is the playing with ball Rohan?
(d) The playing Rohan is with ball.

Directions (Qs. 11 to 16): Rearrange the letters to form a meaningful word.

11. SGALS

(a) sglas (b) glass (c) lasgs (d) none of these.

12. COCLK

(a) clock (b) clkco (c) kolck (d) all of these

13. IGHLT

(a) thgli (b) light (c) ighlt (d) hgilt

14. EVELOPEN

(a) poenleve (b) openvele (c) envelope (d) lpoenenve

15. GOWL

(a) glow (b) wolg (c) logw (d) glwo

16. PAHYP

(a) happy (b) pahpy (c) ahypp (d) hyapp

17. Doll making is (a) / crafts of (b) / one of the (c) / ancient India (d). **[2018]**

(a) abcd (b) bcda (c) acbd (d) dcba

18. are celebrated (a) / festivals (b) / the country (c) / all over (d). **[2018]**

(a) abcd (b) badc (c) cabd (d) dacb

LEVEL-2

1. Unscramble the words and tell how many of these are animals?
Edr, lecyc, odg, peprslis, htba, ionl, evac,etmcopur, pheletan

(a) 0 (b) 2 (c) 3 (d) 1

2. Rearrange the sentences to form a story.

1. One day it was very hot.
2. A crow was flying in the sky for a long time.
3. The crow felt thirsty.
4. But he did not get water from anywhere.
5. At last he saw a pot of water.
6. The water in the pot was very low.

7. The crow saw some pebbles around the pot of water.
8. He dropped those pebbles in the pot of water.
9. The water rose up and the crow drank the water.
10. The crow flew away after drinking the water.

(a) 1,2,3,4,5,6,7,8,9,10 (b) 2,3,1,6,4,8,10,9,5,7
(c) 2,4,6,3,7,9,1,5,8,10 (d) 5,8,1,2,4,10,9,7,3,6

Directions (Qs. 3 to 11): Unscramble the letters to form the name of a vegetable.

3. **BABEGAC**
(a) no change (b) cabbage (c) bagecab (d) egababc

4. **LFOEWRAULIC**
(a) cauliflower (b) oulicloefwr (c) not possible (d) werlofouicl

5. **INJARBL**
(a) jalribn (b) lajirbn (c) brinjal (d) ajlirnb

6. **TOPATO**
(a) apoott (b) tootap (c) potato (d) none of these

7. **UTRPIN**
(a) turnip (b) urnpit (c) irptun (d) nurtip

8. **ERGDYILAFN**
(a) edrgafnliay (b) lady finger (c) inregdalyf (d) not possible

9. **IOONN**
(a) onion (b) oonin (c) innoo (d) oinno

10. **RROACT**
(a) rcoatr (b) carrot (c) torrac (d) rotacr

11. **SEAP**
(a) eaps (b) eaps (c) peas (d) aesp

Directions (Qs. 12 to 19): Choose the answer of the question after arranging the given jumbled letters.

12. **What can we sing?**
GONSS
(a) Essay (b) Speech (c) Songs (d) Applications

13. **We operate the television with its__________.**
TOMERE
(a) Paste (b) Remote
(c) Car (d) Pencil

14. My mom cuts vegetables with________.

FIKNE

(a) Pen (b) Coffee (c) Computer (d) Knife

15. Who am I?

I can sail through the water.

OATB

(a) Cycle (b) Paper (c) Boat (d) None of these

16. Which day comes after Tuesday?

Denwesady

(a) Friday (b) Monday (c) Wednesday (d) Sunday

17. A train runs on________

CARTK

(a) Road (b) River (c) Track (d) Belt

18. Read the paragraph and tell what is the correct sequence of the events ? (2015)

Last Sunday after completing my homework, I went to my aunt's home. I took a bus to reach my aunt's home. There I met my uncle and aunt. We had our lunch together. In the evening my uncle showed me his beautiful garden. Then we had our evening tea together. After some time I took a leave from them and returned to my home.

1. I took a bus to go to my aunt's house.
2. my uncle showed his garden to me.
3. I finished my home work.
4. we had our lunch.

(a) 3421 (b) 1324 (c) 3142 (d) 3214

19. Arrange the following words to make a proper sentence.

gave a mother . red her apple baby the

(a) The mother gave her baby a red apple.

(b) Mother gave a her . red apple baby the.

(c) Apple baby gave a mother her the . red.

(d) . red her apple baby the gave a mother.

Directions (Qs. 20 to 24): Choose the correct number sequence to make a proper sentence.

20. To/(1) eat/(2) apple/(3) baby/(4). the/(5) the/(6) tried/(7)

(Tricky, 2015)

(a) 5 4 7 1 2 6 3 (b) 1 2 3 4 5 6 7 (c) 3 2 1 4 5 6 7 (d) 7 6 5 4 3 2 1

21. **Mouth/(1) was/(2) small/(3) his/(4) too/(5)** **(Tricky, 2016)**

(a) 1 2 3 4 5 (b) 4 1 2 5 3 (c) 2 5 3 4 1 (d) 5 4 3 2 1

22. **Didn't/(1) and/(2) have/(3) any/(4) he/(5) teeth/(6) (Tricky)**

(a) 1 2 3 4 5 6 (b) 3 2 5 6 1 4 (c) 2 5 1 3 2 6 (d) 6 5 4 3 2 1

23. **the/(1) his/(2) brother/(3) took/(4) apple/(5)**

(a) 1 2 3 4 5 (b) 4 2 5 3 1 (c) 5 4 3 2 1 (d) 2 3 4 1 5

24. **Arrange the jumbled letters given below to make a meaningful wor(d)**
K S P I E P R **[2022]**

(a) Skipepr (b) Spikper (c) Skipper (d) Sppiker

RESPONSE GRID

LEVEL 1

1. a b c d	2. a b c d	3. a b c d	4. a b c d	5. a b c d
6. a b c d	7. a b c d	8. a b c d	9. a b c d	10. a b c d
11. a b c d	12. a b c d	13. a b c d	14. a b c d	15. a b c d
16. a b c d	17. a b c d	18. a b c d		

LEVEL 2

1. a b c d	2. a b c d	3. a b c d	4. a b c d	5. a b c d
6. a b c d	7. a b c d	8. a b c d	9. a b c d	10. a b c d
11. a b c d	12. a b c d	13. a b c d	14. a b c d	15. a b c d
16. a b c d	17. a b c d	18. a b c d	19. a b c d	20. a b c d
21. a b c d	22. a b c d	23. a b c d	24. a b c d	

Solutions with Explanation

LEVEL-1

1. **(a)** **2.** **(c)** **3.** **(b)**

4. **(d)** The correct sequence is --- We should pray to God daily.

5. **(b)** **6.** **(a)** **7.** **(b)** **8.** **(d)** **9.** **(a)** **10.** **(a)** **11.** **(b)** **12.** **(a)**
13. **(b)** **14.** **(c)** **15.** **(a)** **16.** **(a)**

17. **(c)** acbd

18. **(b)** badc

LEVEL-2

1. (c) dog, lion and elephant
   (answer-red, cycle, dog, slippers, bath, lion, cave, computer, elephant)
2. (a)
   1. One day it was very hot.
   2. A crow was flying in the sky for a long time.
   3. The crow felt thirsty.
   4. But he did not get water from anywhere.
   5. At last he saw a pot of water.
   6. The water in the pot was very low.
   7. The crow saw some pebbles around the pot of water.
   8. He dropped those pebbles in the pot of water.
   9. The water rose up and the crow drank the water.
   10. The crow flew away after drinking the water.

3. (b) 4. (a) 5. (c) 6. (c) 7. (a) 8. (b) 9. (a) 10. (b)

11. (c)
12. (c) songs
13. (b) remote
14. (d) knife
15. (c) Boat
16. (c) Wednesday
17. (c) track
18. (c)
19. (a)
20. (a) The baby tried to eat the apple.
21. (b) His mouth was too small.
22. (c) And he didn't have any teeth.
23. (d) His brother took the apple.
24. (c)

3 CHAPTER FOREWORD

Hi folks! In this chapter, we shall learn about names. Everything around us has a name; people, places, things and even our emotions. We call them nouns. Solve the exercise given below to check your knowledge of nouns.

Directions: In the following sentences, identify and write the type of underlined nouns.

1. Peace is what everyone desires. ____________________
2. My shirt is made of cotton. ____________________
3. Gold is an expensive metal. ____________________
4. He ate the whole bunch. ____________________
5. She gained a lot of wisdom over the years. ____________________
6. There was a huge pile of books in the library. ____________________
7. Taj Mahal is made using white marble. ____________________
8. I saw a herd of wild horses. ____________________
9. Protein is required for growth. ____________________
10. This bottle is made of plastic. ____________________

Chapter 3

Noun

LEARNING OBJECTIVES

This lesson will help you to:—

- ❖ understand nouns as a part of speech and their grammatical usage.
- ❖ analyse different kinds of nouns and know distinguishing factors between them.
- ❖ develop the idea of using the nouns in proper context.

Activity

This activity helps students identify nouns and arouses interest in current affairs. The activity can be done individually or in small groups. Each student or group is given an age-appropriate newspaper or magazine article. The student divides a sheet of paper into three sections, labeling the sections singular, plural and possessive. The student lists the nouns in the article under the appropriate section of the chart.

QUICK CONCEPT REVIEW

A noun is the name of a person, place, or thing; Saurav, Kolkata, dog, cottage, gold, platinum, swarm, flight, honesty, patience, etc.

KINDS OF NOUNS

There are five kinds of nouns

1. **Proper Noun:** It is the name of a particular person or place and is always written with a capital letter.

   For example:
   - Ashoka was a great king.
   - The Ganga is a sacred river.
   - The Howrah bridge is situated in Kolkata.

2. **Common Noun:** It is a name which is common to any and every person or thing of the same kind.

   For example:
   - The girl is writing a letter.
   - Lion is the king of jungle.
   - We should always respect our teachers.

3. **Collective Noun:** It denotes a number of persons or things grouped together as one complete whole.

For example:

- Fleet of ships is standing in the harbour.
- Keep the bunch of keys safely with you.
- The Indian cricket team won the World cup in 2011.

4. **Material Noun:** It denotes the matter or substance of which things are made.

   For example:

   - Gold is used to make jewellery.
   - Mason works with bricks and cement.
   - Camels can run easily on sand.

5. **Abstract Noun:** It is the name of some quality, state, feelings or emotions.

   For example:

   - Honesty, bravery, motherhood, patriotism, infancy, etc.

1. **Proper Noun**

The Taj Mahal is situated in Agra

2. **Common Noun**

An elephant can carry heavy logs of wood in its trunk.

3. **Collective Noun**

A herd of cattle is grazing in the field.

4. **Material Noun**

Wood is used to make furniture, doors and windows.

5. **Abstract Noun**

Friendship is our greatest strength.

A. WORDS SHOWING COLLECTION

Collective Noun	Used with the Word
array	words
bevy	girls
bouquet	flowers
chain	mountains
code	laws
gang	robbers
heap	stones
lock	hair
kennel	dogs
nursery	plants
pack	hounds, cards
pile	woods, books, arms
sheaf	corn
shower	bullets, rain
shoal	fish
suit	clothes
yoke	oxen, horses
row	seats
wreath	blossoms, leaves
volley	bows, questions

Misconcept /Concept

Misconcept: Possessive nouns demonstrate ownership or a relationship over something. Possessive nouns will have an apostrophe which indicates the ownership. It is common for individuals to confuse possessive nouns with plural nouns.

Concept: The Possessive answers the question-----whose?. The Possessive Case of a Singular Noun is formed by adding ('s) ; as The girl's pen, the horse's tail, the king's palace. The Possessive Case of a Plural Noun ending in 's' is formed by adding the apostrophe(') only ; as Boys' books, birds' nests, horses' tails. Once you have learned about possessive nouns and completed a series of worksheets, it is beneficial to take a series of quizzes in order to test your understanding and usage of possessive nouns.

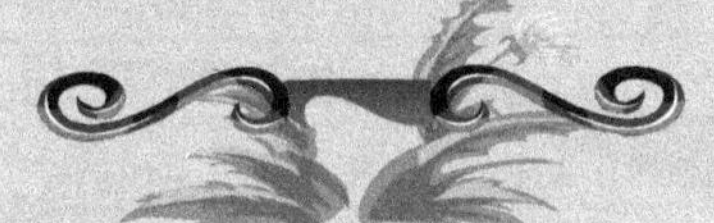

B. FORMATION OF ABSTRACT NOUNS

Words	Abstract Nouns
agent	agency
beggar	beggary
boy	boyhood
dictator	dictatorship
infant	infancy
man	manhood
robber	robbery
speak	speech
slave	slavery
woman	womanhood

Play time

Add a twist to the popular card game. Use index cards to prepare sets of matching common and proper nouns. For instance, "Black Beauty" and "book" would constitute a correct match. Lay the cards face down on a table or floor. Students take turns choosing two cards. If a match is revealed, the student must use the words in a sentence. The student keeps the pair as a score and is allowed to choose again. The game is complete when all of the cards have been paired. The student who collects the most cards wins the game.

C. ONE WORD SUBSTITUTION

SENTENCE	SUBSTITUTION
Official incharge of a museum	curator
One who does not believe in god	atheist
One who collects postage stamps	philatelist
One who goes to a holy place	pilgrim
Man who remains unmarried	bachelor
Woman who remains unmarried	spinster
Person who visits other country for pleasure	tourist
One who writes the life of another person	biographer
One who is a great lover of his country	patriot
One who cheats his own country	traitor

Gender Formation: There are four types of genders.

1. Masculine- Male animal or human.
   Example: Man, deer
2. Feminine- Female animal or human.
   Example: Woman, doe
3. Common- Some words can be used to refer either to masculine or feminine.
   Example: Parent, adult, child

4. Neuter- For non- living things.

   Example: Book, table

Plural Formation: There are various rules to form plurals.

- Add 's' to the singular noun.

  For example: Girl-girls, boy- boys
- Add 'es' to the singular noun which ends with 'ch', 'sh' or 'x'.

  For example: Branch- branches, brush- brushes, tax- taxes.
- Words which have y in the end and there is a consonant before y, y changes into I and then we must add 'es'.

  For example: Baby- babies, lady- ladies.
- We add 'es' to the words ending with o.

  For example: Mango-mangoes.

  But there are exceptions to this rule.

  For example: Photo-photos, Cargo-cargos.
- Words ending with f/fe will change into 'v' and then 'es' is added.

  For example: Thief-thieves, knife-knives.

  But there are exceptions to this rule.

  For example: Handkerchief-handkerchiefs, chief chiefs, safe-safes.
- In few words we add 'en'.

  For example: Child- children, ox- oxen.
- Few words are alike in their singular and plural forms.

  For example: Deer, sheep, salmon, aircraft, spacecraft, series, species.
- Words with numbers before them will be said in singular form but if there is no number written before them they may be said in plural form as well.

  For example: 2 pair of socks, 10 thousand. If there is no number-pairs, thousands, dozens, hundreds.
- Collective noun is said in singular form only.

  For example: Herd, army, bouquet etc.
- There are few objects which are said in plural even if they are singular.

  For example: Scissors, tongs, jeans, trousers, spectacles, etc.
- We do not make plural for abstract noun.

  For example: Honesty, kindness.
- For compound words, we add 's' to the main word.

  For example: Mother-in-law changes to mothers in law, commander in chief changes to commanders-in chief.

Multiple Choice Questions

LEVEL-1

Directions (Qs 1 to 10) : Complete the following sentences by choosing the correct option.

1. **We must show ________ towards animals.**
   (a) honesty (b) action
   (c) kindness (d) cruelty
2. **Are you ________ when you are alone in the dark? [2014]**
   (a) happy (b) nervous
   (c) patient (d) injury
3. **There is no ________ among rotten apples.**
   (a) kind(b) beauty
   (c) fresh (d) choice
4. **There is keen ________ in every trade.**
   (a) market (b) choice
   (c) competition (d) familiarity
5. **Smoking is ________ to health. [2015]**
   (a) injurious (b) difficult
   (c) problem (d) disease
6. **A ________ of people gathered at the meeting.**
   (a) flight (b) herd
   (c) crowd (d) swarm
7. **The farmer took his ________ of cattle for grazing. [2016]**
   (a) bunch (b) mob
   (c) army (d) herd
8. **The ________ of soldiers fought bravely in the battle.**
   (a) army (b) flock
   (c) pack (d) jury
9. **The Himalayas are the highest ______ of snow covered mountains in the world. [2017]**
   (a) volley (b) chain
   (c) row (d) shoal
10. **A ________ of robbers looted the people of the village.**
   (a) jury (b) mob
   (c) herd (d) gang

Directions (Qs. 11 to 15): Choose the correct option to complete the simile.

11. **As black is related to coal so white is related to ________.**
   (a) cotton (b) snow
   (c) ice (d) feather
12. **As bold is referred to leopard so timid is referred to ________. [2015]**
   (a) ostrich (b) lion
   (c) elephant (d) rabbit
13. **As cold is related to ice so hot is related to ________.**
   (a) diamond (b) money
   (c) snow (d) fire
14. **As rich is related to a merchant so poor is related to a ________.**
   (a) poverty (b) beggar
   (c) slums (d) country
15. **As hard is related to stone so soft is related to ________.**
   (a) fur (b) quilt
   (c) mountain (d) grass

Directions (Qs. 16 to 20): Choose the odd one out.

16. **Mumbai, Lucknow, Metropolitan, Patna.**
   (a) Mumbai (b) Lucknow
   (c) Metropolitan (d) Patna
17. **Garland, Zebra, Giraffe, Crocodile. [2015]**
   (a) Garland (b) Zebra
   (c) Giraffe (d) Crocodile
18. **Petrol, Diesel, Truck, Kerosene. [2016]**
   (a) Petrol (b) Diesel
   (c) Truck (d) Kerosene

19. **Swarm, Flock, Team, Cricket.**
   (a) Swarm (b) Flock
   (c) Team (d) Cricket

20. **Action, Kindness, Bouquet, Patience.**
   (a) Action (b) Kindness
   (c) Bouquet (d) Patience

21. **Choose the odd one out.** **[2018]**
   (a) Lion (b) animal
   (c) book (d) honesty

22. **Choose the odd one out.** **[2018]**
   (a) flock (b) sheep
   (c) crowd (d) herd

23. **Complete the following sentences by choosing the correct option.**
   To err is ________ to forgive is divine. **[2019]**
   (a) human (b) humane
   (c) humanity (d) men

24. **Smoking is injurious to ________** **[2019]**
   (a) Injury (b) health
   (c) men (d) wealth

25. **My ________ is going to London for business.** **[2022]**
   (a) parents (b) friends
   (c) father (d) uncles

LEVEL-2

1. **Match the animals with the food they eat.**

List I		List II	
A.	snake	1.	rat
B.	lion	2.	fish
C.	eagle	3.	deer
D.	crane	4.	frog

	A	B	C	D
(a)	1	2	3	4
(b)	2	3	4	1
(c)	3	4	1	2
(d)	4	3	1	2

2. **Match the materials with the articles.** **[Tricky]**

List I		List II	
A.	LPG	1.	fire
B.	coal	2.	truck
C.	wood	3.	Gas stove
D.	diesel	4.	steam engine

	A	B	C	D
(a)	4	2	1	3
(b)	3	4	1	2
(c)	1	3	4	2
(d)	2	1	3	4

3. **Match the objects with the places where they are made.**

List I		List II	
A.	leather	1.	dockyard
B.	ships	2.	tannery
C.	wine	3.	orchard
D.	fruits	4.	brewery

	A	B	C	D
(a)	1	2	3	4
(b)	2	3	4	1
(c)	2	1	4	3
(d)	3	4	1	2

4. **Match the collective nouns with the words.**

List I		List II	
A.	flight	1.	laws
B.	row	2.	wolves
C.	pack	3.	seats
D.	code	4.	stairs

	A	B	C	D
(a)	4	3	2	1
(b)	4	1	3	2
(c)	2	3	4	1
(d)	2	4	1	3

5. Match the phrases with the given words.

List I		List II	
A.	luggage is kept in	1.	resort
B.	place visited for enjoyment	2.	theatre
C.	wild animals are kept in	3.	cloak room
D.	place visited for watching play	4.	menagerie

	A	B	C	D
(a)	2	1	3	4
(b)	1	3	4	2
(c)	3	4	1	2
(d)	3	1	4	2

6. Read the statements and choose the correct option as correct or incorrect.

Statement A: Infant is a common noun but infancy is an abstract noun.

Statement B: A sentence starting with a common noun is proper.

Statement C: Fleet is a collective noun but ship is a common noun.

Statement D: Common nouns can sometimes be used as proper nouns.

(a) A and B are correct.

(b) B and D are correct.

(c) C and D are correct.

(d) A and C are correct.

7. Read the statements and choose the correct option as correct or incorrect.

Statement A: Proper, common, material and collective nouns come under concrete noun.

Statement B: A proper noun may be used as a common noun.

Statement C: Gold is a material noun but jewellery is an abstract noun.

Statement D: Kennel is a collective noun but dog is a material noun.

(a) A and B are correct.

(b) B and D are correct.

(c) C and D are correct.

(d) A and C are correct.

Directions (Qs. 8 to 12): Choose the correct noun represented by the pictures given below.

8.

Bible

(a) material noun

(b) common noun

(c) proper noun

(d) abstract noun

9.

(a) common noun

(b) collective noun

(c) abstract noun

(d) proper noun

10.

(a) proper noun
(b) abstract noun
(c) material noun
(d) common noun

11.

(a) material noun
(b) proper noun
(c) common noun
(d) abstract noun

12.

(a) common noun
(b) collective noun
(c) abstract noun
(d) proper noun

13. **Read the statements and choose the correct option. [Tricky]**
(A) "DEER" and "SHEEP" are singular nouns but are also used in plural sense.
(B) "THE" should not be used before an abstract noun.

(a) TT (b) TF
(c) FT (d) FF

Directions (Qs. 14 to 17): Read the passage and answer the following questions.

Christopher Columbus was born in Genoa, Italy in 1451. While spending most of his early years at sea, Columbus began to believe that he could find a shortcut to the Indies by sailing west across the Atlantic Ocean. Unfortunately, the King of Portugal refused to finance such a trip, and Columbus was forced to present his idea to the King and Queen of Spain. In 1492, King Ferdinand and Queen Isabella agreed to pay for his trip. They gave him a crew and three ships, the Nina, Pinta and Santa Maria. Columbus sailed aboard the Santa Maria.

The trip was long and hard. Many sailors grew restless and wanted to turn around. After two months at sea, land was finally sighted. The ships docked on the island of Hispaniola. Columbus named the native people he saw "Indians", because he believed he had found the shortcut he was looking for. In actuality, Columbus found North America, a brand new continent at that time. Columbus, however, couldn't be convinced. He died with the belief he had found the shortcut to the Indies. Soon, however, other explorers and nations understood the importance of his discoveries.

14. **Where was Christopher Columbus born?**
(a) The New World (b) Portugal
(c) Spain (d) Italy

15. **Which of the following was NOT one of his ships?**
(a) Nina (b) Isabella
(c) Pinta (d) Santa Maria

16. **In the last but one line of this passage, which word is the abstract noun?**
(a) died (b) belief
(c) shortcut (d) Indies

17. Which is NOT true?

(a) Columbus was born in Italy.

(b) Columbus received three ships and a crew from the King and Queen of Spain.

(c) Columbus found a shortcut to the Indies.

(d) The journey across the Atlantic took two months

Directions (Qs. 18 to 25): Read the passage and fill up the blanks with correct option.

Green is a beautiful colour! In nature, the 18.______ that you walk on is green and the 19.______ that you see on trees are usually green. Most of the plants that you see are green too! Frogs are green and many grasshoppers are green too. Turtles are different shades of green.

Did you know that you can make green 20.______ by mixing blue and yellow? Because you can make green my mixing two primary colours, it is called a secondary colour. Green is also the name used to describe the movement to make products that do not harm the 21.______. Green products are often those made from recycled 22.______ or those that are safe to throw out in the 23.______.

18. (a) shoes (b) road (c) grass (d) floor

19. (a) nest (b) birds (c) flowers (d) leaves

20. (a) paint (b) house (c) gate (d) path

21. (a) stars (b) sun (c) earth (d) moon

22. (a) ornaments (b) materials (c) garments (d) leather

23. (a) road (b) garden (c) park (d) trash

24. Choose the correct option for noun comparisons.

COMPARISON	NOUN
	Rose
	Hare
	Rock
	tiger

(a) firm, fierce, fast, fair

(b) fair, firm, fast, fierce

(c) fair, fast, firm, fierce

(d) fierce, firm, fast, fair

25. Choose the correct option for the collective nouns.

WORD	COLLECTIVE NOUN
	Girls
	Plants
	Fish
	leaves

(a) nursery, bevy, wreath, shoal

(b) wreath, bevy, shoal, nursery

(c) bevy, shoal, nursery, wreath

(d) bevy, nursery, shoal, wreath

26. Choose the correct option for animal habitats. [2016]

HABITAT	ANIMAL
	Tiger
	Spider
	Eagles
	Cows

(a) lair, cobweb, eyrie, byre

(b) eyrie, lair, cobweb, byres

(c) byres, cobweb, lair, eyrie

(d) cobweb, lair, byres, eyrie

27. **There are a few Proper, Common, Material, Collective and Abstract noun are hidden in the grid. Find them and then answer the questions below.**

A	M	A	X	P	Q	W	E	R	T	Y	U	I	O	P	L	K	J	H	G
Z	Y	X	V	C	R	O	W	D	W	N	B	V	C	X	Z	A	S	D	F
M	I	H	J	K	K	G	A	N	G	M	M	U	K	F	X	Q	S	C	V
H	M	I	Q	C	M	V	T	X	P	Q	E	Y	O	U	T	H	R	T	Y
U	C	A	M	A	U	P	E	T	R	O	L	F	L	O	C	K	J	Y	H
S	H	T	T	U	M	B	R	E	L	L	A	A	K	R	H	G	V	E	C
B	I	G	A	C	B	U	N	C	H	E	N	N	A	I	A	F	H	Y	A
C	L	B	B	W	A	C	T	I	O	N	D	R	T	N	I	H	I	D	V
G	D	E	L	H	I	E	V	H	N	J	D	H	A	B	R	C	K	L	Z
J	H	N	E	R	X	V	G	H	E	S	F	T	H	V	Z	S	F	R	G
G	O	H	X	E	N	M	I	A	S	Q	W	E	R	T	Y	U	I	O	P
S	O	Y	A	S	D	F	G	H	T	K	L	K	C	V	N	M	Q	R	C
J	D	U	P	Q	W	E	R	T	Y	U	I	O	P	A	S	D	F	G	H
B	R	J	O	U	T	Y	F	F	O	M	N	B	V	C	X	Z	L	K	J
T	F	M	W	D	G	U	Z	S	F	G	H	N	C	T	G	D	S	H	A

The total number of nouns in the grid is

(a) 18 (b) 20 (c) 22 (d) 14

Directions (Qs. 28 to 37): Considering the grid answer the following questions.

28. **Consider the statements and mark it true or false.**

Statement A: Umbrella is a collective noun.

Statement B: Chair is a common noun.

Statement C: Bunch is a collective noun.

Statement D: Youth is a proper noun.

(a) TFTF (b) FTTF
(c) TTFF (d) FFTT

29. **How many collective and abstract nouns are there?**

(a) 8 (b) 9
(c) 7 (d) 5

30. **Consider the statements and mark it true or false.** **[2013]**

1. Common nouns---umbrella, fan, chair, table

2. Material noun--- flock, crowd, gang, bunch

(a) TF (b) FT
(c) TT (d) FF

31. **Rohit: I'm in the cricket team this year!** **[2020]**

Raman: Wow! ____________.

(a) Never mind
(b) Congratulations
(c) Whatever
(d) You play cricket

32. **I thought you are _________ with this concept.** **[2021]**

(a) known (b) familiar
(c) equal (d) voluntary

33. **Garima : My bag is as light as a/an __________.** **[2022]**

(a) feather (b) bolt
(c) elephant (d) bed

34. How many common nouns have been used in the following sentence?
Raju told his friend that his father wanted him to be an engineer but he wanted to be an architect. [2022]
(a) Six (b) Three
(c) Five (d) Four

35. One who presents a radio/television programme [2022]
(a) Actor (b) Analyst
(c) Mediator (d) Anchor

36. A community of people smaller than a village [2022]
(a) Hangar (b) Hamlet
(c) Hutch (d) Hinterland

37. Enthusiastic clapping by audiences as a sign of their approval [2022]
(a) Laurel (b) Inundate
(c) Ovation (d) Metapho

RESPONSE GRID

LEVEL 1

1. a b c d	2. a b c d	3. a b c d	4. a b c d	5. a b c d
6. a b c d	7. a b c d	8. a b c d	9. a b c d	10. a b c d
11. a b c d	12. a b c d	13. a b c d	14. a b c d	15. a b c d
16. a b c d	17. a b c d	18. a b c d	19. a b c d	20. a b c d
21. a b c d	22. a b c d	23. a b c d	24. a b c d	25. a b c d

LEVEL 2

1. a b c d	2. a b c d	3. a b c d	4. a b c d	5. a b c d
6. a b c d	7. a b c d	8. a b c d	9. a b c d	10. a b c d
11. a b c d	12. a b c d	13. a b c d	14. a b c d	15. a b c d
16. a b c d	17. a b c d	18. a b c d	19. a b c d	20. a b c d
21. a b c d	22. a b c d	23. a b c d	24. a b c d	25. a b c d
26. a b c d	27. a b c d	28. a b c d	29. a b c d	30. a b c d
31. a b c d	32. a b c d	33. a b c d	34. a b c d	35. a b c d
36. a b c d	37. a b c d			

Solutions with Explanation

LEVEL-1

1. **(c)** **2.** **(b)** **3.** **(d)** **4.** **(c)**
5. **(a)** **6.** **(c)** **7.** **(d)** **8.** **(a)**
9. **(b)** **10.** **(d)** **11.** **(b)** snow
12. **(d)** rabbit **13.** **(d)** fire
14. **(b)** beggar **15.** **(a)** fur
16. **(c)** Metropolitan is a common noun and all other are proper nouns
17. **(a)** Garland is a collective noun and all other are common nouns

18. (c) Truck is a common noun and all other are material nouns
19. (d) Cricket is a common noun and all other are collective nouns
20. (c) Bouquet is a collective noun and all other are abstract nouns
21. (d) 22. (b) 23. (a)
24. (b) health 25. (c) father

LEVEL-2

1. (d) 2. (b) 3. (c) 4. (a)
5. (d) 6. (d) 7. (a)
8. (c) The Bible is a holy book of Christians, so it is a proper noun
9. (b) fleet of ships is a collective noun
10. (d) horse is a common noun
11. (a) petrol is a material noun
12. (b) a bunch of keys is a collective noun
13. (a) "deer" and "sheep" are used in both singular and plural form.

We do not use **the** before abstract noun. Example-

The honesty is the best policy-----wrong

Honesty is the best policy-----right

14. (d) 15. (b) 16. (b) 17. (c)
18. (c) 19. (d) 20. (a) 21. (c)
22. (b) 23. (d) 24. (c) 25. (d)
26. (a)

27. (b)

				C	R	O	W	D											
						G	A	N	G				K						
					M		T					Y	O	U	T	H			
	C				U	P	E	T	R	O	L	F	L	O	C	K			
	H		T	U	M	B	R	E	L	L	A	A	K		H				
	I		A		B	U	N	C	H		N	N	A		A				
	L		B		A	C	T	I	O	N	D		T		I				
	D	E	L	H	I				N				A		R				
	H		E						E										
	O								S										
	O								T										
	D								Y										

Proper nouns---Delhi, Mumbai, Kolkata, Chennai
Common nouns---umbrella, fan, chair, table
Material nouns---petrol, land, water, air
Collective nouns---flock, crowd, gang, bunch
Abstract nouns---childhood, honesty, action, youth

28. (b) 29. (a) 30. (a)
31. (b) Congratulations
32. (b) familiar
33. (a) feather
34. (d) 35. (d) 36. (b) 37. (c)

4 CHAPTER FOREWORD

Hello! Lets learn about pronouns. We cannot use nouns in every sentence we write or speak. It sounds boring. We use pronouns to avoid repetition. Here's a little exercise for you to begin.

Directions: Rewrite the following sentences using correct pronouns.

1. Maitreyi is a smart girl. He comes first in class.

   ____

2. Did your cat jump over the wall? He broke his leg.

   ____

3. Mohan and Sohan ate all the chocolates. He didn't give to anyone.

   ____

4. My name is Kunal. She study in class 4th.

   ____

5. The queen was looking for the crown. He was very worried.

   ____

6. The thieves found the way to escape. We stole lots of ornaments.

   ____

7. The people cleared the tree. The tree was blocking the road.

   ____

8. The little boy went to bed early. You is feeling sleepy.

   ____

9. The baby was sleeping. You just had food.

   ____

10. The lion is the king of the jungle. She is my favourite animal.

    ____

Chapter 4 Pronoun

LEARNING OBJECTIVE

This lesson will help you to:—

- know about pronouns and differentiate between various types of pronouns.

QUICK CONCEPT REVIEW

Pronouns are words like I, it, which, who, that, his, herself. They are used 'in place of' (pro) a noun. To avoid repetition, we use a pronoun for the second mentions of the same person or thing.

For example:

I saw the dog. I think it was chewing your shoe.

Now, let's study the different kinds of pronouns.

1. **Personal Pronouns:** Personal pronouns represent people or things.

   The personal pronouns are: I, you, he, she, it, we, they, me, him, her, us, them.

   Personal pronouns are further divided into 3 persons-

   1. First person- the person speaking- I, we.
   2. Second person- person spoken to- you.
   3. Third person- person spoken of- he, she it, they.

2. **Possessive Pronouns:** Possessive pronouns indicate that something belongs to somebody/ something.

   The possessive pronouns are: mine, yours, his, hers, ours, theirs.

   For example:
   - This place is theirs.
   - This book is mine.
   - The prize will be his.

3. **Reflexive Pronouns:** "Reflexive" means "going back to itself."

   Reflexive pronouns show that the action affects the person who performs the action. Reflexive pronouns end in "-self" (singular) or "-selves" (plural).

   The reflexive pronouns are: myself, yourself, himself, herself, itself, ourselves, themselves.

   For example:
   - He cut himself while shaving.
   - I sent myself to bed.
   - He could hurt himself.

4. **Demonstrative Pronouns:** "Demonstrative" means "showing, making something clear."

   Demonstrative pronouns point to things.

   The demonstrative pronouns are: this, that, these, those.

   Use "this" and "these" to talk about things that are near in space or in time.

   Use "that" and "those" to talk about things that are farther away in space or time.

   For example:

   - This is the report I want.
   - That is a big ship.

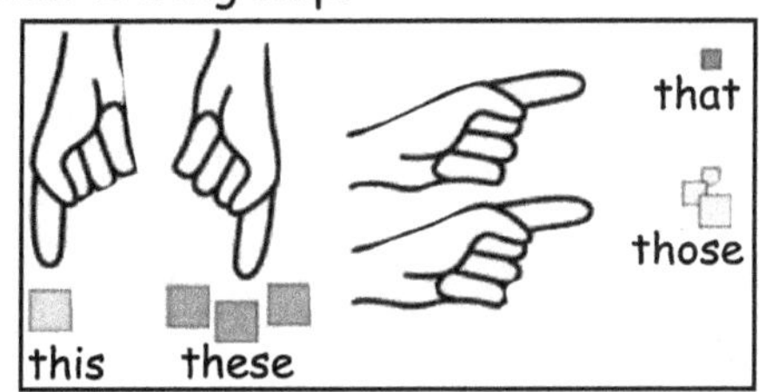

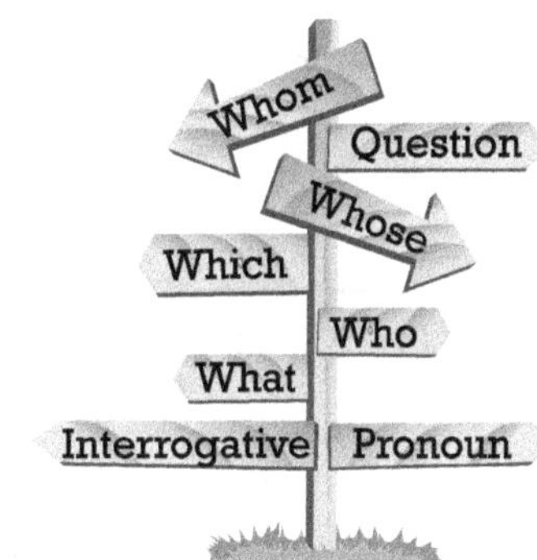

5. **Interrogative Pronouns:** "Interrogative" means "used in questions."

   Interrogative pronouns are used to ask questions.

   The interrogative pronouns are: who, whom, which, what, whose, whoever, whatever, whichever, whom ever.

   Use "who" and "whom" to talk about people.

   Use "which" and "what" to talk about animals and things.

   For example:

   - Who is your father?
   - Whom did you speak to?

PLAY TIME

Material Required: lots of picture cards (a boy, a girl, a thing etc, basically nouns) with matching pronoun flash cards. (his, her, him, them, it etc.)

Place all the cards on the table face-down (or posted on the board in a similar way). The picture cards and pronoun cards are to be placed separately. The class can be divided into two groups. The groups take turns turning over the cards. Each player in the group gets a chance to turn over two cards- one from the picture card section and the other from the pronoun card's section. If they do not match, they have to be turned back again so everybody else cannot see. If they match, they stay as they are, with the pictures facing front and the child explains as to which kind of pronoun that is.

Multiple Choice Questions

LEVEL-1

Directions (Qs. 1 to 3): Find the odd one out.

1. (a) He (b) Ourselves (c) She (d) It
2. (a) Myself (b) Yourself (c) That (d) Herself
3. (a) Who (b) Whom (c) What (d) She

Directions (Qs. 4 to 8): Choose the interrogative pronoun that best completes each sentence.

4. **__________ is the girl in the blue dress?**
   (a) Who (b) Whom (c) What (d) Which
5. **__________ hat is this?**
   (a) Who (b) Whose (c) Who's (d) Which
6. **__________ is the name of the team in red?**
   (a) What (b) Which (c) Who (d) Whose
7. **With __________ does your brother work?**
   (a) who (b) whom (c) what (d) which
8. **__________ does your mom like to play on the guitar?**
   (a) What (b) Which (c) Whom (d) Who

Directions (Qs. 9 to 12): Replace the underlined words with correct pronoun.

9. **I met <u>Mary, Lily, and Paula</u> at the party.**
   (a) their (b) them (c) her (d) hers
10. **Mom bought <u>Jack and I</u> a new DVD Player.**
    (a) our (b) us (c) mine (d) we
11. **She forgot to invite <u>Salma</u> to the function.**
    (a) her (b) she (c) it (d) he
12. **Someone stole <u>Mr. and Mrs. Baker's</u> car.**
    (a) they (b) them (c) their (d) there
13. **Which of he following alternatives to the underlined portion would not be acceptable?**
    When I travel to Barcelona <u>which will be my last trip this year</u>. I will start writing up my diary again.
    (a) which will be my last trip this year (b) (which will be my last trip this year)
    (c) which will be my last trip this year (d) which will be my last trip this year;
14. **Find the odd one out.** **[2019]**
    (a) we (b) they (c) you (d) she

15. Choose the correct pronoun for the sentence.

    Someone has stolen my book. [2019]

    (a) reflexive (b) demonstrative (c) indefinite (d) personal

16. Jayati had a big lunch. ________ might not want to eat dinner. [2020]

    (a) It (b) She (c) I (d) Me

17. Richa is crying because the bag we lost in the fair was ________. [2021]

    (a) her (b) its (c) hers (d) our

18. They lost _______ suitcase at the railway station. [2022]

    (a) there (b) they (c) them (d) their

19. Fill in the blank with the correct pronoun.

    This is the boy ______ stood first last year. [2022]

    (a) which (b) whom (c) whose (d) who

LEVEL-2

Directions (Qs 1 to 7): Fill in the blanks with a suitable option.

1. __________ (Walt Disney) may be best known for creating Mickey Mouse.

   (a) She (b) He (c) They (d) It

2. __________ however, (Disney) had many other achievements during his lifetime.

   (a) He (b) She (c) It (d) They

3. __________ some of (the achievements) include creating the first cartoon with sound.

   (a) His (b) Her (c) These (d) It

4. __________ (Cartoon characters) made Disney famous around the world.

   (a) Them (b) Those (c) That (d) Him

5. __________ (The Disney studio) also made the first feature-length animated movies.

   (a) It (b) He (c) She (d) They

6. __________ (animated film) was called Snow White and the Seven Dwarfs.

   (a) This (b) That (c) It (d) Him

7. In the 1950's, __________ (Disney and his partners) began to make films with live actors, too.

   (a) Him (b) We (c) Us (d) They

Directions (Qs. 8 to 14): Identify the underlined pronoun in each statement and choose under which category it fall.

8. I thought <u>you</u> knew <u>him</u>.

   (a) Demonstrative (b) Personal (c) Possessive (d) Reflexive

9. **These books are ours.**

(a) Demonstrative (b) Personal (c) Possessive (d) Reflexive

10. **We explained how it worked for us.**

(a) Demonstrative (b) Personal (c) Possessive (d) Reflexive

11. **That building is theirs.**

(a) Demonstrative (b) Personal (c) Possessive (d) Reflexive

12. **I fell down and hurt myself.**

(a) Demonstrative (b) Personal (c) Possessive (d) Reflexive

13. **This is my house and that is my uncle's house.**

(a) Demonstrative (b) Personal (c) Possessive (d) Reflexive

14. **You don't need much food to feed those.**

(a) Demonstrative (b) Personal (c) Possessive (d) Reflexive

Directions (Qs. 15 and 16): Tick the statement that is incorrect.

15. (a) Personal pronouns represent people or things.

(b) The demonstrative pronouns are: I, you, he and she.

(c) Interrogative pronouns are used to ask questions.

(d) The reflexive pronouns are: myself, yourself, himself.

16. **Statement A:** The word "pronoun" comes from "pro" (in the meaning of "substitute") + "noun."

Statement B: "Who" and "whom" are used to talk about animals.

Statement C: Reflexive pronouns are used to ask questions.

Statement D: "Relative" means "connected with something."

(a) TFTF (b) FTFT (c) FTTF (d) TFFT

17. **Which option shows personal pronouns?**

(a) That, this, these, those (b) Who, what, where, which

(c) You, she, he they (d) Myself, yourself, herself, ourselves

18. **Which option shows interrogative pronouns?**

(a) Who, what, where, which (b) That, this, these, those

(c) Him, your, mine (d) Everybody, anybody, somebody

Directions (Qs. 19 to 26): Identify the underlined pronoun from the sentences.

19. **Mary herself will prepare the food.**

(a) personal (b) interrogative

(c) possessive (d) reflexive

20. Your sister asked me which <u>that</u> liked better.

(a) personal, interrogative
(b) interrogative, possessive
(c) possessive, interrogative
(d) reflexive, possessive

21. <u>I</u> spoke to him yesterday.

(a) personal
(b) interrogative
(c) possessive
(d) reflexive

22. <u>I</u> believe this pen is <u>his</u>; it is not mine.

(a) personal, interrogative
(b) interrogative, possessive
(c) personal, possessive
(d) reflexive, possessive

23. <u>I</u> think these are <u>ours</u>.

(a) personal, interrogative
(b) interrogative, possessive
(c) personal, possessive
(d) reflexive, possessive

24. Which of these dresses do <u>you</u> like?

(a) personal, interrogative
(b) interrogative, possessive
(c) personal, possessive
(d) reflexive, possessive

25. <u>They</u> built this house <u>themselves</u>.

(a) personal, interrogative
(b) interrogative, possessive
(c) personal, possessive
(d) personal, reflexive

26. <u>Anybody</u> can do <u>that</u>.

(a) demonstrative, indefinite
(b) interrogative
(c) possessive
(d) reflexive

Directions (Qs. 27 to 36): Fill in the blanks with suitable possessive.

Ray was desperate. He had only 40 minutes to get to the studio to host the morning 'Chat Show' but (27)___ car would not start. "Mum," he yelled, May I borrow (28)___ car today? (29)____won't move!"

"(30)___ water and electricity bills have to be paid and (31)___ father has no time to do it, also I need to go to the post office," replied his mother.

Ray said, "Mum, I'll be in trouble if I don't get to the studio quickly. They can't begin the programme without (32)___ host."

"Can't any of your friends give you lift?" She asked.

Ray replied, "My friends are still asleep in (33)___ beds this early in the morning! (34)____ job isn't like (35)___. I work irregular hours. They work from nine to five."

His mother gave in. "The car is (36)___ temporarily, only for this morning. In the meantime, I'll call a mechanic to look at your car."

27. (a) my (b) your (c) his (d) him

	(a)	(b)	(c)	(d)
28.	my	your	his	him
29.	my	your	his	mine
30.	my	your	our	mine
31.	my	your	our	mine
32.	their	your	our	mine
33.	their	your	our	mine
34.	your	their	our	mine
35.	my	your	our	mine
36.	my	yours	his	him

Directions (Qs. 37 & 38): Use the correct reflexive pronoun to complete the following sentences.

37. **Meena pinched _________ to make sure that she was not dreaming.**
    (a) himself (b) herself (c) yourself (d) themselves

38. **The little ones enjoyed _________ enormously at the party.**
    (a) himself (b) herself (c) yourself (d) themselves

RESPONSE GRID

LEVEL 1

1. a b c d 2. a b c d 3. a b c d 4. a b c d 5. a b c d
6. a b c d 7. a b c d 8. a b c d 9. a b c d 10. a b c d
11. a b c d 12. a b c d 13. a b c d 14. a b c d 15. a b c d
16. a b c d 17. a b c d 18. a b c d 19. a b c d

LEVEL 2

1. a b c d 2. a b c d 3. a b c d 4. a b c d 5. a b c d
6. a b c d 7. a b c d 8. a b c d 9. a b c d 10. a b c d
11. a b c d 12. a b c d 13. a b c d 14. a b c d 15. a b c d
16. a b c d 17. a b c d 18. a b c d 19. a b c d 20. a b c d
21. a b c d 22. a b c d 23. a b c d 24. a b c d 25. a b c d
26. a b c d 27. a b c d 28. a b c d 29. a b c d 30. a b c d
31. a b c d 32. a b c d 33. a b c d 34. a b c d 35. a b c d
36. a b c d 37. a b c d 38. a b c d

Solutions with Explanation

LEVEL-1

1. (b) (as all others are personal pronouns, while ourselves is a reflexive pronoun.)
2. (c) (as all others are possessive pronouns, while 'that' is a demonstrative pronoun.)
3. (d) (as all others are interrogative pronouns, while she is a personal pronoun.)

4. (a) 5. (b) 6. (a) 7. (b) 8. (a) 9. (b) them
10. (b) us 11. (a) her 12. (c) their 13. (a) 14. (d) 15. (c)
16. (b) She 17. (c) hers 18. (d) their 19. (d)

LEVEL-2

1. (b) personal pronoun as personal pronouns represent people or things.
2. (a) personal pronoun as personal pronouns represent people or things.
3. (a) personal pronouns as personal pronouns represent people or things.
4. (b) Demonstrative pronoun as "Demonstrative" means "showing, making something clear."
5. (a) Personal as personal pronouns represent people or things.
6. (b) Demonstrative pronoun as "Demonstrative" means "showing, making something clear."
7. (d) Personal as personal pronouns represent people or things.
8. (b) (as you and him are representing people.)
9. (c) (as ours shows possession.)
10. (b) (as we, us, it represent people or things.)
11. (c) (as theirs shows possession.)
12. (d) (as myself represents going back to itself.)
13. (a) (as this, that show and demonstrate something.)
14. (a) as those shows or demonstrates something.)
15. (b) The demonstrative pronouns are: this, that, these, those.
16. (d) A and D statements are true.

17. (c) 18. (a) 19. (d) 20. (a) 21. (a) 22. (c) 23. (c) 24. (a)
25. (d) 26. (a) 27. (c) 28. (b) 29. (d) 30. (c) 31. (b) 32. (a)
33. (a) 34. (b) 35. (d) 36. (b) 37. (b) 38. (d)

5 CHAPTER FOREWORD

Simon says "jump". Simon says dance... you must have guessed by now that the next chapter is indeed about Verbs.

Let's solve the following exercise to check our knowledge.

Directions: Complete the following sentences with the correct form of verbs.

1. I like to ________________ (read)
2. She ________________ to the movies. (go)
3. They ________________ the leaking pipe (repair)
4. The keys are ________________ on the table. (keep)
5. I ________________ the new song. (sing)
6. The Queen ________________ the soldiers. (order)
7. The room was ________________ by him. (clean)
8. The dog ________________ loudly. (bark)
9. He ________________ me a cup of coffee. (give)
10. The rainbow ________________ colourful. (be)

5 Chapter

Verb

LEARNING OBJECTIVES

This lesson will help you to:—

- ❖ learn about verbs.
- ❖ know about Transitive and Intransitive verb.
- ❖ learn the formation and uses of verbs.

QUICK CONCEPT REVIEW

Verbs are important elements of language and grammar. As our life is full of movements so verbs become an integral part of our speech, conversation and writing mode. Verbs determine the position and action of nouns and pronouns.

DEFINITION

Verb is an important part of a sentence. No sentence is complete without it. Verbs are action words. They always express activity, either physical, mental or a state of being.

TYPES OF VERBS

Transitive Verbs

These are verbs that pass over from the doer or subject to some object. As the word indicates- "transitive - passing over".

For example :

<u>The teacher</u> <u>explained</u> <u>the question</u>.

↓ ↓ ↓

subject verb object

- Zainab gave the gift to her mother.
- Can you lend me your notebook, please?

Most transitive verbs take a single object. But some transitive verbs such as 'give, ask, offer, promise, tell', etc. take two objects after them. An indirect object

Real Life Example

A verb is a critical element of any sentence. It is an action word that says something about the subject of the sentence. For example, in the sentence, "The dog ran home," "ran" is the verb because it tells what the dog is doing.

Examples

A.

Talking

Sunny is talking to his sister.

B.

Reading

Peter is reading his book.

which denotes the 'person to whom' something is given or for whom something is done, is usually the name of some thing.

For example :

- His father gave him a rupee
- Rahul borrowed the Science book from his classmate.

Who is doing the action? — Rahul (Subject)

What is the action being done? — borrowed (Verb)

What did Rahul borrow? — Science book (direct object)

From whom did he borrow? — his classmate (indirect object)

Intransitive Verbs

An intransitive verb is a verb that denotes an action which does not pass over to an object or which expresses a state of being.

For example:

- He ran a long distance.
- The baby sleeps.
- There is a flaw in the diamond.

Auxiliary Verbs

These are also known as helping verbs and are used together with a main verb to show the tense or form a question. Commonly used auxiliary verbs include- is, am, are, do, does, did, have, has, had, etc.

For example:

- Rita is writing a letter.
- Does he have the new address?

CHARTS

A. Formation of Verbs from Nouns

Nouns	Verbs
justice	justify
light	lighten
terror	terrify
memory	memorise
sale	sell
red	redden
life	live
horror	horrify
belief	believe
class	classify

Activity

Try writing two sentences showing transitive verbs and circle the direct and indirect objects.

- ________________
- ________________

Activity

❖ Create verb poems using the name of a person and verbs that describe her. For example, a student might choose to write "Mom" at the top of the page. Underneath, he/she should write the verbs that she does, such as "cares," "cooks" and "works."

Play time

Play verb race with your partner. Select a theme and then write as many verbs as both of you can in one minute. For example, if you select the theme of "Olympics." You may write verbs such as "ski," "fall" and "skate." Give a point to the player who writes the greatest number of verbs.

B. Formation of Verbs from Adjectives

Adjectives	Verbs	Adjectives	Verbs
rich	enrich	large	enlarge
sick	sicken	real	realise
civil	civilise	sure	ensure
fine	refine	high	heighten
fertile	fertilise	wide	widen

C. Movement Identification

Animals	Movement	Animals	Movement
elephants	amble	mice	scamper
monkeys	climb	horses	trot
crows	flap	eagles	swoop
lambs	frisk	ducks	waddle
rabbits	leap	cocks	strut
wolves	lope	bears	lumber
lions	prowl	owls	flit
cats	stalk		

Objects	Movement	Objects	Movement
chains	clank	bells	peal
woods	crackle	flags	flutter
coins	jingle	winds	sigh
fire	creak	waves	ripple
streams	purl	leaves	rustle
babies	lisp	trains	rumble
thunder	rumbles	silks	rustle
aeroplanes	zoom		

Multiple Choice Questions

LEVEL - 1

Directions (Qs. 1 to 10): Choose the verb from the following sentences.

1. **Time changes all things.**
   (a) charges (b) cheats (c) changes (d) chooses
2. **Children are dancing on the stage.** **[2014]**
   (a) driving (b) dancing (c) digging (d) drinking
3. **The policeman arrested the thief.**
   (a) arrested (b) arrived (c) abided (d) arose
4. **We took shelter under a tree.**
   (a) told (b) tore (c) threw (d) took
5. **The fire burns brightly.** **[2015]**
   (a) brings (b) burns (c) begins (d) blows
6. **Cocks crow in the morning.**
   (a) caws (b) clings (c) crow (d) chides
7. **I failed to catch the train on time.**
   (a) fell (b) fought (c) felt (d) failed
8. **The sun rises in the east.**
   (a) rides (b) runs (c) rises (d) rings
9. **Mangoes are good to eat in summer.** **[2016]**
   (a) eat (b) ate (c) eaten (d) smell
10. **Father promised to give me a video-game.**
    (a) pointed (b) pasted (c) promised (d) packed

Directions (Qs. 11 to 15): Complete the analogy.

11. **Lion is to roar, tiger is to ________.** **[2017]**
    (a) growl (b) chatter (c) bark (d) crow
12. **Donkey is to bray, monkey is to ________.**
    (a) growl (b) chatter (c) Bark (d) crow
13. **Cat is to purr, dog is to ________.** **[2015]**
    (a) growl (b) chatter (c) bark (d) crow
14. **Hen is to cackle, cock is to ________.**
    (a) growl (b) chatter (c) bark (d) crow

15. Owl is to hoot, vulture is to __________.

(a) growl (b) chatter (c) bark (d) scream

Directions (Qs. 16 to 20): Find the odd one out.

16. (a) gibber (b) bellow (c) twitter (d) grunt

17. (a) caw (b) howl (c) cackle (d) warble

18. (a) hoot (b) scream (c) quack (d) clang

19. (a) bleat (b) drone (c) hum (d) chirp

20. (a) ring (b) blow (c) creak (d) yell

Directions (Qs. 21 to 25) : Choose the correct word to complete the following sentences.

21. _________ you want a blue and green dress?

(a) Do (b) Does (c) Are (d) Am

22. The chief guest _________ distributing the prizes at that time.

(a) is (b) were (c) was (d) are

23. I _________ having some problem in my throat.

(a) is (b) am (c) are (d) were

24. All the people _________ tired after the party.

(a) has (b) had (c) were (d) was

25. Everyone _________ done his or her homework.

(a) have (b) has (c) am (d) are

26. My parents __________ when I told them I wanted to quit the basketball team. [2018]

(a) churned up (b) taken the biscuit (c) went bananas (d) gulped up

27. Fill in the blanks with suitable verb.

They ________ us yesterday in the party. [2019]

(a) meet (b) met (c) remind (d) see

28. I wonder why Anita hasn't replied to my message. She ________ not have got [2020]

(a) is (b) will (c) could (d) might

29. I always ________ something when I leave my house. [2020]

(a) forgets (b) forgetting (c) forgot (d) forget

30. The meal ________ rice, curry and salad. [2021]

(a) includes (b) include (c) including (d) does includes

31. Ravi : Can you _________ me salt and pepper? [2021]

Soma : Sure, here you go.

(a) send (b) take (c) pass (d) leave

32. **Mike : Everyone is _______ to donate food for the poor.** **[2022]**

(a) requested (b) request (c) requests (d) has request

LEVEL-2

1. **Match the following:**

	List I		List II
A.	Farmers dig the field	1.	to pay the customer.
B.	Teacher teaches us to follow	2.	at our doorstep.
C.	Postman delivers our letters	3.	the grammatical rules.
D.	Banker counts money	4.	to grow crops.

	A	B	C	D
(a)	1	4	2	3
(b)	2	3	4	1
(c)	4	3	2	1
(d)	3	4	2	1

2. **Choose the correct statements.**

Statement A: The soldiers fought bravely. (transitive)

Statement B: The beggar sat by the roadside. (transitive)

Statement C: The boy writes a letter. (intransitive)

Statement D: The children shout loudly. (intransitive)

(a) A and B are correct. (b) B and C are correct.

(c) Only D is correct. (d) A and C are correct.

3. **Which of these pictures suggests the verb "pick" ?**

A.   B.  C.  D. 

(a) A (b) D (c) B (d) C

4. **Which of these pictures suggests the verb "set" ?**

A. 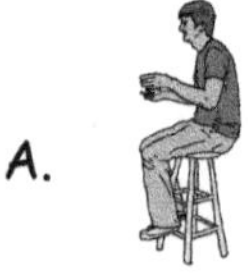 B.  C.  D. 

(a) B (b) D (c) A (d) C

5. **Which of these pictures suggests the verb "wash" ?**

A.  B.  C.  D.

(a) B (b) C (c) A (d) D

Directions (Qs. 6 to 10): Read the passage carefully and answer the following questions.

The horse is a very useful animal. It is found in almost every country. It feeds on grass or gram. It is therefore, used for riding over long distances. It is used in the cities for carrying luggages by cart. An Arabian horse is world famous. It is used by the military to carry soldiers. It is also used in sports. Horse racing and polo are very popular sports in which horse plays a part.

6. **What does the horse feed on?**

   (a) Grains (b) Beans (c) Gram (d) Pulses

7. **How is the horse used in cities?**

   (a) Travelling long distances (b) Selling vegetables

   (c) Carrying people (d) Carrying luggages

8. **How is Arabian horse used in military?**

   (a) Carry soldiers (b) Carry ammunitions

   (c) Carry food (d) Carry guns

9. **Name the game where the horses play a part.**

   (a) Soccer (b) Tennis (c) Golf (d) Polo

10. **Write the past tense of ' find' by picking up from the passage.**

    (a) Feed (b) Fond (c) Found (d) Food

11. **Read the statements and choose the correct option.**

    Statement A: Transitive verb--- The planets move round the sun.

    Statement B: Intransitive verb--- The wind blew slowly.

    (a) TT (b) TF (c) FT (d) FF

Directions (Qs. 12 to 17): Read the following passage and fill in the blanks.

A learned Pundit once (12)____ the court of Akbar. He told the king and his courtiers that he had mastery over many different languages. The Pundit could (13)____ many languages fluently. He challenged everybody at the court to name his mother tongue. When everyone (14)____, the challenge was taken up by Birbal. That night, Birbal went quietly to the Pundit's room when he was asleep. He (15)___ into the Pundit's ear and tickled it with a feather. The pundit, half (16)___, cried out suddenly and (17)___ out words in his mother tongue.

12. (a) came (b) visited (c) went (d) searched
13. (a) talk (b) cry (c) laugh (d) speak
14. (a) found (b) told (c) failed (d) passed
15. (a) whispered (b) shouted (c) cried (d) laughed
16. (a) arise (b) awoken (c) awake (d) arisen
17. (a) read (b) wrote (c) told (d) shouted

Directions (Qs. 18 to 22) : Read the following riddles and choose the correct option.

18.Likes to help people and takes care of their smiles.

(a) surgeon (b) hairdresser (c) dentist (d) none

19.Works in the fields with plants and animals.

(a) farmer (b) botanist (c) zoologist (d) horticulturist

20.Surrounded by books and people in tranquility.

(a) storekeeper (b) teacher (c) student (d) librarian

21.I study the weather and work with maps and charts.

(a) meterologist (b) scientist (c) geneticist (d) none

22.You seek my help to take care of your skin, nail and hair.

(a) climatologist (b) dermatologist (c) astrologist (d) none

23. **Count how many verbs are there in the sentence.**

Mom will distribute the pie evenly between my sisters and myself.

(a) 2 (b) 3 (c) 1 (d) None

24. **Count how many verbs are there in the sentence.**

My dream is for every person to fulfil his or her goals.

(a) 3 (b) 2 (c) 1 (d) None

Directions (Qs. 25 to 29): In English the largest number of verbs start with "S" ? Find them out.

25. **S_e**

(a) See (b) Say (c) Shine (d) Show

26. **Sh_k_**

(a) Shake (b) Shine (c) Show (d) Shrink

27. **Sh_w**

(a) Shine (b) Show (c) Shrink (d) Slide

28. **S_e_k**

(a) Shrink (b) Slide (c) Speak (d) Sting

29. **Sw_ng**

(a) Sting (b) Steal (c) Swim (d) Swing

Directions (Qs. 30 to 35) : Choose the verb from the given options.

30. (a) Able (b) Enable (c) Ability (d) Abled

31. (a) Character (b) Characteristic (c) Characterise (d) Characterisation

32. (a) Success (b) Successful (c) Succeed (d) Successor

33. (a) Sweet (b) Sweeten (c) Sweetness (d) Sweetner

34. (a) Vacancy (b) Vacant (c) Vacate (d) Vacation

35. (a) Lightning (b) Light (c) Lighter (d) Enlighten

36. **Rohit : I forgot to switch off the heater.** **[2021]**

Beena : Oh! We ________ go back and switch it off.

(a) can (b) need (c) must (d) dare

Directions (Q. No. 37 and 38): Choose the correct option to fill in the blank.

37. **I love the way your baby brother ________ your actions.** **[2021]**

(a) mimic (b) mimics (c) copy (d) copying

38. **Shasha ________ the drowning girl bravely.** **[2021]**

(a) help (b) save (c) rescued (d) worried

39. **Fill in the blanks with the correct form of verbs.** **[2022]**

I _______ to meet him yesterday but he _______ to talk to me.

(a) went, refuses (b) goes, refuses (c) went, refused (d) gone, refused

RESPONSE GRID

LEVEL 1

1. a b c d	2. a b c d	3. a b c d	4. a b c d	5. a b c d
6. a b c d	7. a b c d	8. a b c d	9. a b c d	10. a b c d
11. a b c d	12. a b c d	13. a b c d	14. a b c d	15. a b c d
16. a b c d	17. a b c d	18. a b c d	19. a b c d	20. a b c d
21. a b c d	22. a b c d	23. a b c d	24. a b c d	25. a b c d
26. a b c d	27. a b c d	28. a b c d	29. a b c d	30. a b c d
31. a b c d	32. a b c d			

LEVEL 2

1. a b c d	2. a b c d	3. a b c d	4. a b c d	5. a b c d
6. a b c d	7. a b c d	8. a b c d	9. a b c d	10. a b c d
11. a b c d	12. a b c d	13. a b c d	14. a b c d	15. a b c d
16. a b c d	17. a b c d	18. a b c d	19. a b c d	20. a b c d
21. a b c d	22. a b c d	23. a b c d	24. a b c d	25. a b c d
26. a b c d	27. a b c d	28. a b c d	29. a b c d	30. a b c d
31. a b c d	32. a b c d	33. a b c d	34. a b c d	35. a b c d
36. a b c d	37. a b c d	38. a b c d	39. a b c d	

Solutions with Explanation

LEVEL - 1

1. **(c)** **2.** **(b)** **3.** **(a)** **4.** **(d)** **5.** **(b)** **6.** **(c)** **7.** **(d)** **8.** **(c)** **9.** **(a)**
10. **(c)**
11. **(a)** growl
12. **(b)** chatter
13. **(c)** bark
14. **(d)** crow
15. **(d)** scream.
16. **(c)** twitter
17. **(b)** howl
18. **(d)** clang
19. **(b)** drone
20. **(d)** yell

21. (a) 22. (c) 23. (b) 24. (c) 25. (b) 26. (c) 27. (b)

28. (d) might

29. (d) forget

30. (a) includes

31. (c) pass

32. (a) requested

LEVEL - 2

1. (c)
2. (c) As (A) is intransitive because it has no object. (C) is transitive because it has an object 'letter'.
3. (d) 4. (b) 5. (c) 6. (c) 7. (d) 8. (a) 9. (d) 10. (c)
11. (c) there is no object in any of the sentences.
12. (b) 13. (d) 14. (c) 15. (a) 16. (c) 17. (d) 18. (c) 19. (a)
20. (d) 21. (a) 22. (b) 23. (a) 24. (b) 25. (a) 26. (a) 27. (b)
28. (c) 29. (d) 30. (b) 31. (c) 32. (c) 33. (b) 34. (c) 35. (d)
36. (c) must
37. (c) copy
38. (c) rescued
39. (c)

6 CHAPTER FOREWORD

Hmm! Verb is an action, Tense tells us the time, then what do we call the part of speech that tells how an action is being done? "Adverbs"; that's the answer. Let's learn about adverbs.

I. Directions : Circle the adverbs given in the following sentences.

1. The potter's wheel moved speedily.
2. A group of children watched patiently.
3. The man walked slowly towards the bus stop.
4. The glass of the window fell everywhere.
5. It would be finished soon.
6. Rita always sits here with me.
7. Please answer quickly. I am in a hurry.
8. The teacher arrived early.
9. The children heard the story quietly.
10. I suddenly remembered that I forgot to bring an umbrella.

II. Directions : Complete the sentences using appropriate adverbs. Take a clue from words given in the bracket.

1. The girls sang the song ______________________ (sweet)
2. The lady waited for the bus ______________________ (patient)
3. They visit their grandparents ______________________ (regular)
4. He spoke very ______________________ (soft)
5. I ______________________ have coffee. (normal)
6. I ______________________ walk to the college. (often)
7. He ______________________ ate his breakfast. (hurried)
8. You need to run ______________________ (steady)
9. He won't say it ______________________(repeated)
10. The boys were talking very ______________________ (loud)

Chapter 6

Adverb

LEARNING OBJECTIVES

This lesson will help you to:—

- learn the use of adverbs in sentence construction and in the expression of English language.
- learn to differentiate adverb from other parts of speech and observe how and to what extent adverbs modify them.

QUICK CONCEPT REVIEW

What is an Adverb?

An adverb is a word that tells us more about a verb.

It "qualifies" or "modifies" a verb (The man ran quickly). In the following examples, the adverb is in bold and the verb that it modifies is in italics.

- John *speaks* **loudly**. (How does John speak?)
- **Afterwards** she *smoked* a cigarette. (When did she smoke?)

But adverbs can also modify adjectives (Tara is really beautiful), or even other adverbs (It works very well).

Look at these examples:

- Modify an adjective:
  - He is really handsome. (How handsome is he?)
  - That was extremely kind of you.
- Modify another adverb:
  - She drives incredibly slowly. (How slowly does she drive?)
  - He drives extremely fast.

ADVERB FORMATION

We make many adverbs by adding -ly to an adjective, for example:

- Quick (adjective) > quickly (adverb).

❖ Careful (adjective) > carefully (adverb).

❖ Beautiful (adjective) > beautifully (adverb).

There are some basic rules about spelling for -ly adverbs. See the table below:

Adjective ending	Do this	Adjective	Adverb
most adjectives	add -ly	quick nice sole careful	quickly nicely solely carefully
-able or -ible	change -e to -y	regrettable horrible	regrettably horribly
-y	change -y to -ily	happy	happily
-ic	change -ic to -ically	economic	economically

But not all words that end in -ly are adverbs. The words friendly, lovely, lonely and neighbourly, for example, are all adjectives.

And some adverbs have no particular form. Look at these examples:

❖ Well, fast, very, never, always, often, still

KINDS OF ADVERBS

Here you can see the basic kinds of adverbs.

Adverbs of Manner

Adverbs of manner tell us the manner or way in which something happens. They answer the question "how?". Adverbs of manner mainly modify verbs.

❖ He speaks slowly. (How does he speak?)

❖ They helped us cheerfully. (How did they help us?)

❖ James Bond drives his cars fast. (How does James Bond drive his cars?)

Adverbs of Place

Adverbs of place tell us the place where something happens. They answer the question "where?". Adverbs of Place mainly modify verbs.

❖ Please sit here. (Where should I sit?)

❖ They looked everywhere. (Where did they look?)

❖ Two cars were parked outside. (Where were two cars parked?)

Adverbs of Time

Adverbs of time tell us something about the time that something happens. Adverbs of time mainly modify verbs.

They can answer the question "when?":

- ❖ He came yesterday. (When did he come?)
- ❖ I want it now. (When do I want it?)

Or they can answer the question "how often?":

- ❖ They deliver the newspaper daily. (How often do they deliver the newspaper?)
- ❖ We sometimes watch a movie. (How often do we watch a movie?)

Adverbs of Degree/ Frequency

Adverbs of degree tell us the degree or extent to which something happens. They answer the question "how much?" or "to what degree?". Adverbs of degree can modify verbs, adjectives and other adverbs.

- ❖ She entirely agrees with him. (How much does she agree with him?)
- ❖ Mary is very beautiful. (To what degree is Mary beautiful? How beautiful is Mary?)
- ❖ He drove quite dangerously. (To what degree did he drive dangerously? How dangerously did he drive?)

Multiple Choice Questions

LEVEL-1

Directions (Qs. 1 to 7): Fill blanks in the following sentences with an adverb and state its kind.

1. **Miss Kapoor sings ________.**
   (a) tomorrow (b) song (c) sweetly (d) dirty
2. **The umbrella was kept ________.** **[2014]**
   (a) often (b) yesterday (c) rarely (d) there
3. **Uncle Sam ________ goes to the club.**
   (a) rarely (b) tomorrow (c) beautifully (d) fast
4. **Pintu ran ________ to catch the ball.**
   (a) quickly (b) entirely (c) really (d) nearly
5. **Teddy went to the circus ________.** **[2015]**
   (a) rarely (b) beautifully (c) fast (d) yesterday
6. **Karan will buy some meat ________.**
   (a) thick (b) tomorrow (c) roasted (d) where
7. **Piggy ________ makes mistakes.**
   (a) rarely (b) yesterday (c) there (d) wisely

Directions (Qs. 8 to 17): Choose the correct adverbs in the following sentences.

8. **A load of salmon arrived on the docks ________.**
   (a) cheaply (b) beautifully (c) frequently (d) yesterday.
9. **People who shop ________ can save a great deal of money.** **[2016]**
   (a) wisely (b) beautifully (c) tomorrow (d) never
10. **Denise ________ goes to sales.**
    (a) tomorrow (b) always (c) fast (d) yesterday
11. **Our space probe landed ________ on the moon today.**
    (a) frequently (b) trouble (c) softly (d) never
12. **In the past, she has been ________ lucky with her buys.** **[2017]**
    (a) rare (b) very (c) unlucky (d) never
13. **For example, she bought a ________ new tent at the outdoors store.**
    (a) nearly (b) very (c) extremely (d) beautifully
14. **She is ________ skilful in both spending and saving money.**
    (a) cheaply (b) amazingly (c) tomorrow (d) never

15. ________ suddenly, the horse bolted across the field.
(a) Quite (b) Very (c) Rarely (d) Never

16. On the other hand, where can you get a ________ tasty ice cream cone?
(a) yesterday (b) frequently (c) really (d) tastily

17. The boys were ________ nice to the new student.
(a) extremely (b) beautifully (c) here (d) sweetly

18. I like to happily go and visit my friends who live by the sea. [2018]
(a) I like to (b) happily go and visit
(c) my friends who (d) live by the sea

19. Tell the type of underlined adverb:
He speaks slowly. [2018]
(a) Adverb of place (b) Adverb of manner
(c) Adverb of time (d) Adverb of frequency

20. Tell the type of underlined adverb:
He came yesterday. [2018]
(a) Adverb of place (b) Adverb of manner
(c) Adverb of time (d) Adverb of frequency

21. Find the adverb in the following sentences.
They often go to Shimla. [2019]
(a) They (b) often (c) go (d) Shimla

22. Mohan told us a very interesting story. [2019]
(a) Mohan (b) told (c) very (d) interesting

23. I _______ sing while I am having a shower. [2020]
(a) already (b) occasional (c) always (d) annually

LEVEL-2

Directions (Qs. 1 to 7) : Choose the correct option that identifies the type of underlined adverb.

1. I always have my breakfast at eight.
(a) Adverb of manner (b) Adverb of time
(c) Adverb of degree (d) Adverb of frequency

2. The cat crept in slowly.
(a) Adverb of manner (b) Adverb of time
(c) Adverb of degree (d) Adverb of frequency

3. **I <u>never</u> realised how easy English is** **[2014]**
   (a) Adverb of manner (b) Adverb of time
   (c) Adverb of degree (d) Adverb of frequency
4. **You should try <u>harder</u>.**
   (a) Adverb of manner (b) Adverb of time
   (c) Adverb of degree (d) Adverb of frequency
5. **He did the work <u>well</u>.** **[2013]**
   (a) Adverb of manner (b) Adverb of time
   (c) Adverb of degree (d) Adverb of frequency
6. **Please wait <u>outside</u>.** **[2015]**
   (a) Adverb of manner (b) Adverb of place
   (c) Adverb of degree (d) Adverb of frequency
7. **Sitara <u>proudly</u> received the award.** **[2016]**
   (a) Adverb of manner (b) Adverb of place
   (c) Adverb of degree (d) Adverb of frequency

Directions (Qs. 8 to 18): Choose the correct spelling for each adverb.

8. (a) Sweetly (b) Swetlly (c) Sweetlly (d) Sweetlie
9. (a) Slowy (b) Slowly (c) Sloly (d) Slouly
10. (a) Wonderfuli (b) Wonderfullly (c) Wonderfully (d) Wonder fully
11. (a) Beautifulli (b) Beautifullly (c) Beautifooly (d) Beautifully
12. (a) Carefuly (b) Carefullly (c) Carefuly (d) Carefully
13. (a) Quiety (b) Quietli (c) Quietlie (d) Quietly
14. (a) Complete (b) Completely (c) Completly (d) Compleetly
15. (a) Angryly (b) Angryli (c) Angrily (d) Angrilie
16. (a) Really (b) Real (c) Reallie (d) Realy
17. (a) Happyly (b) Happily (c) Happilie (d) Happyli
18. (a) Silently (b) Siletly (c) Silntly (d) Silentlie

Directions (Qs. 19 to 23): Find the adverb in the following sentences.

19. **He slowly puts the clock back into its box.**
    (a) back (b) slowly (c) its (d) box
20. **He usually gets good marks in Maths.**
    (a) good (b) grades (c) marks (d) usually

21. I called them yesterday

(a) I (b) yesterday (c) called (d) them

22. Julia quickly ran to the grocery store.

(a) ran (b) grocery (c) quickly (d) store

23. Simon arrives late for most of the meetings.

(a) most (b) meetings (c) arrives (d) late

Directions (Qs. 24 to 33): Read the paragraph and choose the correct adverbs to fill in the blanks.

(24)___ the movie (25)___, we (26)___ walked (27)___ and headed home (28)___ we went (29)___, we (30)___ wiped our feet. I ran (31)___ and since I was ___(32)___ tired. So, I relaxed on my bed and took a nap. When I woke up, my mom had (33)___ brought me some hot chocolate. What a nice day.

24. (a) When (b) Always (c) After (d) Never

25. (a) yesterday (b) before (c) after (d) beautifully

26. (a) wisely (b) briskly (c) fast (d) slow

27. (a) outside (b) inside (c) tomorrow (d) today

28. (a) today (b) rarely (c) always (d) before

29. (a) inside (b) frequently (c) efficiently (d) cheaply

30. (a) rapidly (b) slowly (c) today (d) there

31. (a) upstairs (b) wisely (c) cheaply (d) slowly

32. (a) quite (b) efficiently (c) beautifully (d) never

33. (a) badly (b) lonely (c) carefully (d) lovingly

Directions (Qs. 34 to 43): Complete the passage with suitable adverbs.

Today I helped my mom cook dinner. We ___(34)___ cut the vegetables and ___(35) ___ placed them into a boiling pot of water. Next, mom ___(36)___ browned the chicken and ___(37)___ let it cook through. I ___(38)___ waited for my next job, which was to ___(39) ___ sprinkle spices into the soup. But, I ___(40)___ poured in too much cumin. I ___(41)___told my mom my mistake, and she ___(42)___ told me that as a child, she had ___(43)___ made the same mistake.

34. (a) frequently (b) carefully (c) slowly (d) happily

35. (a) fast (b) slowly (c) accidently (d) gently

36. (a) quickly (b) lonely (c) cheaply (d) lately

37. (a) frequently (b) patiently (c) lately (d) silently

38. (a) really (b) eagerly (c) happily (d) slowly

	(a)	(b)	(c)	(d)
39.	cautiously	completely	lately	loudly
40.	totally	accidently	efficiently	badly
41.	quietly	honestly	stupidly	really
42.	cunningly	sweetly	horribly	badly
43.	coincidently	amazingly	efficiently	beautifully

44. Amidst the pandemic ________ I volunteered at the government hospital. [2021]

(a) before (b) last month
(c) tomorrow (d) annual

45. The baby is sleeping ________. [2022]

(a) always (b) sound
(c) loudly (d) almost

RESPONSE GRID

LEVEL 1

1. a b c d	2. a b c d	3. a b c d	4. a b c d	5. a b c d
6. a b c d	7. a b c d	8. a b c d	9. a b c d	10. a b c d
11. a b c d	12. a b c d	13. a b c d	14. a b c d	15. a b c d
16. a b c d	17. a b c d	18. a b c d	19. a b c d	20. a b c d
21. a b c d	22. a b c d	23. a b c d		

LEVEL 2

1. a b c d	2. a b c d	3. a b c d	4. a b c d	5. a b c d
6. a b c d	7. a b c d	8. a b c d	9. a b c d	10. a b c d
11. a b c d	12. a b c d	13. a b c d	14. a b c d	15. a b c d
16. a b c d	17. a b c d	18. a b c d	19. a b c d	20. a b c d
21. a b c d	22. a b c d	23. a b c d	24. a b c d	25. a b c d
26. a b c d	27. a b c d	28. a b c d	29. a b c d	30. a b c d
31. a b c d	32. a b c d	33. a b c d	34. a b c d	35. a b c d
36. a b c d	37. a b c d	38. a b c d	39. a b c d	40. a b c d
41. a b c d	42. a b c d	43. a b c d	44. a b c d	45. a b c d

Solutions with Explanation

LEVEL-1

1. (c) sweetly- adverb of manner.
2. (d) adverb of place. (there)
3. (a) adverb of frequency. (rarely)
4. (a) adverb of manner. (quickly)
5. (d) adverb of time. (yesterday)
6. (b) adverb of time. (tomorrow)
7. (a) adverb of frequency. (rarely)
8. (d) modifying verb- arrived.
9. (a) modifying verb- shop.
10. (b) modifying verb- goes.
11. (c) modifying verb- landed.
12. (b) modifying adjective- lucky.
13. (a) modifying adjective- new.
14. (b) modifying adjective- skilful.
15. (a) modifying adverb- suddenly.
16. (c) modifying adjective- tasty.
17. (a) modifying adjective- nice.

18. (b)	19. (b)	20. (c)	21. (b)
22. (c)	23. (c) always		

LEVEL-2

1. (d)	2. (a)	3. (d)	4. (a)
5. (a)	6. (b)	7. (a)	8. (a)

9. (b) 10. (c) 11. (d) 12. (d)
13. (d) 14. (b) 15. (c) 16. (a)
17. (b) 18. (a) 19. (b) 20. (d)
21. (b) 22. (c) 23. (d) 24. (c)
25. (a) 26. (b) 27. (a) 28. (d)
29. (a) 30. (a) 31. (a) 32. (a)
33. (d) 34. (b) 35. (b) 36. (a)
37. (b) 38. (b) 39. (a) 40. (b)
41. (b) 42. (b) 43. (a)
44. (b) last month
45. (b) soundly

7 CHAPTER FOREWORD

Hello! Let's learn about tenses. Tense is the form a verb takes to show the time it happened. Now, check your knowledge by solving the exercise given below.

Directions: State the tense of the following sentences.

1. I will have been working with this organisation for six months by the end of next month.
2. They will have solved the quiz on their own.
3. I will have bought the oranges before you reach the market.
4. I will be taking swimming lessons next summer.
5. Sam will take you to the doctor tomorrow.
6. Daniel will have repaired the computer before the next meeting.
7. The teachers will have prepared the test papers before the vacations begin.
8. I will cook tonight.
9. The maid will be clearing the tables for us.
10. Her book will have become famous by the time it reaches other countries.

7

Chapter

Tense

LEARNING OBJECTIVES

This lesson will help you to:—

- ❖ learn about the meaning of tenses.
- ❖ study and learn about the usage of tenses.
- ❖ learn different types of tenses.

Real Life Example

Tenses are an important part of our communication. They make and break the meaning of the words in a sentence. We continuously use the tenses in communicating.

QUICK CONCEPT REVIEW

What are tenses ?

Tenses are used to show the relation between the action or state described by the verb and the time, which is reflected in the form of the verb.

There are three main verb tenses: present, past, and future. Each main tense is divided into simple, continuous, perfect, and perfect continuous tenses. But here, we will be studying only about simple, perfect and continuous tenses.

SIMPLE TENSE

Things to remember about simple tense:

(a) Present tense is the original verb form.

(b) Past tense has a few patterns.

(c) Future tense needs will (shall) + verb.

For example:

- I run a marathon this year. (present)
- I ran a marathon last year. (past)
- I will run a marathon next year. (future)

SIMPLE TENSE

Past	Present	Future
Past simple (commonly called simple past)	Present simple (commonly called simple present)	Future simple (commonly called simple future)
The dog was sick. It rained (yesterday)	The dog is sick. It rains (every day)	The dog will be sick. It will rain (tomorrow)
She (just) went to the market	She goes to the market (as usual)	She will go to the market (soon)

SIMPLE PRESENT

The simple present tense is used to describe an action that is regular, true or normal.

Forms of the predicate verb:

1. BASE (if the subject is I, we, you, they, or any plural)
2. +S (if the subject is he, she, it, or any singular other than I or you)

We use the present tense:

1. For repeated or regular actions in the present time period.

   For example:

   - I take the train to the office.
   - John sleeps eight hours every night during the week.
2. For facts.

   For example:

   - The President of The USA lives in The White House.
   - A dog has four legs.
3. For habits.

   For example:

   - I get up early every day.
   - Carol brushes her teeth twice a day.
4. For things that are always / generally true.

   For example:

   - The Queen of England lives in Buckingham Palace.
   - They speak English at work.

We form the present tense using the base form of the infinitive. In general, in the third person we add 'S' in the third person.

Amazing Facts

- Americans do not use the present perfect tense so much as British speakers. Americans often use the past tense instead. An American might say "Did you have lunch?", where a British person would say "Have you had lunch?"
- For can be used with all tenses. Since is usually used with perfect tenses only.

Historical preview

The evolution of a future and perfect tense represents the most significant innovation of Modern English in comparison to earlier stages of that language. Old English had a two tense system (past and non-past), which is claimed to have been preserved in Modern English by some linguists.

Subject	Verb	The rest of the sentence
I / you / we / they	speak / learn	English at home
he / she / it	speaks / learns	English at home

Negative Sentences in the Simple Present Tense

To make a negative sentence in English we normally use **don't or doesn't** with all verbs except to Be and modal verbs (can, might, should etc.).

- **Affirmative:** You speak French.

  Negative: You don't speak French.

- The following is the word order to construct a basic negative sentence in English in the present tense using **don't or doesn't**.

Subject	don't/ doesn't	Verb*	The Rest of the sentence
I / you / we / they	don't	have / buy	cereal for breakfast
he / she / it	doesn't	eat / like etc.	

SIMPLE PAST TENSE

In the simple past tense, the action is simply mentioned and understood to have taken place in the past. The action started and ended sometime in the past but the time may or may not be mentioned.

Example of positive statement: The boy played cricket yesterday.

Example of negative statement: She didn't talk to Pooja last week.

Example of interrogative statement: Did you complete the work?

- For making positive statements in the simple past tense, use the verb in the past form for all subjects.
- For making negative statements in the simple past tense use 'didn't' or 'did not' and the verb in the base form for all subjects.
- For making questions in the simple past tense, use 'did' and the verb in the base form for all subjects.

SIMPLE FUTURE TENSE

The simple future tense is used when we plan or make a decision to do something. Nothing is said about the time in the future.

Forms of the predicate verb:

1. WILL + BASE
2. AM/IS/ARE + GOING TO + BASE

   Examples of positive statement:

   - You will read the story book tomorrow.
   - You are going to read the story book tomorrow.

   Examples of negative statement:

   - He will not play football next week.
   - He is not going to play football next week.

   Examples of interrogative statement:

   - Will I go to Mumbai next month?
   - Am I going to land in to Mumbai next month?

For making positive statements in the simple future tense, use 'will' or 'going to' and the verb in the base form for all subjects.

For making negative statements in the simple future tense, use 'will not' or 'not going to' and the verb in the base form for all subjects.

> **Misconcept/Concept**
>
> **Misconcept:** Tense and time are synonymous.
>
> **Concept:** The term "tense" is used to refer to a verb form, not to chronological time. Thus tense and time are not synonymous. The word "tense" does not mean "time". These are two different words meaning two different things.

PERFECT TENSE

- ❖ The three perfect tenses in English are the three verb tenses which show action already completed. (The word perfect literally means "made complete" or "completely done.")
- ❖ They are formed by the appropriate tense of the verb 'have' plus the past participle of the verb.

PRESENT PERFECT

- ❖ The structure of the present perfect tense is:

subject +	auxiliary verb +	main verb
	have	past participle

For example:

- You have eaten mine.
- Have they done it?

This tense is called the present perfect tense. There is always a connection with the past and with the present. There are basically three uses of the present perfect tense:

- ❖ experience
- ❖ change
- ❖ continuing situation

We often use the present perfect tense to talk about experience from the past. We are not interested in when you did something. We only want to know if you did it:

For example:

- I have seen ET.
- I have lived in Bangkok.

Connection with past: the event was in the past.

Connection with present: in my head, now, I have a memory of the event; I know something about the event; I have its experience.

❖ We also use the present perfect tense to talk about a change or new information.

For example:

- I have bought a car.
- John has broken his leg.

❖ We often use the present perfect tense to talk about a continuing situation. This is a state that started in the past and continues in the present (and will probably continue into the future). This is a state (not an action). We usually use for or since with this structure.

For example:

- I have worked here since June.
- He has been ill for 2 days.

Connection with past: the situation started in the past.

Connection with present: the situation continues in the present.

For and since with present perfect tense

We often use for and since with the present perfect tense.

❖ We use 'for' to talk about a period of time -5 minutes, 2 weeks, 6 years.

❖ We use 'since' to talk about a point in past time -9 o'clock, 1st January, Monday.

For example:

- I have been here for 20 minutes.
- I have been here since 9 o'clock.
- John hasn't called for 6 months.

PAST PERFECT

It is used to express an action which has occurred in past (usually, a long time ago) and action which has occurred in past before another action in past.

For example:

I had lived in America. (The sense of time in this sentence refers to a completed action in past and especially a long time ago)

STRUCTURE OF SENTENCE

Positive sentence

❖ Subject + auxiliary verb + main verb (past participle) + object.

❖ Subject + had + 3rd form of verb or past participle + object.

For example:

- He had taken the exam last year.
- A thief had stolen my watch.

Negative sentence

❖ Subject + auxiliary verb + NOT + main verb (past participle) + object.

❖ Subject + had + not + 3rd form of verb or past participle + object.

"Not" is written after auxiliary verb in negative sentence.

For example:

- He had not taken the exam last year.
- A thief had not stolen my watch.

Interrogative sentence

❖ Auxiliary verb (had) + subject + main verb (past participle) + object?

An Interrogative sentence starts with an auxiliary verb "had".

For example:

- Had he taken the exam last year?
- Had it rained heavily last month?

FUTURE PERFECT

It is used to express an action which will occur in future and is thought to be completed in future. It expresses a sense of completion of an action which will occur in future.

For example:

"John will have gone tomorrow". It shows a sense of completion of an action (go) which will occur in future (tomorrow).

STRUCTURE OF SENTENCE

Positive sentence

❖ Subject + auxiliary verb + main verb (past participle) + object.

For example:

- She will have finished the work by Wednesday.
- I will have left for home by the time he gets up.

Negative sentence

❖ Subject + Not between auxiliary verbs and main verb (past participle) + object.

For example:

- She will not have finished the work by Wednesday.
- I will not have left for home by the time he gets up.

Interrogative sentence

❖ Auxiliary verb + Subject + auxiliary verb + main verb (past participle) + object.

For example:

- Will she have finished the work by Wednesday?
- Will I have left for home by the time he gets up?

CONTINUOUS TENSE

Present Continuous

It is used to express a continued or ongoing action at present time. It expresses an action which is in progress at the time of speaking.

For example:

A person says, "I am writing a letter". It means that he is in the process of writing a letter right now.

❖ Present continuous tense is also called present progressive tense.

STRUCTURE OF SENTENCE

Positive Sentence

❖ Subject + auxiliary verb + main verb-ing (Present participle) + object

If the subject is "I" then auxiliary verb "am" is used after subject in the sentence.

If the subject is "He, She, It, singular or proper name" then auxiliary verb "is" is used after subject in the sentence.

If subject is "You, They or any plural" then auxiliary verb "are" is used after subject in the sentence.

The participle "ing" is added to the 1st form of verb i.e. going (go) writing (write).

For example:

- I am playing cricket.
- He is driving a car.
- They are reading their lessons.

Negative Sentence

❖ Subject + auxiliary verb + not + main verb-ing (Present participle) + object.

❖ Subject + am/is/are + not + (1st form of verb + ing) + object.

For example:

- I am not playing cricket.
- He is not driving a car.
- They are not reading their lessons.

Interrogative Sentences

❖ Auxiliary verb + Subject + main verb-ing (Present participle) + object.

For example:

- Am I playing cricket?
- Is he driving a car?
- Are they reading their lessons?

PAST CONTINUOUS

It is used to express a continued or ongoing action in past, an ongoing action which occurred in past and completed at some point in past.

For example:

"He was laughing." This sentence shows ongoing action (laughing) of a person which occurred in past.

Past continuous tense is also called past progressive tense.

STRUCTURE OF SENTENCE

Positive sentences

- Subject + auxiliary verb + main verb (present participle) + object.
- Subject + was/were + (1st form of verb or base verb +ing) +object.

  For example:

  - She was crying yesterday.
  - They were climbing on a hill.

Negative sentences

- Subject + auxiliary verb + NOT + main verb (present participle) + object
- Subject + was/were + NOT + (1st form of verb or base verb +ing) +object

  For example:

  - She was not crying yesterday.
  - They were not climbing on a hill.

Interrogative sentences

- Auxiliary verb + subject + main verb (present participle) + object
- Was/were + subject + (1st form of verb or base verb +ing) + object

  For example:

  - Was she crying yesterday?
  - Were they climbing on a hill?

FUTURE CONTINUOUS

It is used to express a continued or an ongoing action in future.

For example:

"I will be waiting for you tomorrow", it conveys ongoing nature of an action (waiting) which will occur in future.

STRUCTURE OF SENTENCE

Positive sentence

- Subject + auxiliary verb + main verb (present participle) + object.
- Subject + will be+ 1st form of verb or base form+ing (present participle) + object.

  For example:

  - I will be waiting for you.
  - You will be feeling well tomorrow.

Negative sentence

- Subject + not between auxiliary verbs+ not + main verb (present participle) + object.
- Subject + will not be + 1st form of verb or base form+ing (present participle) + object.

For example:

- I will not be waiting for you.
- You will not be feeling well tomorrow.

Interrogative sentence

- Auxiliary verb + subject + auxiliary verb + main verb (present participle) + object
- Will + subject + be+ 1st form of verb or base form+ing (present participle) + object

For example:

- Will I be waiting for you?
- Will you be feeling well tomorrow?

Multiple Choice Questions

LEVEL-1

Directions (Qs. 1 to 7) : Complete the following sentences with suitable form of verb.

1. We ______ Mrs Stewart when we were in California.

(a) have met (b) are meeting
(c) will neet (d) met

2. Dia wanted to buy a CD, but she__________ have enough money. [2013]

(a) doesn't (b) didn't
(c) do not (d) had not

3. Sorry, Lisa______ not here at the moment.

(a) am
(b) is
(c) be
(d) none of these

4. My mother ________ 42 years old next saturday. [2014]

(a) will be (b) was
(c) is (d) will have

5. My brother ____________football in the same club as me.

(a) plays (b) played
(c) play (d) is playing

6. I _______ (work) at three o'clock.

(a) was working
(b) worked
(c) were working
(d) am working

7. _________ (eat) by six? [2015]

(a) Will you eat
(b) Will you have eaten
(c) Will you be eating
(d) Won't you eat

Directions. (Qs. 8 and 9): Pick the odd one out

8. (a) She will perform on his wedding.
(b) She came to Delhi yesterday.
(c) She will join her friends tomorrow.
(d) She will shop, eat and enjoy from now.

9. (a) A cat has four legs.
(b) The President of India lives in The Rashtrapati Bhawan.
(c) They went to Punjab yesterday.
(d) They travel to their country house every weekend.

10. 'James is a taxi driver. He drives a taxi. But on Sundays he doesn't drive his taxi. He stays at home.'

The given line is in-
(a) future tense
(b) present tense
(c) past tense
(d) This sentence is grammatically incorrect.

Directions (Qs. 11 to 14): Identify if the following sentences are in past, present or future tense.

11. John writes his name on the chalkboard.
(a) Present
(b) Past
(c) Future
(d) None of these

12. Mary jumped on her bed. [2016]
(a) Present
(b) Past
(c) Future
(d) None of these

13. Akshay plays violin in his room.
(a) Present
(b) Past
(c) Future
(d) None of these

14. Carla will sing in the school today.
(a) Present
(b) Past
(c) Future
(d) None of these

15. Complete the following sentence.
_________ (it/stop) raining by tomorrow morning?
(a) Will it stop
(b) Would it stop
(c) Will it have stopped
(d) Would it have stopped

Directions (Qs. 16 to 30): Fill in the blanks by choosing the options from the box.

will write	saw	will go	will eat
will dance	sang	danced	wrote
went	ate	eat	will see

16. I _________ a song at the concert yesterday.
(a) sang (b) danced
(c) ate (d) saw

17. He _________ a letter to his girlfriend tomorrow.
(a) wrote (b) will write
(c) saw (d) will see

18. I _________ to the library to borrow some books this weekend.
(a) went (b) will dance
(c) will go (d) wrote

19. I _________a movie yesterday.
(a) saw (b) will see
(c) will dance (d) sang

20. I _________ lunch in one hour.
(a) will eat (b) ate
(c) will see (d) will go

21. Choose the part of the sentence that has an error.
The most suprising thing that happened while I was away was that my pet fish all reproducing and now I have more than I can handle. [2018]
(a) The most surprising thing that happened
(b) while I was away was that my
(c) pet fish all reproducing and now
(d) I have more than I can handle

22. We are all _________ on playing together this time next week at Sam's house. [2019]
(a) being planned (b) planned
(c) to plan (d) planning

23. I am surprised at how much effort we have _________ in over the past few months. [2019]
(a) had to put
(b) gone over
(c) done and dusted
(d) seen or had

24. By the end of the semester we __________ studying the same thing in history for two years. [2019]
(a) are (b) will be
(c) had been (d) will have been

25. I think that the wind is much too strong ________ a kite today. [2020]
(a) flying (b) to fly
(c) to flying (d) fly

26. You _________ practise tonight, won't you? [2020]
(a) will (b) would
(c) shall d) can

27. The boy ________ up the tree, so that the bear couldn't see him. [2021]
(a) climb (b) climbs
(c) climbed (d) climbing

28. Rahul : Sumit plays football __________ . [2021]
(a) tomorrow (b) every evening
(c) day (d) than

29. Sachin : Did Hari _______ it with you?
Shama : No, he didn't. [2021]
(a) discuss (b) discussed
(c) discusses (d) discussing

30. Shivani likes to _________ the guitar and the piano. [2022]
(a) play (b) played
(c) plays (d) playing

LEVEL-2

1. Match the following verbs in their present tense with their past tense.

List I (Present tense)		List II (Past tense)	
A.	pull	1.	ate
B.	see	2.	waited
C.	eat	3.	pulled
D.	wait	4.	saw

	A	B	C	D
(a)	2	3	1	4
(b)	3	4	1	2
(c)	2	4	3	1
(d)	1	3	2	4

Directions (Qs. 2 and 3): Read the statements and find the correct option.

2. **Statement A:** The amount of time she spent doing her homework, paid off.
Statement B: As soon as I got home, I done my laundry.
(a) A is correct.
(b) B is correct.
(c) A and B are correct.
(d) A and B are incorrect.

3. **Statement A:** We put "ing" in the present simple tense.
Statement B: When we have to tell about daily routine we talk in the present simple tense.
(a) Only A is true.
(b) Only B is true.
(c) Both A and B are true.
(d) Both A and B are false.

Directions (Qs. 4 to 9): Complete the sentences below by changing the form of the verb in (bracket) to past tense. Then complete the puzzle.

4. **(Across 1) The floor was ________ (sweep) clean.**
   (a) swept (b) sweeped
   (c) sweep (d) sweap
5. **(Down 2) Macy ________ (wrap) the gift with a beautiful bow.**
   (a) wraps (b) wrapped
   (c) wrapper (d) wrapping
6. **(Across 3) Peter ________ (repair) the race cars before every competition.**
   (a) repair (b) repairs
   (c) repaired (d) repairing
7. **(Down 4) Yesterday, Mia ________ (read) a novel.**
   (a) read (b) reading
   (c) reads (d) red
8. **(Across 5) Susan ________ (jump) high in the air.**
   (a) jumps (b) jumper
   (c) jump (d) jumped
9. **Match the following sentences with the correct tenses.**

	List I		List II
A.	He will be coming to meet you on Saturday.	1.	Past
B.	She is humming her favourite song.	2.	Future
C.	I ate bananas.	3.	Present

	A	B	C		A	B	C
(a)	2	3	1	(b)	1	3	2
(c)	3	2	1	(d)	2	1	3

Directions (Qs. 10 to 15): Fill in the spaces with the correct form of the verb in present continuous tense.

10. **Billy (do) ________ his homework now. We are going to watch a movie/ when he is finished.**
    (a) is doing (b) will do
    (c) was doing (d) can do
11. **Dr. Mason is busy. He (see) ________ a patient right now. He will see you in twenty minutes.**
    (a) will see (b) is seeing
    (c) will seeing (d) was seeing
12. **Andrea and Alejandro (take) ________ a walk. The fresh air feels great.**
    (a) will take
    (b) will taking
    (c) is taking
    (d) are taking
13. **Right now, I (buy) ________ groceries. I need eggs, milk, and bread.**
    (a) will buy (b) am buying
    (c) can buy (d) am buy
14. **We (eat) ________ dinner. It tastes good. Can you pass me the salt, please?**
    (a) won't eat
    (b) can eat
    (c) will eat
    (d) are eating
15. **My car (move) ________ down the hill. I forgot to engage the parking break. Somebody please help me!**
    (a) will move
    (b) was moving
    (c) is moving
    (d) will be moving

Directions (Qs. 16 to 23): Fill in the spaces with the correct form of the verb in () in simple past perfect tense.

16. **It (jump) ________ out of its cage just before we arrived at the zoo!**
    (a) jumped
    (b) had jumped
    (c) have jumped
    (d) will jump

17. **When I arrived at the cinema, the film ________ (start).**
    (a) have started
    (b) was started
    (c) had started
    (d) had start.
18. **We were late for the plane because we ________ (forgot) our passports.**
    (a) had forgot
    (b) had forgotten
    (c) forget
    (d) have forget
19. **The garden was dead because it________ (be) dry all summer.**
    (a) had been (b) has been
    (c) will be (d) been
20. **What ________ served for breakfast?**
    (a) do you usually have
    (b) are you usually having
    (c) have you usually
    (d) had been
21. **Who ______________ this building? It is extremely beautiful to look at.**
    (a) was designed
    (b) is designed
    (c) had designed
    (d) has designed
22. **I too want to domesticate a dog. Where ________ you ________ your dog from?**
    (a) has, get (b) is, got
    (c) was, got (d) had, got
23. **The baby's face is really dirty. Where ___________ you ___________ him?**
    (a) was, left (b) is, leave
    (c) are, left (d) had, left

Directions (Qs. 24 to 27): Put the verbs between brackets in the correct form.

24. **What time (the banks/open) ________ in Britain?**
    (a) do the banks open
    (b) will the banks open
    (c) the bank opens
    (d) the banks will open
25. **When ________ (you/read) my book?**
    (a) will you have read
    (b) will you read
    (c) would you read
    (d) did you read
26. **She (not/wake) ________ up early on Sundays.**
    (a) do not wake
    (b) doesn't wake
    (c) don't wake
    (d) doesn't woke
27. **I'm sorry, by next week, they ________ (not/write) the article.**
    (a) won't have written
    (b) won't write
    (c) haven't written
    (d) had not written

Directions (Qs. 28 to 30): Make the correct form of the past simple or the present perfect.

28. **I ________ (see) three police cars this morning.**
    (a) have seen
    (b) will seen.
    (c) saw.
    (d) had seen.
29. **My grandparents only________ (know) each other for a few months before they ________ (get) married.**
    (a) know, get
    (b) knew, got
    (c) knew, get.
    (d) know, get.
30. **I ________ (not/see) the sea before.**
    (a) have seen not
    (b) haven't seen
    (c) has not seen
    (d) didn't see.

Directions (Q. No. 31 and 37): Choose the part of the sentence that error.

31. Don't you have any friends on the other section of the class? [2020]

(a) Don't you have
(b) any friends on
(c) the other section
(d) of the class?

32. Even though Karnal is so close to Panipat, we rare go there on weekends [2020]

(a) Even though Karnal is
(b) so close to Panipat,
(c) we rare go there
(d) on weekends.

33. Harman: __________ sports practice today? [2020]
Sally: Not sure.

(a) Did we had
(b) Does we have
(c) Do we have
(d) Are we have

34. Elif Would you like some more pasta? [2020]

Amal : __________.

(a) I like it a lot.
(b) Enjoy yours!
(c) No, thanks. I'm full.
(d) You make the best pasta.

35. Riaan: Hi Smith, Did you send Hina an invitation? [2020]
Smith: If I found her address, I would __________ her an invitation.

(a) be send (b) sending
(c) send (d) sent

36. Mother: Why did you get such a low grade in Mathematics? I thought you knew all the formulas. [2020]

Son: Yes, but __________ .

(a) I did much silly mistake
(b) I had more silly mistakes
(c) I made some silly mistakes
(d) I don't forget the silly mistakes

37. Choose the correct option to complete the conversation. [2020]
Teacher: Saurabh, why are you late today?
Saurabh: Sir, my bicycle __________.

(a) got punctured
(b) is puncturing
(c) get punctures
(d) has puncturing

Directions (Q. No. 38 to 42): Choose the part of sentence that has an error.

38. Sudden, Ravisha became super polite. [2021]

(a) Sudden
(b) Ravisha became
(c) super polite
(d) No error

39. The next fish trip would be great with our new gear. [2021]

(a) The next fish
(b) trip would be
(c) great with our
(d) new gear.

40. Choose the part of the sentence that has an error. [2021]
These shoes are exactly the same as my.

(a) These shoes (b) are exactly
(c) the same (d) as my.

41. Choose the correct option to complete the conversation. [2021]
Rajni : I have never __________ classical music.
Jyoti : Oh! I love classical music.

(a) being in (b) been
(c) been into (d) be into

42. Ritika __________ seeds in her garden yesterday. [2022]

(a) is sowing (b) was sowing
(c) are sowing (d) were sowing

Directions (Q. No. 43 and 45): Choose the part of the sentence that has an error.

43. Rohit goes to the temple with his mother regular. [2022]

(a) Rohit goes
(b) to the temple
(c) with his
(d) mother regular.

44. This restaurant serves the better Chinese food in the city. [2022]

(a) This restaurant
(b) serves the
(c) better Chiense food
(d) in the city.

45. Choose the part of the sentence that has an error. [2022]
I will be wait for you at the library.

(a) I will
(b) be wait
(c) for you
(d) at the library.

RESPONSE GRID

LEVEL 1

1. a b c d	2. a b c d	3. a b c d	4. a b c d	5. a b c d
6. a b c d	7. a b c d	8. a b c d	9. a b c d	10. a b c d
11. a b c d	12. a b c d	13. a b c d	14. a b c d	15. a b c d
16. a b c d	17. a b c d	18. a b c d	19. a b c d	20. a b c d
21. a b c d	22. a b c d	23. a b c d	24. a b c d	25. a b c d
26. a b c d	27. a b c d	28. a b c d	29. a b c d	30. a b c d

LEVEL 2

1. a b c d	2. a b c d	3. a b c d	4. a b c d	5. a b c d
6. a b c d	7. a b c d	8. a b c d	9. a b c d	10. a b c d
11. a b c d	12. a b c d	13. a b c d	14. a b c d	15. a b c d
16. a b c d	17. a b c d	18. a b c d	19. a b c d	20. a b c d
21. a b c d	22. a b c d	23. a b c d	24. a b c d	25. a b c d
26. a b c d	27. a b c d	28. a b c d	29. a b c d	30. a b c d
31. a b c d	32. a b c d	33. a b c d	34. a b c d	35. a b c d
36. a b c d	37. a b c d	38. a b c d	39. a b c d	40. a b c d
41. a b c d	42. a b c d	43. a b c d	44. a b c d	45. a b c d

Solutions with Explanation

LEVEL-1

1. (d) We **met** Mrs Stewart when we were in California.
2. (b) Dia wanted to buy a CD, but she **didn't** have enough money.
3. (b) Sorry, Lisa **is** not here at the moment.
4. (a) My mother **will be** 42 years old next Saturday.
5. (a) My brother **plays** football in the same club as me.
6. (a) I **was working at** three o'clock.
7. (b) **Will you have eaten** by six?
8. (b) **'She came to Delhi yesterday'** is the odd one out because it is the only sentence in the options which is in past tense.
9. (c) **'They went to Punjab yesterday'** is the only sentence in the past tense among the simple present tense options.
10. (b) James is a taxi driver. He **drives** a taxi. But on Sundays he **doesn't drive** his taxi. He stays at home.
11. (a) John **writes** his name on the chalkboard.
12. (b) Mary **jumped** on her bed.
13. (a) Akshay **plays** violin in his room.
14. (c) Carla **will sing** in the school today.
15. (c) **Will it have stopped** raining by tomorrow morning?
16. (a) I **sang** a song at the concert yesterday.
17. (b) He **will write** a letter to his girlfriend tomorrow.
18. (c) I **will go** to the library to borrow some books this weekend.
19. (a) I **saw** a movie yesterday.
20. (a) I **will eat** lunch in one hour.
21. (c)
22. (d)
23. (a)
24. (d)
25. (b) to fly
26. (a) will
27. (c) climbed
28. (b) every evening
29. (a) discuss
30. (a) play

LEVEL-2

1. (b)
2. (a) The statement A is correct. Statement B should be- As soon as I got home, I did my laundry.
3. (b) 'Ing' as a suffix can also be used in the future tense.

Solutions (4 to 8):

				1. S	2. W	E	P	T		
					R					
					A					
			3. R	E	P	A	I	4. R	E	D
					P			E		
					E			A		
5. J	U	M	P	E	D			D		

4. (a) The floor was swept clean.
5. (b) Macy wrapped the gift with a beautiful bow.
6. (c) Peter repaired the race cars before every competition.
7. (a) Yesterday, Mia read a novel.
8. (d) Susan jumped high in the air.
9. (a)
10. (a) Billy **is doing** his homework now. We are going to watch a movie when he is finished.
11. (b) Dr. Mason is busy. He **is seeing** a patient right now. He will see you in twenty minutes.

12. (d) Andrea and Alejandro are taking a walk. The fresh air feels great.
13. (b) Right now, **I am buying** groceries. I need eggs, milk, and bread.
14. (d) We **are eating** dinner. It tastes good. Can you pass me the salt, please?
15. (c) My car **is moving** down the hill. I forgot to engage the parking break. Somebody please help me!
16. (b) It **had jumped** out of its cage just before we arrived at the zoo!
17. (c) When I arrived at the cinema, the film **had started**.
18. (b) We were late for the plane because **we had forgotten** our passports.
19. (a) The garden was dead because it **had been** dry all summer.
20. (d) What had been served for breakfast?
21. (c) Who had designed this building? It is extremely beautiful to look at.
22. (d) I too want to domesticate a dog. Where had you got your dog from?
23. (d) The baby's face is really dirty. Where had you left him?
24. (a) What time <u>**do the banks open**</u> in Britain?
25. (a) When **will you have read** my book?
26. (b) She **doesn't wake** up early on Sundays.
27. (a) I'm sorry, by next week, they **won't have written** the article.
28. (a) I **have seen** three police cars this morning.
29. (b) My grandparents only **knew** each other for a few months before they **got** married.
30. (b) I **haven't seen** the sea before.
31. (a) Don't you have
32. (b) so close to Panipat,
33. (c) Do we have
34. (c) No, thanks. I'm full.
35. (c) send
36. (c) I made some silly mistakes
37. (a) got punctured
38. (a) Sudden,
49. (a) The next fish
40. (d) as my
41. (c) been into
42. (b) was sowing
43. (d) mother regular.
44. (c) better Chinese food
45. (b) be wait

8 CHAPTER FOREWORD

Ever wondered, why we say an orange, a book or the sun ? We shall learn about articles in this chapter. Let's solve the exercise to check our understanding.

Directions : Complete the sentences using appropriate articles. If no article is needed write NA.

1. I bought ___________ pair of shoes.
2. He saw ___________ movie last night.
3. We are staying at ___________ hotel.
4. Rekha is ___________ famous actress.
5. Many people do not like ___________ Sushi.
6. We are ___________ Indians.
7. They live in ___________ apartment. ___________ apartment is new.
8. May I have ___________ piece of cake?
9. My teacher told ___________ amazing story today.
10. ___________ night is quiet. Let's take ___________ walk!

8 Chapter

Article

LEARNING OBJECTIVES

This lesson will help you to:—

- ❖ learn about different types of articles.
- ❖ correctly use the articles.

Real Life Example

An article is a kind of adjective which is always used with a noun and it gives some information about it. There are only two kinds of articles definite and indefinite articles. But they are used very often and are important for using English accurately.

QUICK CONCEPT REVIEW

An article is a word (or prefix or suffix) that is used with a noun to indicate the type of reference being made by the noun. Articles specify the grammatical definiteness of the noun, in some languages extending to volume or numerical scope. The articles in the English language are 'the' and 'a/an'.

In languages that employ articles, every common noun, with some exceptions, is expressed with a certain definiteness (e.g., definite or indefinite), just as many languages express every noun with a certain grammatical number (e.g., singular or plural). Every noun must be accompanied by the article, if any, corresponding to its definiteness and the lack of an article (considered a zero article) itself specifies certain definiteness.

Articles are usually characterized as either definite or indefinite.

DEFINITE ARTICLE

A definite article indicates that its noun is a particular one (or ones) identifiable to the listener. It may be something that the speaker has already mentioned, or it may be something uniquely specified.

The definite article in English, for both singular and plural nouns, is **'the'**.

For example:

The park close to my house is large.

RULES TO USE "THE"

1. When we speak about a particular thing or a restatement.

   For example: There is a garden next to my house. The garden has many swings.

2. When we speak about unique things.

   For example: The sun, the stars.

3. When we speak about:
   - **Rivers:** The Ganga, The Yamuna.
   - **Sea:** The Dead Sea, The Caspian Sea.
   - **Mountain Ranges:** The Himalayas, The Andes.
   - **Group of islands:** The Andaman Nicobar islands, The Lakshadeep Islands.
   - **Oceans:** The Pacific Ocean.
   - Countries which have united, republic or kingdom in their names- The USSR, The UK.
4. When there is superlative degree- This is the best we can do.
5. When ordinal numbers are used- The fourth chapter.
6. With musical instruments- the guitar, the flute.
7. When we speak about religious books- The Ramayana, The Quran.
8. When we speak about historical monuments- The Taj Mahal.
9. With newspapers- The Times of India.
10. When we speak about a system or service-
    - How long does it take on the train?
    - I heard it on the radio.

INDEFINITE ARTICLE

An indefinite article indicates that its noun is not. particular one (or ones) identifiable to the listener. **'a'** and **'an'** are indefinite articles

The choice of putting a/an depends on the sound of the vowel.

We put 'a' with the nouns which have a consonant sound at the beginning.

A one rupee note. (since the sound is 'V' when we are saying one, A University. (since the sound is Y)

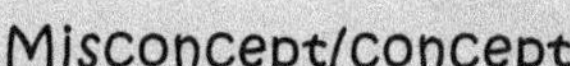

Misconcept: We use article an with vowels.

Concept: The choice between a/ an depends on the sound of the vowel and not the letter we can see. Words like useful, one, European begin with a vowel but instead of the article an, we use the article a before them as they do not begin with a vowel sound. So we say, a useful book, a one rupee note and a European tourist.

We put 'an' with the nouns when the initial sound is that of vowels-a,e,i,o,u.

We use Indefinite article when

1. We use the indefinite article, a/an, with count nouns when the hearer/reader does not know exactly which one we are referring to:

   For example: There is a girl standing there.
2. We use a/an to say what someone is or what job they do:

   For example: My sister is a doctor.
3. We use a/an with a singular noun to say something about all things of that kind:

   For example: A man needs friends. (= All men need friends)
4. We put 'a' with year.

ZERO ARTICLE

The zero article is the absence of an article. In languages having a definite article, the lack of an article specifically indicates that the noun is indefinite. Linguists interested in X-bar theory causally link zero articles to nouns lacking a determiner. In English, the zero article rather than the indefinite is used with plurals and mass nouns, although the word "some" can be used as an indefinite plural article. Eg Visitors end up walking in mud.

RULES

Omission of Articles

1. Do not use any article before the names of countries, person, months and specific places.

   For example:

   Japan, Saleem, Gandhiji, Anna Salai, March, Friday, Christmas.
2. Do not use any article before the names of metals.
   For example:

   Iron and coal are found in England. Gold is very costly.
3. Do not use any article before the names of languages.
   For example:
   - Hindi is a difficult language.
   - We are studying Arabic.
4. Do not use any article before the abstract nouns.
   For example:
   - Truth prevails.
   - Knowledge is power.
   - Love is God.

- Honesty is the best policy.
- Poverty is the worst crisis.
- Wisdom will win.
- Absence is not tolerated.
- Strength never fails.
- Wisdom is the gift of heaven.
- Cleanliness is next to Godliness.

5. Do not use any article before the names of games.

   For example:

   - I play tennis.
   - They play football.
   - Baseball is famous in USA.
   - Chess is played by intelligent people.

6. Do not use any article before the names of relatives.

   For example:

   - Father has gone out.
   - Aunt wants you to see her.
   - Mother is the symbol of love.
   - Sister means affection.

7. We don't use any article before names of continents and countries.

   For example:

   Asia, Norway, Sri Lanka

8. When we want to mention the buildings which are for school, hospital, court, church, prison, market, etc., we use as well as omit <u>the</u>.

   For example:

   - The injured man was taken to hospital.
   - The Minister visited the hospital.
   - The murderer was sent to prison.
   - The Wall of the prison must be very high.

9. Do not use any article before the names of foods and festivals.

   For example:

   - Breakfast is at eight o'clock.
   - He takes sugar with his tea.
   - We celebrate Holi in the month of March.

Note : We use the, before the names of countries or States which include words like republic, union, kingdom, states . **Example:** The United Kingdom, The United States of America

Play time

A game you can play to master articles! Write 20 different nouns or adjective-noun pairs beginning with vowels and consonants on separate chits of paper. The chits are shuffled and thrown in the centre. Each player picks up a chit and says the word aloud along with the article that should go with it.

Points are scored on the basis of right answers and the time taken to say the word which should not be more than 3 seconds. The words can be cock, blanket, engine, old story, haunted house, best speaker, moon, earth, duck, Bible, year, sweetest fruit, etc.

Multiple Choice Questions

LEVEL-1

Directions (Qs. 1 to 21): Choose the correct option.

1. I want ______ apple from that basket. [2011]
   (a) a (b) an (c) the (d) none
2. The church on _______ corner is progressive.
   (a) a (b) an (c) the (d) none
3. Miss Lin speaks _______ Chinese.
   (a) a (b) an (c) the (d) none
4. I borrowed _____ pencil from your pile of pencils and pens. [2012]
   (a) a (b) an (c) the (d) none
5. One of ______ students said, "The professor is late today."
   (a) a (b) an (c) the (d) none
6. Eli likes to play _______volleyball.
   (a) a (b) an (c) the (d) none
7. I bought ______ umbrella to go out in the rain. [2013]
   (a) a (b) an (c) the (d) none
8. My daughter is learning to play_______ violin at her school.
   (a) a (b) an (c) the (d) none
9. Please give me _____ cake that is on the counter.
   (a) a (b) an (c) the (d) none
10. I lived on ______ Main Street when I first came to town. [2015]
    (a) a (b) an (c) the (d) none
11. Albany is the capital of ________New York State.
    (a) a (b) an (c) the (d) none
12. My husband's family speaks _______Polish.
    (a) a (b) an (c) the (d) none
13. An apple _____ day keeps the doctor away. [2017]
    (a) a (b) an (c) the (d) none
14. _____ ink in my pen is red.
    (a) a (b) an (c) the (d) none
15. Our neighbours have _____ cat and a dog.
    (a) a (b) an (c) the (d) none

16. Choose the correct answer from the given options.
Ravi and Mohan live in ________ village. **[2018]**

(a) a (b) an (c) the (d) none

17. This is ________ book I read yesterday. **[2018]**

(a) a (b) the (c) an (d) none

18. Shan is late by ________ hour today. **[2018]**

(a) a (b) an (c) the (d) none

19. Jacob takes _______ shower every morning. **[2021]**

(a) a (b) an (c) the (d) no article

20. John's grandfather is ________ European citizen. **[2022]**

(a) a (b) an (c) the (d) no article

21. Fill in the blank with an appropriate article.
There is ______ university in my city. **[2022]**

(a) a (b) an (c) the (d) None of these

LEVEL-2

Directions (Qs. 1 and 2): Choose the correct article for the following tables.

1.

______________	bingo game
______________	historian
______________	opera
______________	honourable discharge

(a) a, an, a, an (b) a, a, an, an (c) a, an, an, a (d) an, a, a, an

2.

______________	up stairway
______________	usual feeling
______________	paper clip
______________	early bird

(a) an, a, an, a (b) a, an, an, a (c) a, a, an, an (d) an, a, a, an

Directions (Qs. 3 to 5): Choose the correct statement from following sets of statements.

3. **Statement A** : I like the blue T-shirt over there better than the red one.

Statement B : Where is a book I lent you last week?

Statement C : Their car does 150 miles an hour.

Statement D : Do you still live in the Bristol?

(a) A and B are correct. (b) B and D are correct.

(c) C and D are correct. (d) A and C are correct.

4. **Statement A** : The tomatoes are 99 pence kilo. **[2014]**

Statement B : Is your mother working in an old office building?

Statement C : What do you usually have for the breakfast?

Statement D : Carol's father works as an electrician.

(a) A and B are correct. (b) B and D are correct.

(c) C and D are correct. (d) A and C are correct.

5. **Statement A** : Ben has a terrible headache.

Statement B : After this tour you have the whole afternoon free to explore the city.

Statement C : My grandmother likes the flowers very much.

Statement D : I love flowers in your garden.

(a) A and B are correct. (b) B and D are correct.

(c) C and D are correct. (d) A and C are correct.

Directions (Qs. 6 to 11): Read the following passage and fill in the blanks.

I have ____(6)____ horse of my own. I call her pretty girl. She is ____(7)____ intelligent animal, but she is not ____(8)____thoroughbred horse. I could never enter her in ____(9)____ race, even if I wanted to. But I do not want to. She is ____(10)____companion, for my own pleasure. I took her swimming ____(11)____day or two ago.

6. (a) a (b) an (c) the (d) no article

7. (a) a (b) an (c) the (d) no article

8. (a) a (b) an (c) the (d) no article

9. (a) a (b) an (c) the (d) no article

10. (a) a (b) an (c) the (d) no article

11. (a) a (b) an (c) the (d) no article

Directions (Qs. 12 to 14): Read the following sets of sentences and mark the correct option.

12. **(A) See you on Wednesday.**

(B) I always listen to the radio in the morning.

(a) TT (b) TF (c) FT (d) FF

13. **(A) Alex goes to work by x bus.**

(B) Don't be late for the school.

(a) TT (b) TF (c) FT (d) FF

14. **(A) Listen! Dennis is playing a trumpet.**

(B) We often see our cousins over (no article) Easter.

(a) TT (b) TF (c) FT (d) FF

15. Match the following:

	List I		List II
A.	We have a	1.	cinema.
B.	Is fencing a popular sport	2.	beautiful garden which is full of roses.
C.	Can you give me an	3.	in the world? No, it isn't.
D.	They're at the	4.	envelope, please?

	A	B	C	D
(a)	1	2	3	4
(b)	2	3	4	1
(c)	3	4	1	2
(d)	4	3	1	2

Directions (Qs. 16 to 25): Choose the correct answer from the given options.

16. Please wait for ________ hour for the test results.

(a) a (b) an (c) the (d) none

17. India is the second most populous country in ________ world. **[2016]**

(a) a (b) an (c) the (d) none

18. Amit is ________ M.B.A. from Rajdhani University.

(a) a (b) an (c) the (d) none

19. Do you have ________ pen?

(a) a (b) an (c) the (d) none

20. Is this ________ pen given by Mr. Singh?

(a) a (b) an (c) the (d) none

21. How do I go to ________ Lajpat Nagar?

(a) a (b) an (c) the (d) none

22. Mr. Reddy is wearing ________ blue shirt.

(a) a (b) an (c) the (d) none

23. This is ________ unique coin. **[2017]**

(a) a (b) an (c) the (d) none

24. I saw ________ elephant on the road today.

(a) a (b) an (c) the (d) none

25. The headmaster was talking to ________ parents.

(a) a (b) an (c) the (d) none

RESPONSE GRID

LEVEL 1

1. a b c d	2. a b c d	3. a b c d	4. a b c d	5. a b c d
6. a b c d	7. a b c d	8. a b c d	9. a b c d	10. a b c d
11. a b c d	12. a b c d	13. a b c d	14. a b c d	15. a b c d
16. a b c d	17. a b c d	18. a b c d	19. a b c d	20. a b c d
21. a b c d				

LEVEL 2

1. a b c d	2. a b c d	3. a b c d	4. a b c d	5. a b c d
6. a b c d	7. a b c d	8. a b c d	9. a b c d	10. a b c d
11. a b c d	12. a b c d	13. a b c d	14. a b c d	15. a b c d
16. a b c d	17. a b c d	18. a b c d	19. a b c d	20. a b c d
21. a b c d	22. a b c d	23. a b c d	24. a b c d	25. a b c d

Solutions with Explanation

LEVEL-1

1. (b) 2. (c) 3. (d) 4. (a) 5. (c) 6. (d) 7. (b) 8. (c) 9. (c) 10. (d)

11. (d) 12. (d) 13. (a) 14. (c) 15. (a) 16. (a) 17. (b) 18. (b)

19. (a) a **20. (b)** an **21. (a)**

LEVEL-2

1. (b) 2. (d)

3. (d) B. Where is the book I lent you last week?

D. Do you still live in (no article) Bristol?

4. (b) A. The tomatoes are 99 pence a kilo.

C. What do you usually have for (no article) breakfast?

5. **(a)** C. My grandmother likes (no article) flowers very much.

D. I love the flowers in your garden.

6. **(a)** **7.** **(b)** **8.** **(a)** **9.** **(a)**

10. **(a)** **11.** **(a)** **12.** **(a)**

13. **(b)** Don't be late for (no article) school.

14. **(c)** Listen! Dennis is playing the trumpet.

15. **(b)** **16.** **(b)** **17.** **(c)** **18.** **(b)**

19. **(a)** **20.** **(c)** **21.** **(d)** **22.** **(a)**

23. **(c)** **24.** **(b)** **25.** **(c)**

9 CHAPTER FOREWORD

The words we use to describe people, things, emotions etc. are all adjectives. In this chapter, we shall learn about adjectives.

Let's begin by solving the excercise given.

Directions: Underline the adjectives and circle the noun it describes, in the following sentences.

1. He wrote an amazing play.
2. I will have a red apple and some milk for breakfast.
3. Who broke that window?
4. Whose coat are you wearing?
5. They cleaned their house before winter.
6. My father bought a new computer.
7. Both the sisters are going to Australia.
8. Give me a few pennies.
9. This short story has a happy ending.
10. The peon gave you his file.

Chapter 9

Adjective

LEARNING OBJECTIVES

This lesson will help you to:—

- learn about adjectives.
- understand the degrees of adjectives.

QUICK CONCEPT REVIEW

An adjective is a describing word. It describes a noun or pronoun and is placed before it.

Example: A tall boy, a fat lady.

Can you figure out the adjective in the sentence below?

Mr. Gupta is a kind man.

What describes Mr. Gupta?

He is kind. So, 'kind' is an adjective.

KINDS OF ADJECTIVES

1. **Adjective of quality:** It denotes a particular kind of noun. It asks the question-'of what kind' from the noun it describes.

   Example: a brave lady. (What kind of lady? A brave lady).

2. **Adjective of quantity**: It describes the degree or quantity of a noun. It asks the question-'how much' from the noun it describes.

   Example: There is some tea left. (How much tea is left? Some tea).

3. **Adjective of number**: It shows exact number of a noun or pronoun. It asks the question- 'how many' from the noun it describes. There are five boys standing. (How many boys? Five).

   All cardinals (1, 2, 3,....) and ordinals (first, second, third....) come in this category.

Poem on Adjective

On my way to the zoo I saw a bear.
It was a brown bear.
It was an ugly brown bear
It was a wild, ugly, brown bear
It was an angry, wild, ugly, brown bear
It was a hungry, angry, wild, ugly, brown bear
It was an escaped, hungry, angry, wild, ugly, brown bear
And it wanted to eat me!

Amazing Facts

- Some adjectives that start with **aq** .
- Aquatic: means living or growing in, on, or near the water.
- Aqueous: means something relating to or similar to, or dissolved in water.
- The cards have been paired. The student who collects the most cards wins the game.

4. **Demonstrative adjective**: They point out. This, that, these, those are demonstrative adjectives.

   Example: This man, that book, these pens, those kites.
5. **Possessive adjective:** It shows possession.

   Example: My dress, his father, their house.
6. **Interrogative adjective:** It is used to ask question.

   Example: Whose book is this? Which car did you buy? What colour is his balloon?

Important Tip

An interrogative adjective is followed by a noun while an interrogative pronoun stands as an independent subject, as:

Whose book is this? (Interrogative adjective)

Whose is this book? (Interrogative pronoun)

DEGREES OF COMPARISON

There are three degrees of comparison:

1. **Positive degree**: The adjective in its first form is called as positive degree. This means it is not compared with anything or anyone. Example- Raghu is a tall boy.
2. **Comparative degree:** When two things are compared. Example- Sanjeev is taller than Ramesh.
3. **Superlative degree:** When more than two things are compared. Example- He is the tallest boy in the class.

Rules to form degree of adjectives:

1. When adjective is a mono syllabic word we add 'er' to change it into comparative and 'est' to change into superlative degree.

   Example: tall-taller-tallest

   P C S
2. When adjective ends with 'e', we add 'r' to change it into comparative and 'st' to change into superlative degree.

   Example: brave-braver-bravest

   P C S
3. When adjective ends with 'y', we first change 'y' into 'I' and then we add 'er' to change it into comparative and 'est' to change into superlative degree.

Example: easy-easier-easiest

P C S

4. When adjective ends with a consonant and has a vowel before it, the consonant gets doubled then we add 'er' to change it into comparative and 'est' to change into superlative degree.

   Example: red-redder-reddest

   P C S

5. When adjective is a bi syllabic word (that means we can break it into parts-eg-beautiful= beauty+ ful) we add 'more' to change it into comparative and 'most to change into superlative degree.

   Example: beautiful-more beautiful-most beautiful

   P C S

Points to Remember

In comparative degree, use 'than' after the comparative form of the adjective.

Use 'the' before the superlative forms of adjectives.

We do not compare few adjectives like- perfect, square, round, eternal, unique.

ORDER OF ADJECTIVES

When describing something, we need to follow an order.

Below is the list to be used in sequence.

- Opinion
- Size
- Age
- Shape
- Colour
- Origin
- Material
- Purpose

For example:

- That is a nice little old white brick house.
- I have always wanted an expensive Italian sports car.

Multiple Choice Questions

LEVEL-1

Directions (Qs. 1 to 10): Choose the correct adjectives.

1. **Please, can I have a clean plate? This one is very _____.**
   (a) bad (b) dirty (c) ugly (d) dark
2. **Please put the light on. It's very _____ in here.** **[2013]**
   (a) weak (b) bad (c) thin (d) dark
3. **I need some new shoes. These ones are really ___.**
   (a) full (b) weak (c) old (d) sad
4. **I couldn't eat anything more. I was completely _____.**
   (a) full (b) empty (c) thin (d) strong
5. **I don't like that photo. It looks really _____.**
   (a) closed (b) ugly (c) difficult (d) open
6. **I'm quite heavy now, but when I was younger I was very _____.** **[2014]**
   (a) thin (b) short (c) small (d) high
7. **Don't sit on the grass. It's still ___ because it was raining earlier today.**
   (a) wet (b) low (c) dry (d) light
8. **It's a very ___ story. It made me cry when I read it.**
   (a) clean (b) bad (c) sad (d) weak
9. **It's not _____ to remember all the new words when you are learning a language.**
   (a) slow (b) easy (c) empty (d) light **[2015]**
10. **In my country, a few people are very rich, but many people are _____.**
    (a) poor (b) weak (c) low (d) fast

Directions (Qs. 11 to 15) : Find out the adjectives from the options given below.

11. (a) Beauty (b) Beautiful (c) Beautician (d) Beautify
12. (a) Brave (b) Bravery (c) Braveness (d) Bravely
13. (a) Wonder (b) Wonderful (c) Wonderfully (d) Wonderfulness
14. (a) Calmness (b) Calmy (c) Calm (d) none of these
15. (a) Care (b) Carelessly (c) Carefully (d) Careful
16. **My project will sink or swim depending on how well I present it in ________ coming class tomorrow.** **[2019]**
    (a) Big (b) farther (c) high (d) next
17. **I saw many ________________ animals at the zoo** **[2019]**
    (a) some (b) Strangely (c) Stranger (d) Strange

18. I put up a really __________ tent for my brother and it will probably blow down if there is any wind. [2019]

(a) aching (b) dramatic (c) flimsy (d) backward

19. Do you know of ________ clubs in the school that I could join? [2020]

(a) every (b) many (c) any (d) a little

20. Ajay's _______ nature made him very unpopular. [2021]

(a) mature (b) kind (c) arrogant (d) calm

21. My uncle donates money to this <u>charity</u> every month. [2022]

(a) Noun (b) Pronoun (c) Verb (d) Adjective

22. Dustin : Have you ________ to school today? [2022]

Jane: Yes, I have.

(a) go (b) went (c) been (d) goes

23. Fill in the blank with the correct degree of adjective.

The Ganga is the ________ of all rivers. [2022]

(a) holy (b) holier (c) holiest (d) more holiest

LEVEL-2

Directions (Qs. 1 to 5): Choose the correct order of adjectives and complete the following sentences.

1. He was wearing a ________ shirt. [2014]

(a) dirty old flannel (b) flannel old dirty
(c) old dirty flannel (d) flannel dirty old

2. Pass me the ________ cups.

(a) plastic big blue (b) big blue plastic
(c) big plastic blue (d) plastic blue big

3. All the girls fell in love with the ________ teacher.

(a) handsome new American (b) American new handsome
(c) new handsome American (d) American handsome new

4. I used to drive ________ car.

(a) a blue old German (b) an old German blue
(c) an old blue German (d) old blue a German

5. He recently married a ________ woman.

(a) young beautiful Greek (b) beautiful young Greek
(c) beautiful Greek young (d) young Greek beautiful

6. This is a ________ movie. [2014]

(a) new Italian wonderful (b) wonderful Italian new
(c) wonderful new Italian (d) Italian new wonderful

7. **She is a ________ supermodel.**
   (a) beautiful slim Brazilian
   (b) Brazilian beautiful slim
   (c) slim Brazilian beautiful
   (d) Slim beautiful Brazilian

8. **It's in the ________ container.** **[2016]**
   (a) large blue metal
   (b) blue large metal
   (c) blue metal large
   (d) metal blue large

9. **He sat behind a ________ desk.**
   (a) big wooden brown
   (b) big brown wooden
   (c) wooden big brown
   (d) brown big wooden

10. **She gave him a ________ vase.**
   (a) small Egyptian black
   (b) black Egyptian small
   (c) small black Egyptian
   (d) Egyptian black small

Directions (Qs. 11 to 13): Match the following List I with List II.

11.

	List I		List II
A.	This is a nice cat.	1.	but father gave me an even better one last weekend.
B.	Here is Emily. She's six years old.	2.	Bungee jumping is more dangerous than skateboarding.
C.	In the last holidays I read a good book,	3.	Her brother is nine, so he is older.
D.	Skateboarding is a dangerous hobby.	4.	It's much nicer than my friend's cat.

	A	B	C	D
(a)	1	2	3	4
(b)	2	3	4	1
(c)	3	4	1	2
(d)	4	3	1	2

12.

	List I		List II
A.	This is a difficult exercise. But the exercise with an asterisk (*)	1.	grandparents' house is even smaller than ours.
B.	This magazine is cheap	2.	This joke was the funniest joke I've ever heard.
C.	We live in a small house, but my	3.	is the most difficult exercise on the worksheet.
D.	Yesterday John told me a funny joke.	4.	but that one is cheaper.

	A	B	C	D
(a)	1	2	3	4
(b)	2	3	4	1
(c)	3	4	1	2
(d)	4	3	1	2

13.

List I		List II	
A.	My father is heavy.	1.	but his sister is more successful than Stan.
B.	The test in Geography was easy,	2.	My uncle is much heavier than my father.
C.	Florida is sunny.	3.	but the test in Biology was easier.
D.	Stan is a successful sportsman	4.	Do you know the sunniest place in the USA?

	A	B	C	D
(a)	1	2	3	4
(b)	2	3	4	1
(c)	3	4	1	2
(d)	4	3	1	2

Directions (Qs. 14 to 16): Choose the correct statements.

14. **Statement A:** We saw many animals at the zoo.
Statement B: The old man hasn't got many hairs on his head.
Statement C: There isn't much sugar in my coffee.
Statement D: How much oranges did you put in the box?
(a) A and B are correct. (b) B and D are correct.
(c) C and D are correct. (d) A and C are correct.

15. **Statement A:** Can you please buy a few apples?
Statement B: We need a little water.
Statement C: I take a few sugar with my coffee.
Statement D: I have a few money left.
(a) A and B are correct. (b) B and D are correct.
(c) C and D are correct. (d) A and C are correct.

16. **Statement A:** I don't know some of them.
Statement B: She has some money.
Statement C: I know any of them.
Statement D: Do you know any of these singers?
(a) A and B are correct (b) B and D are correct
(c) C and D are correct (d) A and C are correct

Directions (Qs. 17 and 18): Fill the table with correct options.

17.

My mother has a soft voice,	but my teacher's voice is ______ than my mother's.
I live in a large family,	but my grandfather lived in a ______ family.
We have only little time for this exercise,	but in the examination we'll have even ______ time.
Lucy is clever,	but Carol is ______ than Lucy.

(a) less, larger, cleverer, softer
(b) larger, softer, less, cleverer
(c) softer, larger, less, cleverer
(d) softer, less, cleverer, larger

18.

He is a ________	charming doctor.
I plan on wearing my ________	black coat.
This is a well _______	French painting from the 18th century.
She was wearing a ________	green dress.

(a) young, long, known, beautiful
(b) known, long, young, beautiful
(c) long, young, beautiful, known
(d) young, known, long, beautiful

Directions (Qs. 19 and 20): Choose the correct option with true/false.

19. A. I have little interest in classical music.

B. We need less furniture in this dance hall than in the big one.

(a) TT (b) TF (c) FT (d) FF

20. A. She dedicates little time to her homework than to her hobbies.

B. This will take little time to finish than the last time we tried.

(a) TT (b) TF (c) FT (d) FF

Directions (Qs. 21 to 30): Read the paragraph and answer the following questions.

People often have decided where they wanted to live based on the natural resources that were available in the area. Natural resources are things that are useful to people and come from the earth. Materials for building shelter are natural resources. So are food sources such as fruits and vegetables, animals that could be caught or hunted and water.

A region's climate and landforms let certain things grow in different areas. They also determine which organisms will be able to survive there. Regions with very rich soil make good farming communities. Poor soil may send farmers looking for better conditions. However, areas with poor soil may attract those who have other purposes for the land. Poor soil doesn't matter if you want to build a factory or if the land has grass for ranching.

Each area attracts people based on their interests and purposes. Areas that support many different interests will naturally have larger populations. While you may not think of the mountains, lakes, or oceans as natural resources, they are. Villages and cities built near water sources have been the most successful. People who want to catch fish for a living can do that by the ocean, but cannot in the desert. People living near water can use it to meet their daily needs. Water can also be used to transport goods to other areas to be sold.

Places that are difficult to reach will naturally have fewer people living in them. Places that are high on mountain tops are not very desirable to some people. Neither are places that are In the middle of hot, dry deserts.

For too long, humans have destroyed resources. We have been using up those that cannot be easily replaced. Renewable resources are those that can be replaced easily. We are fortunate to have many resources that are renewable, such as sun, wind, water and trees. We need to focus more on using renewable resources. This will protect our planet from further harm.

Find out the Synonyms of the following adjectives.

21. USEFUL
(a) useless (b) wonderful (c) helpful (d) harmless

22. NATURAL
(a) unusual (b) normal (c) artificial (d) delicate

23. POOR **[2017]**
(a) pity (b) charity (c) needful (d) rich

24. DIFFERENT
(a) similar (b) separate (c) diverse (d) satisfy

25. LARGER
(a) huge (b) tiny (c) smaller (d) better

26. SUCCESSFUL
(a) failure (b) honesty (c) wisdom (d) victorious

27. DIFFICULT
(a) complex (b) easy (c) sharp (d) blunt

28. DESIRABLE **[2015]**
(a) disgrace (b) ancient (c) modern (d) popular

29. FORTUNATE
(a) unlucky (b) lucky (c) sorrow (d) famous

30. RENEWABLE **[2016]**
(a) remodel (b) repeat (c) retract (d) renown

Directions (Qs. 31 to 40): Find out the Antonyms of the following Adjectives.

31. CAUTIOUS
(a) careless (b) prevent (c) reckless (d) alert

32. BIGGEST **[2014]**
(a) large (b) smallest (c) widest (d) largest

33. SAFE
(a) dangerous (b) secure (c) harmless (d) protected

34. **EASY**

(a) simple (b) effortless (c) difficult (d) fine

35. **OPTIMISTIC** **[2016]**

(a) hopeful (b) confident (c) positive (d) pessimistic

36. **ANXIOUS**

(a) relaxed (b) nervous (c) uneasy (d) careful

37. **SURPRISING**

(a) astonishing (b) predictable (c) amazing (d) shocking

38. **IMPOVERISHED** **[2017]**

(a) wealthy (b) healthy (c) poverty (d) wisdom

39. **FASCINATING**

(a) charming (b) dull (c) attractive (d) interesting

40. **GENEROUS**

(a) kind (b) liberal (c) selfish (d) charitable

Directions (Qs 41 to 45) : Identify the adjectives from the given sentence.

41. **Jupiter is the largest planet in the solar system.**

(a) Jupiter (b) the (c) largest (d) planet

42. **You are very smart.**

(a) You (b) are (c) very smart (d) none

43. **I was very lucky to get a place in the team.**

(a) was (b) very lucky (c) get (d) place

44. **Have you met any actor?**

(a) Have (b) you (c) met (d) any

45. **There is no sugar in the coffee.**

(a) no (b) sugar (c) in (d) coffee

46. **You start the engine of a car by turning _______ key.** **[2020]**

(a) an (b) some (c) the (d) all

47. **Even today many people are guided by _________ moral values.** **[2020]**

(a) superficially (b) abstruse

(c) probation (d) religiously

48. This is the _______ movie I have ever seen. **[2022]**

(a) tame (b) good

(c) best (d) worse

RESPONSE GRID

LEVEL 1

1. a b c d 2. a b c d 3. a b c d 4. a b c d 5. a b c d
6. a b c d 7. a b c d 8. a b c d 9. a b c d 10. a b c d
11. a b c d 12. a b c d 13. a b c d 14. a b c d 15. a b c d
16. a b c d 17. a b c d 18. a b c d 19. a b c d 20. a b c d
21. a b c d 22. a b c d 23. a b c d

LEVEL 2

1. a b c d 2. a b c d 3. a b c d 4. a b c d 5. a b c d
6. a b c d 7. a b c d 8. a b c d 9. a b c d 10. a b c d
11. a b c d 12. a b c d 13. a b c d 14. a b c d 15. a b c d
16. a b c d 17. a b c d 18. a b c d 19. a b c d 20. a b c d
21. a b c d 22. a b c d 23. a b c d 24. a b c d 25. a b c d
26. a b c d 27. a b c d 28. a b c d 29. a b c d 30. a b c d
31. a b c d 32. a b c d 33. a b c d 34. a b c d 35. a b c d
36. a b c d 37. a b c d 38. a b c d 39. a b c d 40. a b c d
41. a b c d 42. a b c d 43. a b c d 44. a b c d 45. a b c d
46. a b c d 47. a b c d 48. a b c d

Solutions with Explanation

LEVEL-1

1. (b) **2. (d)** **3. (c)** **4. (a)** **5. (b)** **6. (a)**

7. (a) **8. (c)** **9. (b)** **10. (a)** **11. (b)** **12. (a)**

13. (b) **14. (c)** **15. (d)** **16. (d)** next **17. (d)** **18. (c)**

19. (c) any **20. (c)** arrogant

21. (a) Noun **22. (b)** went **23. (c)**

LEVEL-2

1. (a)	2. (b)	3. (a)	4. (c)	5. (b)	6. (c)
7. (a)	8. (a)	9. (b)	10. (c)	11. (d)	12. (c)

13. (b)

14. (d) B. The old man hasn't got much hair on his head.

D. How many oranges did you put in the box?

15. (a) C. I take a little sugar with my coffee.

D. I have a little money left.

16. (b) A. I don't know any of them.

C. I know some of them.

17. (c) 18. (a) 19. (a)

20. (d) A. She dedicates less time to her homework than to her hobbies.

B. This will take less time to finish than the last time we tried.

21. (c)	22. (b)	23. (c)	24. (c)	25. (a)	26. (d)
27. (a)	28. (d)	29. (b)	30. (a)	31. (c)	32. (b)
33. (a)	34. (c)	35. (d)	36. (a)	37. (b)	38. (a)
39. (b)	40. (c)	41. (c)	42. (c)	43. (c)	44. (d)

45. (a) 46. (c) the

47. (b) abstruse

48. (c) best

10 CHAPTER FOREWORD

We use addition to add numbers. How do we add words or sentences?

We use conjunctions. Lets learn more about them.

since | for | yet | and | but | until | because | however

Directions : Complete the paragraph using conjunction.

Pooja has a Judo match tomorrow ______________ she is tensed. She has been practising very hard ______________ the past 6 months. Her mother is trying to calm her ______________ she is not listening. Her mother advised her not to worry ______________ take a nap. She didn't finish her lunch too ______________ she was thinking about the match. Pooja is worried ______________ she was not well ______________ the past few days. Her brother ______________ father are also trying to calm her. Her father advised her to practise meditation ______________ not to think too much. Her brother went to the market to buy chocolates for her ______________ the shop was closed.

Chapter 10

Conjunction

LEARNING OBJECTIVES

This lesson will help you to:—

- understand conjunctions.
- learn to use conjunctions.

QUICK CONCEPT REVIEW

What is Conjunction?

- A conjunction is a word used to connect.
  - words, phrases or clauses within sentences
  - one sentence to another sentences
- It is also known as a connector.
- It is a part of speech.

You must have heard the poem Jack and Jill.

Let us recall:

"Jack and Jill went up the hill
To fetch a pail of water
Jack fell down and broke his crown
And Jill came tumbling after".

You can observe that there is a word which joins the words Jack-Jill. It also connects two actions or ideas→ Jack fell down and broke his crown.

This is the work of a conjunction.

A conjunction is a word that is used to combine or join sentences,words or group of words.

For example :

Meeta has a red, green, blue and purple skirt.

Here, the conjunction and joins all related words.

And, but, or and **so** are the most common conjunctions.

Let us see some more examples:

- The teacher might select Aman or Mohit for the play. Here, the conjunction or suggests a choice.
- My mother loves dogs but she dislikes cats. Here, the conjunction but joins two different ideas.

Conjunctions like so, unless and because indicate cause and effect.

There are some conjunctions that always come in pairs to join sentences.

Either... or → when we need to make a choice between two things.

Neither.... nor → when we need to make a choice between two things and it means none of the two.

Both...and → it is used to join the same word- forms.

When two sentences have the same subject, you can combine the predicates with the word *and.*

For example:

- The bird flew over my head.
- The bird landed on the roof.

This can be written as:

The bird flew over my head and landed on the roof.

For example: → He visited not only Agra but also Delhi.

Here's a fun way to remember conjunctions.

For example:

- She came to my house and baked a cake with me.
- My cat is hungry because I forgot to feed her.
- I told her to rewrite her work but she refused.
- Mother asked me to clean the room or she will punish me.

THE COORDINATING CONJUCTIONS

> **Point to Remember**
> Use a plural verb if two singular nouns are joined by 'and'.

COORDINATING CONJUNCTIONS

Coordinating conjunctions are conjunctions that join sentence elements that are the same. They can join words, phrases, and clauses.

For example:

- Cookies and milk
- into the house and out of the door
- He came and she left.

List of coordinating conjunctions- For, And, Nor, But, Or, Yet, So

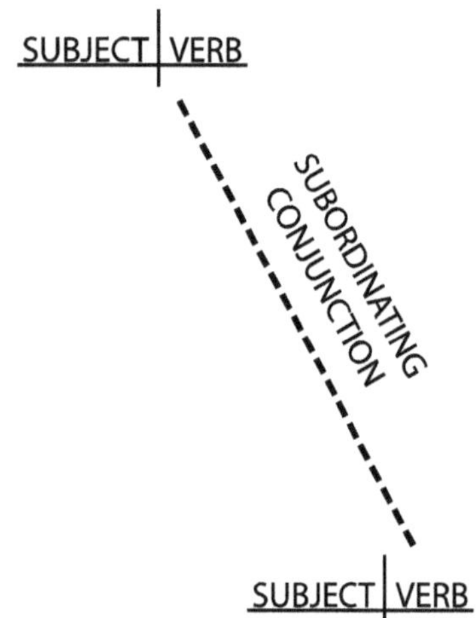

SUBORDINATING CONJUNCTIONS

Subordinating conjunctions are conjunctions that join dependent clauses to independent clauses.

For example: I will eat broccoli after I eat this cookie.

There are many subordinating conjunctions, so keep in mind that this list does not include all of them!

List of subordinating conjunctions

Because, Unless, When, Where, Why, Wherever, Who, That, How, Since, Whether, Unless, Until, As, If, As if, While, Before, After, Although, Provided that, As long as, As though, In order that, So that, Than, Though, Whenever

Multiple Choice Questions

LEVEL-1

Directions (Qs. 1 to 4): Tick the word which is not a conjunction.

1. (a) but (b) When (c) Yes (d) Yet
2. (a) If (b) Before (c) That (d) Unless **[2014]**
3. (a) Either...or (b) Neither...nor (c) Between (d) Both...and
4. (a) Some (b) Till (c) Until (d) Than

Directions (Qs. 5 to 8): Tick the odd pair.

5. (a) This and that (b) Day and night
   (c) Girl and boy (d) Pots and spoons
6. (a) Salt and pepper (b) Soft and silky **[2015]**
   (c) These and those (d) Trousers and socks
7. (a) Hot and cold (b) Winter and summer
   (c) Fat and smart (d) Socks and shoes
8. (a) Mother and father (b) Bread and pickles **[2016]**
   (c) Uncle and aunt (d) Cup and saucer

Directions (Qs. 9 to 14): Tick the most suitable conjunction to complete the sentence.

9. **Meera prefers water ______________ soft drinks.**
   (a) so (b) to (c) if (d) and
10. **You can sit ______________ stand.** **[2013]**
    (a) and (b) or (c) but (d) so
11. **She hugged ______________ her mom ______________ dad.**
    (a) whether...or (b) both...and (c) either...or (d) neither...nor
12. **Put on ______________ your jacket ______________ your coat.** **[2017]**
    (a) whether...or (b) both...and (c) either...or (d) neither...nor
13. **I skipped lunch, ______________ I was unwell.**
    (a) of (b) for (c) so (d) as
14. **It was hot, ______________ I carried a bottle of water.**
    (a) so (b) but (c) as (d) because

15. **Choose the right conjunction to join the sentence correctly.**

    I can fail ________ pass in this exam. **[2018]**

    (a) And (b) but (c) if (d) or

16. **Rohan was absent __________ he was not well.** **[2018]**

    (a) Because (b) if (c) that (d) until

17. **Find the conjunction from the words given below.** **[2019]**

    (a) between (b) slowly (c) or (d) at

18. **Find the conjunction from the words given below.** **[2019]**

    (a) House (b) nor (c) not (d) never

19. **We went to the market ________ shopped for eatables.** **[2021]**

    (a) but (b) yet

    (c) because (d) and

LEVEL-2

Directions (Qs. 1 to 4): Choose the correct option which joins the following pairs of sentences.

1. **I drew a picture. My brother coloured it.**

   (a) I drew a picture so my brother coloured it.

   (b) I drew a picture but my brother colured it.

   (c) I drew a picture and my brother coloured it.

   (d) I drew a picture or my brother coloured it.

2. **There was a table in the room. There were no chairs in the room.**

   (a) There was a table in the room and there were no chairs in the room.

   (b) There was a table in the room but there were no chairs in the room.

   (c) There was a table in the room as there were no chairs in the room.

   (d) There was neither a table nor a chair in the room.

3. **Tina wants to come back from the hostel. She is homesick.**

   (a) Tina wants to come back from the hostel because she is homesick.

   (b) Tina wants to come back from the hostel but she is home sick.

   (c) Tina wants to come back from the hostel so she is homesick.

   (d) Tina wants to come back from the hostel yet she is homesick.

4. **There is no milk. We cannot have tea.**
   - (a) There is no milk until we cannot have tea.
   - (b) There is no milk so we cannot have tea.
   - (c) There is no milk if we cannot have tea.
   - (d) There is no milk as we cannot have tea.

Directions (Qs. 5 to 8): Read the poem and fill up the blanks.

Binu tried to write a poem on her pet cat but she got confused while using conjunctions to join the words/group of words. Can you complete the poem for her?

I love little pussy,
Her coat is so warm,
___(5)___ I don't hurt her,
She 'll do me no harm.
___(6)___ I'll not pull her tail,
___(7)___ drive her away,
___(8)___ pussy and I,
Very gently will play.

5. (a) but (b) as (c) so (d) and
6. (a) but (b) so (c) or (d) and
7. (a) and (b) but (c) or (d) so
8. (a) but (b) and (c) or (d) so

Directions (Qs. 9 to 12): Spot the hidden conjunction in the right option.

9. (a) borulit (b) robulit (c) bulirot (d) bilotir
10. (a) pinasma (b) pinaams (c) paminsa (d) pimansa
11. (a) blandres (b) bnladnre (c) betralnd (d) berlatdn
12. (a) pothenry (b) pohtenry (c) photnery (d) ponhetry

Directions (Qs. 13 to 16): Choose the right conjunction to join the sentence correctly.

13. **I am not well _____ I can't come to work.**
    (a) because (b) as (c) so (d) or
14. **I can speak English _____ French.** **[2016]**
    (a) after (b) though (c) as well as (d) or
15. **I am glad ______ you like it.** **[2017]**
    (a) though (b) until (c) that (d) so
16. **You must hurry ________ you will miss the train.**
    (a) but (b) although (c) so (d) or

Directions (Qs. 17 to 20): Choose the right conjunction from the clue given below.

17. If you have two of something of the same kind you use this:

(a) that (b) for (c) so (d) and

18. When you have to make a choice between two you use this:

(a) then (b) if (c) or (d) but

19. When Ronnie has to give a reason to his teacher for being absent, he will use the conjunction

(a) until (b) because (c) unless (d) before

20. If you don't like pumpkin and bitter gourd, you will use the following conjunction to express yourself:

(a) either...or (b) neither....nor (c) or (d) whether....or

Directions (Qs. 21 to 23): Find the word which is a conjunction.

21. (a) yes (b) yet (c) never (d) your

22. (a) but (b) below (c) alter (d) some

23. (a) so (b) for (c) either (d) all of the above

Direction (Qs. 24 to 26): Read the sentences and choose the correct option.

24. A. I will come if you promise to drop me home. **[Tricky, 2014]**

B. I will come or you promise to drop me home.

C. I will come for you promise to drop me home.

D. I will come but you promise to drop me home.

(a) TTTF (b) TFFF (c) TTFF (d) FFTT

25. A. The house is small whether cozy.

B. The house is small unless cozy.

C. The house is small because cozy.

D. The house is small but cozy.

(a) FFFT (b) TTTF (c) FTFT (d) TFTF

26. A. We had to cancel the picnic but it was raining.

B. We had to cancel the picnic because it was raining.

C. We had to cancel the picnic unless it was raining.

D. We had to cancel the picnic or it was raining.

(a) TFTF (b) FTFT (c) FTFF (d) TFFF

27. I like it ________ my teacher uses coloured chalk on the blackboard. [2020]

(a) what (b) which (c) when (d) who

28. Would you like to come with us ________ stay at home? [2022]

(a) but (b) and (c) or (d) because

29. Which one of the following conjunctions joins the two given sentences correctly? [2022]

The teacher likes Prixit. He is sincere.

(a) The teacher likes Prixit, so he is sincere.

(b) The teacher likes Prixit because he is sincere.

(c) The teacher likes Prixit yet he is sincere.

(d) The teacher likes Prixit although he is sincere.

RESPONSE GRID

LEVEL 1

1. a b c d	2. a b c d	3. a b c d	4. a b c d	5. a b c d
6. a b c d	7. a b c d	8. a b c d	9. a b c d	10. a b c d
11. a b c d	12. a b c d	13. a b c d	14. a b c d	15. a b c d
16. a b c d	17. a b c d	18. a b c d	19. a b c d	

LEVEL 2

1. a b c d	2. a b c d	3. a b c d	4. a b c d	5. a b c d
6. a b c d	7. a b c d	8. a b c d	9. a b c d	10. a b c d
11. a b c d	12. a b c d	13. a b c d	14. a b c d	15. a b c d
16. a b c d	17. a b c d	18. a b c d	19. a b c d	20. a b c d
21. a b c d	22. a b c d	23. a b c d	24. a b c d	25. a b c d
26. a b c d	27. a b c d	28. a b c d	29. a b c d	

Solutions with Explanation

LEVEL-1

1. (c) 'Yes' is not a conjunction.
2. (b) 'before' is a preposition
3. (c) between; it's a preposition
4. (a) 'some' is a determiner
5. (d) pots and pans go together
6. (d) socks and shoes go together
7. (c) slim and smart go together
8. (b) bread and butter go together
9. (b) it shows comparison between water and soft drinks.
10. (b) it denotes choice
11. (b) both...and ; as it joins same word form
12. (c) expresses choice
13. (d) expresses reason
14. (a) as it expresses reason

15. (d) 16. (a) 17. (c)

18. (b) 19. (d) and

LEVEL-2

1. (c) joins two actions
2. (b) points to the contrast; tables but no chairs.
3. (a) expresses reason
4. (b) expresses effect
5. (b) reasons the action
6. (b) as it means therefore
7. (a) expresses choice
8. (a) expresses contrast between the two sentences
9. (a) contains OR
10. (a) contains AS
11. (a) contains AND

12. **(a)** contains THEN

13. **(c)** shows consequences/effect

14. **(c)** another option for 'and'

15. **(c)** expresses cause-effect relation

16. **(d)** shows choice between hurrying up or missing the train.

17. **(d)** and joins similar word forms.

18. **(c)** or expresses choice

19. **(b)** because; gives reason

20. **(b)** neither...nor; means none of the two

21. **(b)**	**22.** **(a)**	**23.** **(d)**	**24.** **(b)**
25. **(a)**	**26.** **(c)**	**27.** **(c)** when	**28.** **(b)** and
29. **(b)**			

11 CHAPTER FOREWORD

Hey kids! In this chapter, we shall learn about prepositions. These are the words that link nouns, pronouns or phrases to other words within a sentence.

Directions: Complete the following sentences using prepositions.

1. The mother is looking __________ her daughter.
2. The family is sitting __________ the dining table having dinner.
3. I haven't been there __________ last summmer.
4. Ravi is holding a bat __________ his hand.
5. Do be there __________ 9 O'clock.
6. What are you doing __________ Saturday?.
7. Jane sat __________ the mirror to dress.
8. I will meet you __________ the evening.
9. The flight was __________ time.

11
Chapter

Preposition

LEARNING OBJECTIVES

This lesson will help you to:—

- understand prepositions.
- know different types of preposition.
- learn how to use prepositions appropriately.

QUICK CONCEPT REVIEW

Read the given sentence

The man is sitting **on** the chair.

Here the word 'on' shows the relation that the 'man' and the 'chair' have with each other. You would also notice that it is placed before the noun 'chair', so;

A word that is placed or positioned before a noun or a pronoun to show the relation between two nouns or pronouns in a sentence is known as a preposition. The word literally means 'positioned before' something.

Examples:

1. The boy is standing on the box.
2. The boy is sitting in the box.
3. The boy is jumping over the box.
4. The boy is hiding behind the box.
5. The boy is lying under the box.
6. The boy is standing in front of the box.

Activity:

Create your comic books.

You can design a character or characters for a comic book strip. You can work individually or as a group of three or four. You all can individually or in group, come up with a "preposition character" -- a person, animal or object that will travel through the comic strip with preposition words. For example, one of you may come up with a bird-like creature called "Beaky." The first comic box may start with Beaky "inside" a tree pecking her way "out." As the comic continues, Beaky can peck her way "through" the tree and prune herself "on" a limb. Encourage humour and creativity with both the drawings and text of the comic. For example, you may write the prepositional phrase underneath the box to describe the action, or have the character speak for herself.

On

In

Over

Behind

Under

In front of

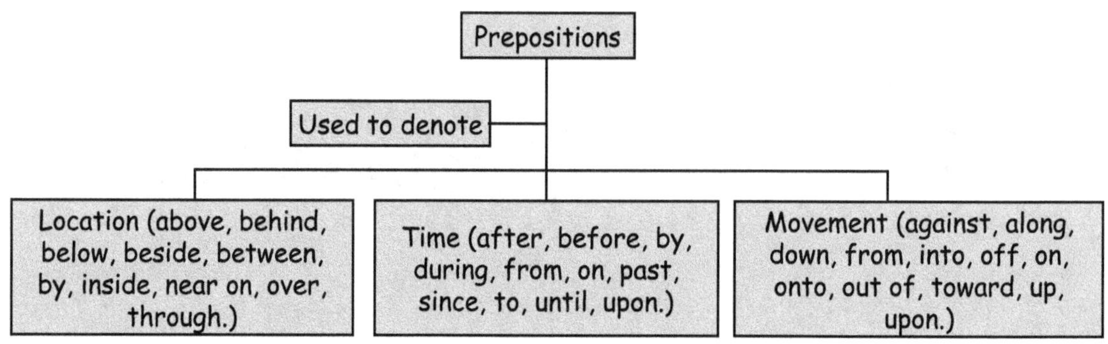

SPECIAL USES OF SOME PREPOSITIONS

Prepositions	When Used	Examples
FOR	_duration of time _distance _purpose	_We walk for an hour everyday. _I walked for 3 kilometres. _Neha bought a book for me.
FROM	_place of origin _cause _source	_She comes from Patna. _He is suffering from fever. _I have heard about the accident from my friend.
SINCE	_from a time in the past until now	_I have been living in Kolkata since 2012.
BETWEEN	_used when referring to two persons or things	_The old man distributed his money between his two sons.
AMONG	_within a group of more than two persons or things	_The money was shared among the five friends.
BEHIND	_at the back of	_The cat ran away and hid behind the bushes.
OVER	_above; higher than _covering	_The picture is hanging over the bookshelf. _Please spread the blanket over the bed.
UNDER	_beneath	_The rat is hiding under the cupboard.
WITH	_accompanying _having; containing _manner _by means of	_She lives with her grandmother. _I have filled the bag with clothes. _He lifted the box with difficulty. _She pasted the pictures with glue.
ABOUT	_on the subject matter of _approximately	_This is a story about three friends. _He is about 10 years old.

Poem on Prepositions

Airplanes
Across the sky
Around the clouds
Around the birds
Above the ground
Into the airport
Inside are people
Through the clouds
On the runway
In the rain
Away we go

Important Tips

Words like "by, with", "since, from", "between, among", " on, upon" all indicate the direction of word that follows, either in physical terms or in terms of giving and receiving. "By" is used after verbs in the passive to express the agent or doer of the action expressed by the verb, "With" is used with the instrument with which the action is done. "Since" is used to denote a point of time used in past tense whereas "From" can be used also for present and future tense. "Between" is used in speaking of two persons or things; "Among" refers to more than two persons or things. "On" is often used in speaking of things at rest; "Upon" is generally used in speaking of things in motion.

Multiple Choice Questions

LEVEL-1

Directions (Qs. 1 to 10): Carefully look at the picture given below and find answers for the following.

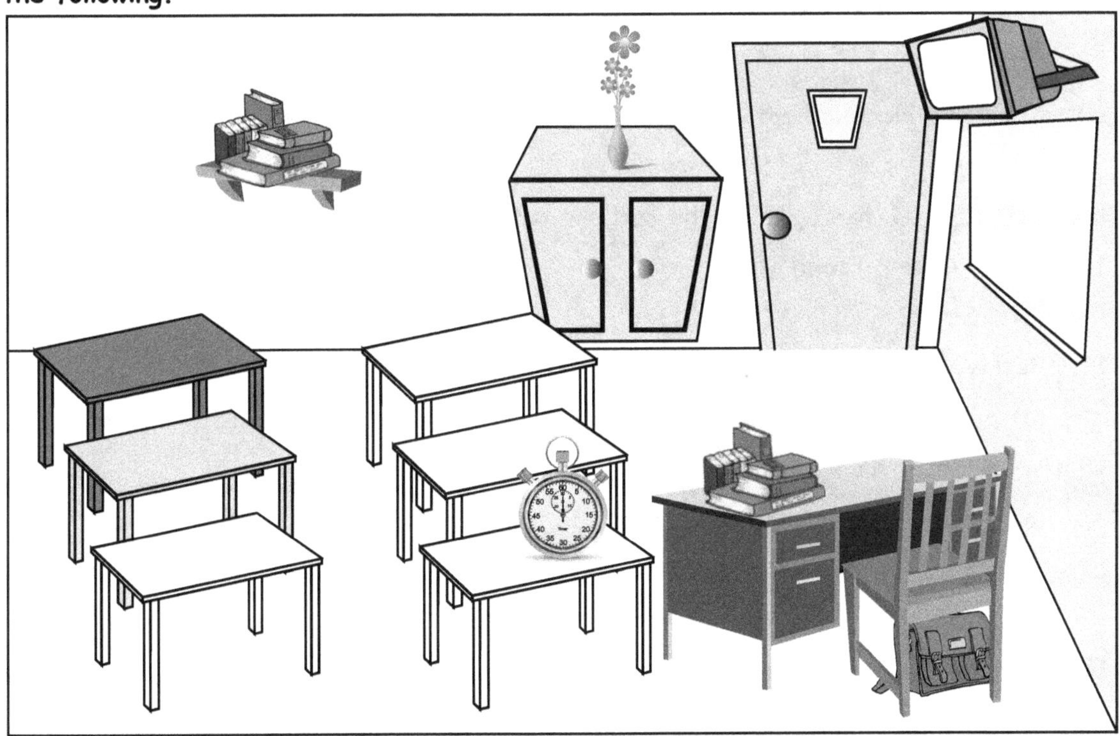

1. **This is the picture ________ a classroom.**
   (a) for (b) to (c) of (d) at
2. **There is a peepdoor ________ the door.**
   (a) of (b) on (c) in (d) between
3. **A small television is fixed ________ the whiteboard.**
   (a) across (b) around (c) among (d) above
4. **The bag is lying ________ the chair.**
   (a) under (b) near (c) behind (d) beside
5. **The flower vase is kept ________ the cupboard.**
   (a) inside (b) towards (c) over (d) with
6. **The grey desk is lying ________ the dark grey and the white desk.**
   (a) among (b) beside (c) about (d) between
7. **The book-rack is fitted ________ the cupboard.**
   (a) upon (b) near (c) across (d) with
8. **The teacher's desk is kept ________ front of the chair.**
   (a) at (b) in (c) to (d) on
9. **The cupboard stands ________ the door of the classroom.**
   (a) between (b) behind (c) beside (d) before
10. **The table clock is kept ________ the desk.**
    (a) on (b) at (c) in (d) to

Directions (Qs. 11 to 15): Find the odd one out. **[Critical Thinking]**

11. **Since, Often, From, Upon**
    (a) Since (b) Often (c) From (d) Upon
12. **Beside, Behind, Seldom, Infront**
    (a) Beside (b) Behind (c) Seldom (d) infront
13. **With, Into, Among, Soon** **[2013]**
    (a) With (b) Into (c) Among (d) Soon
14. **Together, Before, Towards, After** **[2014]**
    (a) Together (b) Before (c) Towards (d) After
15. **Outside, Near, Rather, Inside**
    (a) Outside (b) Near (c) Rather (d) Inside

16. The most difficult part of get up early is when you feet touch the cold floor. [2018]

(a) The most difficult part (b) of get up early

(c) is when your feet (d) touch the cold floor

17. Find the preposition from the sentences given below. [2019]

The animals are killed by men.

(a) The (b) animals (c) killed (d) by

18. I walked through the forest. [2019]

(a) I (b) walked (c) through (d) forest

19. She didn't take part ________ the dance competition. [2021]

(a) in (b) at (c) on (d) for

20. Mom said that she would be back ________ an hour. [2022]

(a) with (b) within (c) on (d) of

21. Don't wear shoes <u>inside</u> the house. [2022]

(a) Adverb (b) Preposition (c) Verb (d) Noun

22. Will : I am going ________ a swim. Are you coming? [2022]

Lucas : Yes, I am.

(a) to (b) on (c) for (d) in

23. Choose the correct option to complete the conversation. [2022]

Mother : I am heading ________ to the market. Take care of yourself.

(a) out (b) of (c) up (d) with

24. Fill in the blank with an appropriate preposition.
The medicine cured him _______ the disease. [2022]

(a) from (b) to (c) of (d) with

LEVEL-2

Directions (Qs. 1 and 2): Match the following List I with List II.

1. **[Critical Thinking]**

	List I		List II
A.	This train travels	1.	box with a screwdriver.
B.	When it is heated	2.	sleep during the day.
C.	Nocturnal animals usually	3.	water changes into steam.
D.	Ravi opened the	4.	from Delhi to Kolkata

	A	B	C	D
(a)	1	2	3	4
(b)	3	4	1	2
(c)	4	3	2	1
(d)	2	1	4	3

2. [Critical Thinking]

	List I		List II
A.	What is he	1.	for the lost umbrella.
B.	Please explain to me	2.	upon doing it.
C.	We searched	3.	talking about?
D.	He insisted	4.	what this means.

	A	B	C	D
(a)	1	2	3	4
(b)	3	4	1	2
(c)	4	3	2	1
(d)	2	1	4	3

Directions (Qs. 3 and 4): Read the sentences and choose the correct option.

3. **A. The cat sprang upon the table.** **[2013]**

   B. I have been unwell by Monday.

   C. He has been sleeping for the last three hours.

   D. We sat over the ground.

   (a) A and B are correct. (b) A and C are correct.

   (c) B and C are correct. (d) C and D are correct.

4. **A. We went to the picnic with our teacher.**

   B. The man walked for five miles.

   C. Tina solved the puzzle by patience.

   D. Mother bought a dress in me.

   (a) A and B are correct (b) A and C are correct

   (c) B and C are correct (d) C and D are correct

Directions (Qs. 5 to 7): Choose the correct option.

5.  **The rat is standing ________the box.** **[2016]**

   (a) after (b) before (c) beside (d) behind

6. The cow jumps ________ the moon. [2015]

(a) on (b) into (c) in (d) over

7. The dog is holding the bone ________its mouth.

(a) outside (b) in (c) towards (d) forward

Directions (Qs. 8 to 11): Read the passage and fill up the blanks with correct option.
One day, an old man and a young man came to the king's court ___(8)___ justice. The young man's case was that the old man had borrowed some money ___(9)___ him to buy a cow, but he never paid the money back. The old man replied that he had paid the money back ___(10)___ full. The king then asked the young man if he would be satisfied if the old man was willing ___(11)___ swear a solemn oath that he had paid his debt. The young man at first said that an oath is not enough, but then he agreed.

8. (a) of (b) on (c) for (d) from

9. (b) to (b) from (c) of (d) with

10. (a) in (b) for (c) at (d) by

11. (a) with (b) on (c) in (d) to

12. **How many prepositions can you find in this poem?**

Diving

by Jon H.

Up the cool metal steps
On top of the long board
With the water below
Among the boisterous spectators are parents.
Off the board I jump
Within seconds I have made a clean dive into the pool
Towards the scoreboard I gaze
On it I see a perfect score
After all the training. I have succeeded
"Yes".

(a) 7 (b) 9 (c) 11 (d) 12

Directions (13 to 22): Choose the correct option.

13. My best friend, John, is named ______ his great-grandfather.

(a) after (b) to (c) about (d) from

14. Grandpa stayed up ______ two in the morning. **[2015]**

(a) since (b) for (c) until (d) after

15. My parents have been married ______ forty-nine years.

(a) since (b) for (c) until (d) after

16. He usually travels to Bengaluru _______ train.

(a) by (b) at (c) with (d) from

17. You frequently see this kind of violence ____ television. **[2016]**

(a) with (b) in (c) on (d) from

18. I told Mom we'd be home ______ an hour or so.

(a) to (b) in (c) at (d) with

19. I was visiting my best friend _____ the hospital. **[2017]**

(a) of (b) on (c) in (d) with

20. The professor _______ South Africa amazed the American students with her stories.

(a) from (b) of (c) in (d) with

21. I'll see you ____ home when I get there.

(a) in (b) by (c) at (d) from

22. It's been snowing ________ Christmas morning.

(a) since (b) for (c) until (d) in

Directions (Qs. 23 to 25): Choose preposition from the following sentences.

23. The teacher told us about the planets. **[2014]**

(a) about (b) across (c) beside (d) behind

24. We walked across the field.

(a) about (b) across (c) beside (d) behind

25. The tiger is hiding behind the bushes. **[2013]**

(a) about (b) across (c) beside (d) behind

RESPONSE GRID

LEVEL 1

1. a b c d	2. a b c d	3. a b c d	4. a b c d	5. a b c d
6. a b c d	7. a b c d	8. a b c d	9. a b c d	10. a b c d
11. a b c d	12. a b c d	13. a b c d	14. a b c d	15. a b c d
16. a b c d	17. a b c d	18. a b c d	19. a b c d	20. a b c d
21. a b c d	22. a b c d	23. a b c d	24. a b c d	

LEVEL 2

1. a b c d	2. a b c d	3. a b c d	4. a b c d	5. a b c d
6. a b c d	7. a b c d	8. a b c d	9. a b c d	10. a b c d
11. a b c d	12. a b c d	13. a b c d	14. a b c d	15. a b c d
16. a b c d	17. a b c d	18. a b c d	19. a b c d	20. a b c d
21. a b c d	22. a b c d	23. a b c d	24. a b c d	25. a b c d

Solutions with Explanation

LEVEL-1

1. (c)
2. (b)
3. (d)
4. (a)
5. (c)
6. (d)
7. (b)
8. (b)
9. (c)
10. (a)
11. (d) upon
12. (c) Seldom
13. (d) Soon
14. (a) Together
15. (c) Rather (all are adverbs)
16. (b)
17. (d)
18. (c) through
19. (a) in
20. (b) within
21. (a) Adverb
22. (c) for
23. (a) out
24. (c)

LEVEL-2

1. (c) 2. (b)

3. (b) B. I have been unwell since Monday.

D. We sat on the ground.

4. (a) C. Tina solved the puzzle with patience.

D. Mother bought a dress for me.

5. (c) 6. (d) 7. (b) 8. (c)

9. (b) 10. (a) 11. (d)

12. (d) 12. up, on, of, with, below, among, off, within, into, towards, on, after.

13. (a) 14. (c) 15. (b) 16. (a)

17. (c) 18. (b) 19. (c) 20. (a)

21. (c) 22. (a) 23. (a) 24. (b)

25. (d)

12 CHAPTER FOREWORD

Ever thought what would happen if we did not use Punctuation marks? Without them, the meaning of the sentences would change. In this chapter, we shall learn about the correct use of Punctuation.

Directions : Rewrite the paragraph using the punctuation marks (full stop, question mark, inverted commas or comma.)

It is proved that animals are our friends we establish intimacy with them by keeping them as our pets sometimes they are kept in cages there are some pets who are allowed to stay with us freely dogs cats parrots and rabbits are some of our favourite pets people also like to keep turtles and hamsters chipmunks and dolphins dog is a faithful animal it plays the role of a watchman while cats are kept as pets to keep the mice away parrots and goldfish are mostly favoured for their attractive features though the role of pets has reduced most of the people keep pets for show and pleasure

____

Chapter **12**

Punctuation

LEARNING OBJECTIVES

This lesson will help you to:—

- ❖ understand punctuation.
- ❖ learn about different types of punctuations.
- ❖ know about usage of punctuations.

Real Life Example

Learning punctuation is an important skill, especially if you are doing a lot of writing assignments in school. Punctuation is used to create sense, clarity and stress in sentences.

QUICK CONCEPT REVIEW

Learning English punctuation is an important skill of acquiring a complete grammatical knowledge. Punctuation is used to create sense, clarity and stress in sentences. It means the right use of putting in **points** or **stops** in writing. The following are the principal stops.

- ❖ Full Stop or Period (.)
- ❖ Comma (,)
- ❖ Semicolon (;)
- ❖ Colon (:)
- ❖ Note of Interrogation or Question Marks (?)
- ❖ Note of Exclamation or Exclamation Marks (!)
- ❖ Dash (_)
- ❖ Parenthesis ( )
- ❖ Inverted Commas or Quotation Marks ("   ")

FULL STOPS AND COMMAS

Full stops are used at the end of a sentence to inform the reader that the sentence is finished and that he should take a moment before reading the next one.

For example:

- Honesty is the best policy.
- Please shut the door.
- The teacher is teaching the pupils.

A comma informs the reader to pause before continuing the sentence. Unlike a period, the sentence is not over but simply being paused for a moment.

For example:

- Health , wealth and peace go together.
- I bought bread, butter, eggs and milk from the market.

Historical preview

Early uses of punctuation in English literature included the works of poets, playwrights and writers to help clarify the statements otherwise they would have been confused statements. It wasn't until the 17th century that the complete roster of punctuation we use today, was created.

QUESTION AND EXCLAMATION MARKS

Like a full stop, a question mark finishes a sentence. Unlike a full stop, a question mark turns the sentence into a question rather than a statement.

For example:

- What are you writing in your copy?
- He said, "Who is there?"

An exclamation point also ends a sentence like a full stop, but the sentence is turned into an exclamation rather than a simple statement. Readers should read a sentence with an exclamation mark with excitement.

For example:

- Bravo! We have won the match.
- Alas! His dog is dead.

COLONS AND SEMICOLONS

A semicolon connects two free-standing but related sentences where the conjunction has been left out. Semicolons are typically used before introduction words such as namely, however, therefore, that is, for example or for instance.

For example: God gave her peace; her land reposed.

A colon is used before a sentence that expands on the previous one. Colons are often used before listing items.

For example: Shakespeare says: "Sweet are the uses of adversity."

APOSTROPHES AND PARENTHESES

An apostrophe is used in a contraction in place of the letter that has been removed. "It's" uses an apostrophe to replace the "i" in "is." "It's" is a contraction of "it is." Parentheses are used to enclose clarifying statements. Someone might use parentheses (if they thought it was necessary) to help clarify or expand on a sentence. if the words in the parentheses were not included and if parentheses are used in a narrative, the sentence must also make sense.

DASH

It is used to indicate an abrupt stop or change of thought or to resume a scattered subject.

For example: Friends, companions, relatives---all deserted him

Multiple Choice Questions

LEVEL-1

Directions (Qs. 1 and 2): Choose the suitable option for the sentences.

1. **Shakespeare says:- Sweet are the uses of adversity.**

   (a) semi colon (b) quotation mark
   (c) comma (d) exclamation mark

2. **This is Priyas grammar book.**

   (a) apostrophe (b) colon (c) quotation mark (d) comma

Directions (Qs. 3 to 7): Tick the word that needs a capital letter.

3. **my father will return next week.** **[2012]**

   (a) my (b) will (c) next (d) week

4. **oh, mom, you don't understand me.**

   (a) mom (b) understand (c) me (d) oh

5. **tomorrow grandmother leaves for dehradun.** **[2014]**

   (a) grandmother (b) tomorrow
   (c) dehradun (d) both (b) and (c)

6. **did sis want to go with us?**

   (a) want (b) did (c) with (d) us

7. **today mother and I will finish the painting.**

   (a) today (b) mother (c) and (d) will

Directions (Qs. 8 to 12) : Complete the following sentences with the correct punctuation.

8. **Is the lion a brave animal**

   (a) Is the lion a brave animal? (b) Is the Lion a Brave animal?
   (c) Is the Lion a brave animal! (d) Is the lion a Brave animal.

9. **Anu had no money in her purse**

    (a) Anu had no money in her purse.
    (b) Anu had no money in Her Purse.
    (c) Anu had no money in her purse?
    (d) Anu had no money in her purse!

10. **How wonderful the weather is**

    (a) how wonderful the weather is?
    (b) How wonderful the weather is!
    (c) How wonderful the weather is?
    (d) How wonderful! the weather is.

11. **Add milk cream cocoa powder in the eggless cake**

    (a) add Milk cream cocoa powder in the Eggless cake
    (b) Add milk, cream, cocoa powder in the eggless cake.
    (c) Add milk cream Cocoa Powder in the Eggless Cake.
    (d) Add Milk, cream cocoa powder in the eggless cake.

12. **No i will not do this**

    (a) No, i will not do this?
    (b) No, I will not do this.
    (c) No, I will not, do this.
    (d) no I will not do this

13. **Find the number of punctuations missing in the given below sentences** **[2018]**

    Hurrah I have won the prize

    (a) one (b) two (c) three (d) four

14. **My favourite colors are red yellow and green** **[2018]**

    (a) one (b) two (c) three (d) four

LEVEL-2

Directions (Qs. 1 to 8): Decide if the exclamation mark is correctly put, then choose the correct answer.

1. **A. Hooray! We are finally free.**

    B. I am sleepy!

    (a) FT (b) TF (c) TT (d) FF

2. **A. My car is old!** **[2012]**

    B. Alas! I lost the match.

    (a) FT (b) TF (c) TT (d) FF

3. A. I am tired!

   B. Where are we going!

   (a) FT (b) TF (c) TT (d) FF

4. A. Does anyone know his name! [2013]

   B. "Hey!" the man yelled, "Please help me".

   (a) FT (b) TF (c) TT (d) FF

5. A. Ouch! I hurt my knee.

   B. Wow!, I just won a lottery.

   (a) FT (b) TF (c) TT (d) FF

6. Match the following:

	List I		List II
A.	The teacher asked Rohan	1.	"Arrange your books in your bag according to the routine."
B.	Father said to me,	2.	"Next month I will buy the doll house for you."
C.	The major ordered his soldiers,	3.	"Why did you not complete your work?"
D.	Mother said to me	4.	"Stand in attention."

	A	B	C	D
(a)	3	2	4	1
(b)	4	1	3	2
(c)	2	3	1	4
(d)	4	3	2	1

7. Choose the correct option.

   A. High and low; rich and poor; wise and foolish; must all die.

   B. Study to acquire a habit of thinking; no study is more important.

   C. How are we ever to get there , is the question ?

   D. What a terrible fire this is !

   (a) A and B are correct. (b) B and D are correct.

   (c) A and C are correct. (d) C and D are correct.

8. **Read the statements and choose the correct option as true/false.**

   Statement A: The semicolon represents a pause of greater importance than that shown by the comma.

   Statement B: The inverted commas are used only to mark the quotations.

   (a) TT (b) TF (c) FT (d) FF

Directions (Qs. 9 and 10): Find out the number of punctuations in the given passages.

9. **One evening as the sun was setting, a wolf watched his own shadow growing longer and longer, "What a great animal I am!" said the wolf to himself, "How foolish I am to be afraid of the lion whom they call the King of Beasts."**

   (a) 9 (b) 11 (c) 13 (d) 7

10. **He said to me, "Please take your seat here. Oh! How glad I am to see you! Why do you look so sad? Is there anything I can do for you? You can certainly count upon me, I need not assure you."**

    (a) 12 (b) 6 (c) 8 (d) 10

Directions (Qs. 11 to 14): Use commas to separate items in a list of three or more.

11. **(a) My, favourite, colours, are blue, red and pink.**

    (b) My favourite colours are blue red and pink.

    (c) My, favourite colours ,are blue red and pink.

    (d) My favourite colours are blue, red, and pink.

12. **(a) I like to go hiking, fishing, swimming and camping during summer.**

    (b) I like, to go, hiking fishing swimming and camping during summer.

    (c) I, like, to go hiking fishing swimming and camping during summer.

    (d) I like to go hiking, fishing, swimming, and camping during summer.

13. **(a) I, have to clean my, room walk the dog and take out, the trash.**

    (b) I have to clean my room, walk the dog and take out the trash.

    (c) I have to clean my room walk the dog and take out the trash.

    (d) I have, to clean, my room, walk the dog and take, out the trash.

14. (a) The, tree, is very tall, old, and green.

(b) The tree is very tall old and green.

(c) The tree is very tall, old and green.

(d) The tree is, very tall, old and, green.

Direction (Qs. 15 to 18): Decide if the following sentences should end with a question mark or not and choose the correct option.

15. A. What time is it.

B. Do you want another piece of cake.

C. Juan asked if we are going to the mall today.

D. It is 5:00

(a) TTFF (b) FFTT (c) TFTF (d) FTFT

16. A. Maybe class ends at 3:30

B. I am not sure if we need more milk

C. Did the man find his dog

D. The turkey is done cooking

(a) TTFF (b) FFTT (c) FFTF (d) TTFT

17. A. I wonder what time it is

B. Was the movie scary

C. It might be sunny tomorrow

D. Is it 7:00

(a) TTFF (b) FFTT (c) FTFT (d) TFTF

18. A. You love painting

B. Was the trip long

C. I have never seen the doll museum in Delhi.

D. What are you cooking

(a) TTFF (b) FFTT (c) TFTF (d) FTFT

Directions (Qs. 19 to 23): Choose the option that best completes the sentence.

19. ________ a lot more work building a shed than I thought it would be.

(a) It's (b) Its

(c) Its' (d) None of the above

20. I can't remember (who's, whose) book I borrowed last week. **[2014]**

(a) who's (b) whose

(c) whos' (d) none of the above

21. ________ hard to concentrate with all the noise in the classroom

(a) It's
(b) Its
(c) Its'
(d) none of the above

22. The plane landed late and now ________ leaving late, too.

(a) it's
(b) its
(c) its'
(d) none of the above

23. Do we know ________ running in the marathon this weekend? **[2016]**

(a) who's
(b) whose
(c) whos'
(d) none of the above

Directions (Qs. 24 to 26): Add apostrophes where needed.

24. Im glad you werent late getting here because I dont want to miss the movie. **[2017]**

(a) gla'd, gett'ing
(b) I'm, weren't, don't
(c) yo'u, her'e
(d) none of these

25. Dad drove me to the doctors office, so Mom doesnt have to leave her job early.

(a) Da'd
(b) offic'e
(c) doctor's, doesn't
(d) none of the above

26. Carl said that were like his second parents because wed always been there to help him.

(a) we're, we'd
(b) secon'd
(c) tha't, always'
(d) none of the above

RESPONSE GRID

LEVEL 1

1. a b c d 2. a b c d 3. a b c d 4. a b c d 5. a b c d
6. a b c d 7. a b c d 8. a b c d 9. a b c d 10. a b c d
11. a b c d 12. a b c d 13. a b c d 14. a b c d

LEVEL 2

1. a b c d 2. a b c d 3. a b c d 4. a b c d 5. a b c d
6. a b c d 7. a b c d 8. a b c d 9. a b c d 10. a b c d
11. a b c d 12. a b c d 13. a b c d 14. a b c d 15. a b c d
16. a b c d 17. a b c d 18. a b c d 19. a b c d 20. a b c d
21. a b c d 22. a b c d 23. a b c d 24. a b c d 25. a b c d
26. a b c d

Solutions with Explanation

LEVEL-1

1. (b) Shakespeare says:-" Sweet are the uses of adversity."
2. (a) This is Priya's grammar book.

3.	(a)	4.	(d)	5.	(d)	6.	(b)
7.	(a)	8.	(a)	9.	(a)	10.	(b)
11.	(b)	12.	(b)				
13.	(b) two	14.	(b)				

LEVEL-2

1.	(b)	2.	(a)	3.	(d)	4.	(a)
5.	(b)	6.	(a)				

7. (b) A. High and low, rich and poor, wise and foolish, must all die.(comma is used to separate each pair of words connected by 'and')

   C. How are we ever to get there , is the question .(it is a statement)

8. (b) The inverted commas are used to enclose the exact words of a speaker, or a quotation.

9.	(a)	10.	(d)	11.	(d)	12.	(a)
13.	(b)	14.	(c)	15.	(a)	16.	(c)
17.	(c)	18.	(d)	19.	(a)	20.	(b)
21.	(a)	22.	(a)	23.	(a)	24.	(b)
25.	(c)	26.	(a)				

13 CHAPTER FOREWORD

In this chapter, we shall learn about contractions. A contraction is a shorter way to say two words.

For example:

is + not = isn't

Directions : Combine the two words and write the contraction in the corresponding box.

Word 1	Word 2	Contraction
He	will	
can	not	
has	not	
They	would	
Are	not	
Let	us	
We	had	
She	is	

13

Chapter

Contraction

LEARNING OBJECTIVES

This lesson will help you to:—

- ❖ Understand the usage of contractions
- ❖ Analyse the different types of contractions

QUICK CONCEPT REVIEW

Contractions and short forms are used in our everyday life. The words are squeezed by placing an apostrophe (') in place of missing letters.

For example:

- I am - I'm
- Do not - Don't

We do not use double contractions.

For example:

She isn't (correct)

She'sn't (incorrect)

We use contractions in question tags.

For example:

- ❖ You are coming, aren't you?
- ❖ She is pretty, isn't she?

Some commonly used contractions include :

ALPHABETICAL LIST OF CONTRACTIONS

are not = aren't	is not = isn't	we are = we're
cannot = can't	it is = it's	we have = we've
could not = couldn't	it has = it's	we will = we'll
did not = didn't	it will = it'll	we would = we'd
do not = don't	must not = mustn't	we had = we'd
does not = doesn't	she is = she's	were not = weren't
had not = hadn't	she has = she's	what is = what's
have not = haven't	she will = she'll	where is = where's
he is = he's	she would = she'd	who is = who's
he has = he's	she had = she'd	who will = who'll
he will = he'll	should not = shouldn't	*will not = won't
he would = he'd	that is = that's	would not = wouldn't
he had = he'd	there is = there's	you are = you're
here is = here's	they are = they're	you have = you've
I am = I'm	they have = they've	you will = you'll
I have = I've	they will = they'll	you would = you'd
I will = I'll	they would = they'd	you had = you'd
I would = I'd	they had = they'd	Shall not = shan't
I had = I'd	was not = wasn't	*irregular

Multiple Choice Questions

LEVEL-1

Directions (Qs. 1 to 10) : Choose the correct contraction for the given word.

1. **where is**
   (a) where's (b) whe'eis (c) where'is (d) wh'reis
2. **he is**
   (a) he'is (b) he's (c) h'is (d) his
3. **they are**
   (a) they'are (b) theya'e (c) they're (d) they'ar
4. **I would**
   (a) I'd (b) I wou'd (c) I'would (d) none
5. **who is**
   (a) whoes (b) who's (c) w'os (d) none
6. **should not**
   (a) should'not (b) shoul'not (c) shouldn't (d) none
7. **we have**
   (a) we'ave (b) weha'e (c) weh've (d) we've
8. **does not**
   (a) doesn't (b) does'not (c) do'snot (d) do'not
9. **are not**
   (a) are'not (b) aren't (c) ar'not (d) ar'nt
10. **were not**
    (a) were'not (b) wer'not (c) weren't (d) none

Directions (Qs. 11 to 17) : Read the sentences and replace the underlined words using contractions.

11. **<u>I am</u> running on the track.**
    (a) I a'm (b) I'm (c) I'am (d) Ia'm
12. **The suitcase <u>is not</u> big enough.**
    (a) is'not (b) isn'ot (c) isn't (d) none
13. **<u>I would</u> like an icecream.**
    (a) I'd (b) I wou'd (c) I wou'ld (d) I'ould
14. **<u>Do not</u> put your hands out of the window.**
    (a) don'ot (b) do'ot (c) don't (d) d'not
15. **Take off the sweater when <u>you are</u> warm.**
    (a) you're (b) you'are (c) youar' (d) youa're

16. Choose the option that best completes the sentence. **[2018]**

__________ not an easy question.

(a) It's (b) its (c) its' (d) none

17. __________ a big animal. **[2018]**

(a) There (b) there's (c) theirs (d) none

LEVEL-2

Directions (Qs. 1 to 12) : Read the passage and replace the words in the box with their contractions.

[We are] (1) having a birthday party just for me today! This [is not] (2) my real birthday. [It is] (3) May 12th and [I will] (4) be 8 years old. I invited many friends. [They are] (5) all coming, but not Alex. [He is] (6) on a trip with his family and [can not] (7) come. I [do not] (8) know what kind of cake mom got me. [She is] (9) keeping it a surprise and [that is] (10) okay because I like surprises. Dad and mom told me not to peek at my birthday gift and I [have not] , (11) even when I really wanted to. [I am] (12) so excited for today to start. I just wish the sun would come up!

1. (a) were (b) wear (c) we're (d) none
2. (a) isn't (b) isnot' (c) is'ot (d) isno'
3. (a) Its (b) It's (c) It'is (d) none
4. (a) I'll (b) I'ill (c) I'will (d) Iwi'l
5. (a) They'are (b) There (c) They're (d) none
6. (a) His (b) He's (c) He'is (d) him
7. (a) cannot (b) can'nt (c) can't (d) can'ot
8. (a) don't (b) do'ot (c) do'not (d) none
9. (a) She'is (b) She's (c) Sh'is (d) S'heis
10. (a) that is (b) that'is (c) tha'is (d) that's
11. (a) haven't (b) havent' (c) hav'not (d) none
12. (a) I'm (b) I am (c) am (d) none

Directions (Qs. 13 to 15) : Which of the following is not a contraction?

13. (a) could've (b) won't (c) hers (d) you've
14. (a) friend's (b) aren't (c) I've (d) you'd
15. (a) we'd (b) girl's (c) he'll (d) hasn't

Directions (Qs. 16 to 20) : Read the sentences and replace the contractions with the corresponding words.

16. **Those aren't my mittens.**
 (a) th'se (b) are not (c) my (d) are my
17. **He isn't going with us.**
 (a) is not (b) he (c) with (d) us
18. **I'll see you at home.**
 (a) see (b) you (c) I will (d) home
19. **I can't find my coat.**
 (a) I (b) can not (c) find (d) my
20. **She didn't see the movie.**
 (a) she (b) did (c) did not (d) movie

Directions (Qs. 21 to 33) : Fill in the blanks with contractions.

21. **__________ going outside.**
 (a) He's (b) She's (c) They're (d) All three
22. **__________ finished eating.**
 (a) They've (b) He'll (c) Hadn't (d) none
23. **He __________ sing.**
 (a) won't (b) can't (c) can not (d) both a & b
24. **You __________ do that.**
 (a) should'not (b) should not (c) shouldn't (d) none
25. **__________ have fun at the show.**
 (a) We'ill (b) W'll (c) We'll (d) none

26. __________ my book?

(a) Wher's (b) Where's (c) Where'is (d) none

27. They __________ been to the fare.

(a) haven't (b) has'nt (c) didn't (d) can't

28. One __________ intrude in other's privacy.

(a) haven't (b) mustn't (c) we'd (d) aren't

29. __________ always be in my heart.

(a) you'll (b) they (c) I've (d) haven't

30. Hari __________ granted permission to go out.

(a) were (b) wasn't (c) we'll (d) we'd

31. Looks like __________ rain today.

(a) here's (b) that's (c) it'll (d) must not

32. Sumita : I am going to get some coffee. Do you want some? [2021]

Rajan : ___________.

(a) No, I was (b) No, I am good

(c) Yes, I am good (d) Yes, I don't

33. Smith : Do you believe in supernatural things? [2022]

Martin : _________.

(a) Yes, I am not (b) Yes, I don't

(c) No, I don't (d) No, I do

RESPONSE GRID

LEVEL 1

1. a b c d	2. a b c d	3. a b c d	4. a b c d	5. a b c d
6. a b c d	7. a b c d	8. a b c d	9. a b c d	10. a b c d
11. a b c d	12. a b c d	13. a b c d	14. a b c d	15. a b c d
16. a b c d	17. a b c d			

LEVEL 2

1. a b c d	2. a b c d	3. a b c d	4. a b c d	5. a b c d
6. a b c d	7. a b c d	8. a b c d	9. a b c d	10. a b c d
11. a b c d	12. a b c d	13. a b c d	14. a b c d	15. a b c d
16. a b c d	17. a b c d	18. a b c d	19. a b c d	20. a b c d
21. a b c d	22. a b c d	23. a b c d	24. a b c d	25. a b c d
26. a b c d	27. a b c d	28. a b c d	29. a b c d	30. a b c d
31. a b c d	32. a b c d	33. a b c d		

Solutions with Explanation

LEVEL-1

1. (a)	2. (b)	3. (c)	4. (a)	5. (b)
6. (c)	7. (d)	8. (a)	9. (b)	10. (c)
11. (b)	12. (c)	13. (a)	14. (c)	15. (a)
16. (a)	17. (b)			

LEVEL-2

1. (c)	2. (a)	3. (b)	4. (a)	5. (c)
6. (b)	7. (c)	8. (a)	9. (b)	10. (d)
11. (a)	12. (a)	13. (c)	14. (a)	15. (b)
16. (b)	17. (a)	18. (c)	19. (b)	20. (c)
21. (d)	22. (a)	23. (d)	24. (c)	25. (c)
26. (b)	27. (a)	28. (b)	29. (a)	30. (b)
31. (c)				

32. (b) No, I am good

33. (c) No, I don't

14 CHAPTER FOREWORD

Hey Folks! In this chapter we shall learn about synonyms and antonyms. Synonyms are meanings and antonyms are opposites.

Here is a little exercise for you to warm up.

Directions: Match the words given in Column A with their synonyms given in Column B.

Column A	Column B
1. Pursue	i. Unimportant
2. Compatible	ii. Consistent
3. Apt	iii. Follow
4. Trivial	iv. Suitable
5. Monotonous	v. Dull

Directions: Change the underlined word with its antonym. Take help from the clue box.

Sad	Easy	Shortest	Found	Hot	Over	Fast

1. My teacher gives <u>hard</u> homework.
2. Have you <u>lost</u> your pencil?
3. Ben is the <u>tallest</u> boy in our class.
4. Joe is <u>happy</u> about the party.
5. I like <u>cold</u> coffee.

Chapter 14

Synonym & Antonym

LEARNING OBJECTIVES

This lesson will help you to:—

- ❖ Understand the meanings of various words
- ❖ Understand the opposites of various words
- ❖ Differentiate between synonym and antonym

QUICK CONCEPT REVIEW

SYNONYMS

A word or phrase which means exactly or nearly the same as another word or phrase in the same language is called its synonym.

For example:

- The lady **yelled** at the boy.
- The lady **shouted** at the boy.
- The lady **screamed** at the boy.

In the above sentences, ***"yell"***, ***"shout"*** and ***"scream"*** all mean the same i.e. **"a loud sharp cry"**. Hence, they are synonyms.

Using synonyms improves our vocabulary and holds the reader's attention.

Examples:

Once upon a time there was a king who had three sons. The small son was a simple man named Dummling and each one laughed at him. The king did not know which one of his sons to choose as the heir and so he thought to take an exam.

Let's rewrite the passage.

Once upon a time there was a king who had three sons. The youngest son was a simpleton named Dummling and everyone laughed at him. The king did not know which one of his sons to appoint as the successor and so he considered to take a test.

Thus, we see that after writing the passage with synonyms, the story makes for an interesting read.

Here is the list of some common synonyms.

	Words	Synonyms
1.	Speak	talk, tell, chat
2.	exit	door, outlet, leave
3.	funny	comic, witty
4.	present	gift, current, in hand
5.	house	residence, home, address
6.	near	close by, next to
7.	jog	run, train, trot
8.	angry	mad, irate
9.	crate	box, carton
10.	shut	close, lock
11.	tired	weary, sleepy
12.	hard	firm, solid
13.	leap	jump, dive, soar
14.	stone	rock, pebble

15.	Awful	Terrible
16.	Beneficial	Favourable
17.	Contemporary	Modern
18.	Delicious	Scrumptious
19.	Dicey	Risky
20.	Important	Vital
21.	Knowingly	Deliberately
22.	Lethal	Deadly
23.	Madness	Insanity
24.	Mischievous	Prankster
25.	Nugatory	Worthless
26.	Obsolete	Out of date
27.	Preceding	Previous
28.	Begin	Commence
29.	Calm	Tranquil
30.	Dangerous	Perilous
31.	Deceptive	Misleading
32.	Dubious	Doubtful
33.	Jealous	Envious
34.	Lazy	Sluggish
35.	Lucid	Clear
36.	Mendacity	Lying
37.	Notify	Inform
38.	Obdurate	Stubborn
39.	Passable	Satisfactory
40	Foregoing	Antecedent

ANTONYMS

The word which is opposite in the meaning of the other word is called its antonym.

For example:

- The boy was **naughty** but the girl was **polite**.
- The princess was **good** but the witch was **bad**.

In the sentence (a) above, the word **"naughty"** means *one who behaves badly*, while the word *"polite"* means *to show respectful behaviour*. Thus, **naughty is the antonym of polite.**

Similarly, in sentence (b) above, the word **"good"** means "*having desired quality*", while the word "bad" means *"awful"*. Thus, the word **good is the antonym of bad.**

Here is a list of some common antonyms.

	Words	**Antonyms**
1.	come	go
2.	in	out
3.	top	bottom
4.	far	near
5.	wet	dry
6.	before	after
7.	wrong	right
8.	loud	quiet
9.	large	small
10.	buy	sell
11.	open	close
12.	night	day
13.	push	pull
14.	give	take
15.	fast	slow
16.	Accept	refuse
17.	Admit	deny
18.	Alive	dead
19.	Bitter	sweet
20.	Continue	interrupt
21.	Dangerous	safe
22.	Keen	uninterested
23.	Failure	success
24.	Guilty	innocent
25.	Healthy	sick
26.	Husband	wife

27.	Junior	senior
28.	Adult	child
29.	Alike	different
30.	Attack	defend
31.	Cheap	expensive
32.	Courageous	cowardly
33.	Short	tall
34.	tragedy	comedy
35.	Front	rear
36.	Harvest	plant
37.	Humid	dry
38.	Insult	compliment

Multiple Choice Questions

LEVEL-1

Directions (Qs. 1 to 10) : Choose the synonym of the given word.

1. **Do**
   (a) execute (b) establish (c) preserve (d) spend
2. **Hide**
   (a) breeze (b) conceal (c) seize (d) assign
3. **Move**
   (a) engage (b) beget (c) trot (d) neil
4. **Retain**
   (a) rupture (b) wreck (c) withhold (d) cancel
5. **Label**
   (a) finish (b) way (c) aid (d) tag
6. **Tale**
   (a) fable (b) glance (c) leer (d) opinion
7. **Mad**
   (a) disclose (b) deem (c) furious (d) aloof
8. **Unfortunate**
   (a) sinful (b) dejected (c) alarmed (d) timid

9. Injure

(a) inactive (b) hurt (c) ghastly (d) burly

10. Luminous

(a) lustrous (b) relish (c) smart (d) delicate

Directions (Qs. 11 to 20) : Choose the antonym of the given word.

11. Initiate

(a) commence (b) terminate (c) originate (d) launch

12. Enormous

(a) immense (b) great (c) miniature (d) spacious

13. Fraudulent

(a) mistaken (b) incorrect (c) untrue (d) sincere

14. Warm

(a) frosty (b) heated (c) sweltering (d) none of these

15. Entire

(a) total (b) whole (c) null (d) sum

16. Ordinary

(a) offbeat (b) typical (c) usual (d) general

17. Quiet

(a) mute (b) calm (c) deafening (d) peaceful

18. Smart

(a) bright (b) intelligent (c) stupid (d) none

19. Certain

(a) unsure (b) confident (c) particular (d) specific

20. Close

(a) near (b) shut (c) stop (d) away

Directions (Qs. 21 to 25) : Choose the odd one out.

21. (a) Tough (b) Soft (c) Fragile (d) Tender

22. (a) Faithful (b) Loyal (c) Trustworthy (d) Cheat

23. (a) Beautiful (b) Lovely (c) Ugly (d) Graceful

24. (a) Leader (b) Guide (c) Follower (d) Commander

25. (a) Free (b) Locked (c) Open (d) Loose

DIRECTION (For Qs. 26-28) : Choose the correct synonym of the given word:

26. Smoother **[2018]**

(a) Release (b) Enjoy (c) Follow (d) Protrude

27. Benevolent **[2018]**

(a) Unkind (b) Disliked (c) Irreligious (d) Illegal

28. **Shameful** **[2018]**

(a) Deregulated (b) Admirable (c) Undeveloped (d) Bureaucratic

DIRECTION (For Qs. 29-30) : Choose the correct synonym of the given word:

29. **Eliminate** **[2018]**

(a) Encourage (b) Model (c) Remove (d) Gestate

30. **Pause** **[2018]**

(a) Refer (b) Hesitate (c) Concentrate (d) Giant

31. **Choose the correct antonym of the given word:**

Enthralled **[2018]**

(a) Bored (b) Angry (c) Happy (d) Sad

32. **Choose the correct synonym of the given word:**

Dropout **[2018]**

(a) Formalise (b) Ironic (c) End (d) Quitter

33. **Choose the correct antonym of the given word:**

Coerce **[2019]**

(a) Encourage (b) Belittle (c) Betray (d) Celebrate

34. **Insulate** **[2019]**

(a) Cushion (b) Rebuff (c) Entreat (d) Reveal

35. **Euphoric** **[2019]**

(a) Rapturous (b) Enigmatic

(c) Morose (d) Misunderstood

DIRECTION (For Qs. 36-43): Choose the correct antonym of the given word:

36. **Loathe** **[2019]**

(a) Retrieve (b) Admire (c) Endanger (d) Relinquish

37. **Concurrent** **[2019]**

(a) Embellished (b) Divergent (c) Crammed (d) Rapport

38. **Choose the correct synonym of the given word:**

Funnel **[2019]**

(a) Replace (b) Siphon (c) Elongate (d) Obliterate

39. **Choose the correct SYNONYM OF RESENTMENT.** **[2020]**

(a) Grudge (b) Love (c) Discourse (d) Confer

40. **Choose the correct ANTONYM OF TENTATIVE.** **[2020]**

(a) Rear (b) Certain (c) Astern (d) Precede

41. Choose the SYNONYM OF NEGATE. **[2021]**

(a) Refute (b) Allow (c) Enact (d) Support

42. Choose the correct SYNONYM OF MARVELLOUS. **[2022]**

(a) Fantastic (b) Average (c) Normal (d) Materialistic

43. Notify **[2022]**

(a) Conceal (b) Cancel (c) Inform (d) Postpone

LEVEL-2

Directions (Qs. 1 to 8) : Choose the synonym of the underlined word.

1. The teacher is very angry with the students.

(a) calm (b) annoyed (c) quiet (d) cool

2. We went to watch a movie but it was too long.

(a) sticky (b) lengthy (c) big (d) short

3. Pragya's great-grandpa is very old.

(a) friendly (b) big (c) elderly (d) young

4. The doctor asked the patient to be silent.

(a) noisy (b) early (c) sit (d) quiet

5. The boy is plucking the beautiful flowers.

(a) pretty (b) ugly (c) good (d) nice

6. Mother is in a happy mood today.

(a) laughing (b) sad (c) silent (d) joyful

7. The sounds coming from the store were strange.

(a) funny (b) unusual

(c) weird (d) both (b) and (c)

8. The odour of your shoes is most unpleasant.

(a) colour (b) sight (c) smell (d) looks

Directions (Qs. 9 to 15) : Choose the corect prefix to get the opposite of the word given.

9. Ability

(a) Ir (b) In (c) Mis (d) Un

10. Honest

(a) Im (b) Un (c) Dis (d) Il

11. Justice

(a) Il (b) Ir (c) In (d) Im

12. Literate

(a) Dis (b) Mis (c) In (d) Il

13. **Legal**

(a) Il (b) Dis (c) Mis (d) In

14. **Proper**

(a) In (b) Im (c) Un (d) Il

15. **Relevant**

(a) Ir (b) Im (c) Il (d) In

Directions (Qs. 16 to 20) : Choose the antonym of the underlined word.

16. **Rohan is very healthy but his younger brother Sohan is not.**

(a) delicate (b) poor

(c) weak (d) None of these

17. **Everybody wants to succeed because nobody likes failure.**

(a) happy (b) success

(c) joyous (d) None of these

18. **We should not discuss our personal life in public.**

(a) secret (b) private

(c) open (d) None of these

19. **My father is very sick.**

(a) ill (b) fine

(c) healthy (d) None of these

20. **She has the ability to complete her work on time.**

(a) incompetence (b) aptitude

(c) skill (d) None of these

Directions (Qs. 21 to 35) : Read the passage and answer the questions that match the corresponding numbers in the passage.

The detective looked (21) at the doors and windows of the room. (22) He looked at the floor (23). He then decided to ask the maid when the maid had found that the painting on the wall was missing (24). The maid said that she knew nothing (25) about the painting at all.

21. **The synonym of the word is**

(a) saw (b) sea

(c) sway (d) none of these

22. **The opposite of the word is**

(a) him (b) his

(c) she (d) none of these

23. Give the opposite

(a) ground (b) ceiling (c) level (d) none of these

24. The antonym of "missing" used in the paragraph is

(a) detective (b) decided
(c) found (d) none of these

25. Give the meaning

(a) zero (b) everything
(c) all (d) none of these

26. Choose the SYNONYM OF PERPENDICULAR. **[2020]**

(a) Gradual (b) Resilience
(c) Steep (d) Strength

27. Choose the correct ANTONYM OF FABRICATE. **[2020]**

(a) Wreck (b) Construct
(c) Invent (d) Formulate

28. Choose the SYNONYM OF FEARLESS. **[2021]**

(a) Shy (b) Timid
(c) Heroic (d) Weak

29. Choose the ANTONYM OF PUZZLED. **[2021]**

(a) Exhibited (b) Sure
(c) Confused (d) Lost

30. Choose the correct SYNONYM of ENCHANTING **[2022]**

(a) Enlarged (b) Captivating
(c) Responsive (d) Boring

31. Choose the correct ANTONYM of OUTSKIRTS **[2022]**

(a) Edge (b) Bourder
(c) Middle (d) Costumes

32. Oversee **[2022]**

(a) Cheat (b) Follow (c) Neglect (d) Inspect

33. Gaiety **[2022]**

(a) Sadness (b) Happiness (c) Gloom (d) Permanent

34. Protract **[2022]**

(a) Prolong (b) Delay (c) Finish (d) Stretch

35. Moot **[2022]**

(a) Arguable (b) Resolved
(c) Unsettled (d) Both (A) and (C)

RESPONSE GRID

LEVEL 1

1. a b c d	2. a b c d	3. a b c d	4. a b c d	5. a b c d
6. a b c d	7. a b c d	8. a b c d	9. a b c d	10. a b c d
11. a b c d	12. a b c d	13. a b c d	14. a b c d	15. a b c d
16. a b c d	17. a b c d	18. a b c d	19. a b c d	20. a b c d
21. a b c d	22. a b c d	23. a b c d	24. a b c d	25. a b c d
26. a b c d	27. a b c d	28. a b c d	29. a b c d	30. a b c d
31. a b c d	32. a b c d	33. a b c d	34. a b c d	35. a b c d
36. a b c d	37. a b c d	38. a b c d	39. a b c d	40. a b c d
41. a b c d	42. a b c d	43. a b c d		

LEVEL 2

1. a b c d	2. a b c d	3. a b c d	4. a b c d	5. a b c d
6. a b c d	7. a b c d	8. a b c d	9. a b c d	10. a b c d
11. a b c d	12. a b c d	13. a b c d	14. a b c d	15. a b c d
16. a b c d	17. a b c d	18. a b c d	19. a b c d	20. a b c d
21. a b c d	22. a b c d	23. a b c d	24. a b c d	25. a b c d
26. a b c d	27. a b c d	28. a b c d	29. a b c d	30. a b c d
31. a b c d	32. a b c d	33. a b c d	34. a b c d	35. a b c d

Solutions with Explanation

LEVEL-1

1. (a)	2. (b)	3. (c)	4. (c)	5. (d)	6. (a)	7. (c)	8. (b)
9. (b)	10. (a)	11. (b)	12. (c)	13. (d)	14. (a)	15. (c)	16.(a)
17. (c)	18. (c)	19. (a)	20. (d)	21. (a)	22. (d)	23. (c)	24.(c)
25. (b)	26. (a)	27. (a)	28. (b)	29. (c)	30. (b)	31. (a)	32.(d)
33. (a)	34. (a)	35. (a)	36. (b)	37. (b)	38. (c)		

39. (a) Grudge

40. (b) Certain

41. (a) Refute
42. (a) Fantastic
43. (c)

LEVEL-2

1.	(b)	2.	(b)	3.	(c)	4.	(d)	5.	(a)	6.	(d)	7.	(d)	8.	(c)
9.	(b)	10.	(c)	11.	(c)	12.	(d)	13.	(a)	14.	(b)	15.	(a)	16.	(c)
17.	(b)	18.	(b)	19.	(c)	20.	(a)	21.	(a)	22.	(c)	23.	(b)	24.	(c)
25.	(a)														

26. (c) Steep
27. (a) Wreck
28. (c) Heroic
29. (b) Sure
30. (b) Capivating
31. (c) Middle

32. (d) 33. (b) 34. (c) 35. (b)

15 CHAPTER FOREWORD

Hello there! In this chapter, we shall learn about homonyms, homophones and homographs. Sounds confusing? The words which are often confusing have similar pronunciation or spelling. Let us understand this better.

Directions : Read the sentences and fill in the blanks with appropriate words.

1.Every __________ is precious when you are running to win the race.

2.The dress was pretty even the __________ flowers sparkled in the light.

3.Her eyes were filled with __________.

4.Don't __________ that sheet.

5.The wind __________ and we sat by the pool looking at the __________ water.

6.Jane mixed the __________ to bake bread.

7.Rayan picked the __________ from the garden.

8.The tiny __________ on the dress looked cute.

9.Hari played fondly with his __________ and arrow.

10.Gauri __________ that her new room looked awesome.

15 Chapter — Homophones, Homonyms & Homographs

LEARNING OBJECTIVES

This lesson will help you to:—

- Differentiate between words that sound the same but have different spellings.
- Differentiate between words that sound the same but have different meanings.
- Identify the meaning of words with similar spellings and different meanings.

QUICK CONCEPT REVIEW

HOMOPHONES

A homophone is a word that has the same pronunciation as another word but that has a different meaning and spelling.

For example:

- One - won: "One" means the number 1. "Won" is the past tense of win.
- There - Their: "There" is a place or position. "Their" means belonging to people or things.
- Deer - dear: "Deer" means a hoofed animal. "Dear" means expensive or loved one
- Bare - Bear: "Bare" means not covered. "Bear" is an animal.

HOMONYMS

These words have the same spelling and pronunciation but different meanings.

For example:

- Well: It means in good way.
- Well: It also means a shaft dug into the ground to get water.
- Bark: Sound made by dog.
- Bark: Outer covering of a tree trunk.
- Seal: An emblem or symbol

- Seal: A water animal

HOMOGRAPHS

Words which are spelled the same but they may not be pronounced the same are called homographs.

For example:

- Desert: area of land (pronounced - deh - zert)
- Desert: abandon (pronounced as - di - zurt)
- Bass - fish (pronounced as bass)
- Bass - instrument (pronounced as base)

Multiple Choice Questions

LEVEL-1

Directions (Qs. 1 to 10) : Complete the following sentences by choosing the correct option.

1. **Dinner will be ready in about an ________.**

   (a) hour (b) our (c) are (d) R

2. **________ game was postponed because of the rain.**

   (a) are (b) hour (c) our (d) R

3. **Put ________toys away for them.**

   (a) there (b) their (c) they are (d) none of these

4. **I ________ a message to Chris.**

   (a) scent (b) cent (c) sent (d) send

5. **The ________ flew over the plain.**

   (a) plain (b) pane (c) pain (d) plane

6. **We stood on the ________ waiting.**

   (a) stare (b) state (c) stair (d) stead

7. **She only had a ________ of cake as he doesn't eat sweets.**

   (a) peace (b) pie (c) tease (d) piece

8. **The tunic had a pretty ________.**

   (a) yoke (b) yolk (c) yalk (d) none of these

9. **We keep our money in the ________.**

(a) blank (b) space (c) bank (d) none of these

10. **The ________ is drying without water.**

(a) flour (b) flower (c) floor (d) none of these

11. **Choose the homophone of the given word :**
Sell **[2018]**

(a) shell (b) sale (c) cell (d) none

12. **Night** **[2018]**

(a) White (b) neat (c) knight (d) neigh

13. **The word 'told' is the past form of** **[2019]**

(a) tell (b) tale (c) tail (d) tall

14. **The land with unfertile soil is** **[2019]**

(a) dessert (b) desert (c) deserve (d) desolate

LEVEL-2

Directions (Qs. 1 to 5) : Choose the correct word based on the clues given.

1. **Uncovered**

(a) bore (b) bear (c) bare (d) none of these

2. **A table in a church**

(a) alter (b) altar (c) alternate (d) alright

3. **A plant with red roots**

(a) beet (b) beat (c) bee (d) eat

4. **Top of a room**

(a) sealing (b) selling (c) ceiling (d) none of these

5. **Breakfast food**

(a) sequence (b) serial (c) cereal (d) none of these

Directions (Qs. 6 to 10) : Choose the homograph from the options given.

6. (a) content (b) can't (c) conect (d) none
7. (a) balloon (b) bat (c) blue (d) none
8. (a) led (b) load (c) lead (d) light
9. (a) move (b) jump (c) run (d) proceeds
10. (a) row (b) sail (c) sale (d) both a & b

Directions (Qs. 11 to 15) : Choose the homophone of the given words.

11. Cite

(a) set (b) sit (c) site (d) none

12. Coarse

(a) course (b) ofcourse (c) cross (d) rose

13. Gene

(a) jin (b) jean (c) jane (d) gene

14. heal

(a) peal (b) seal (c) deal (d) heel

15. knead

(a) need (b) seed (c) deed (d) mend

Directions (Qs. 16 to 20) : Read the sentences and fill the blanks choosing the correct homophone pair.

16. ________ outfit should I choose to wear to the dance? Last Halloween, I dressed up as a ________.

(a) stitch-click (b) which-witch (c) this-that (d) what-frog

17. I watched the little ant carry ________ piece of bread. I heard my mom laugh and ________ my favourite sound.

(a) Its'-its (b) is-it (c) Its-it's (d) none of these

18. Put this ________ you will be able to find it. Lucky is going to ________ his new shirt.

(a) wear-were (b) where-there (c) were-where (d) where-wear

19. I need to cut my ________ so I can ________ the teacher better.

(a) hair-here (b) here-hear (c) hair-hear (d) none

20. I shall cook ________ when we ________ next time.

(a) met-meat (b) meat-meet (c) met-meet (d) none

Directions (Qs. 21 to 30) : Read the sentences and identify the homophones in the sentence.

21. Susan ate one apple after she won the race.

(a) one-won (b) ate-the (c) apple-race (d) Susan-she

22. I want to buy two dresses.

(a) want-buy (b) to-two (c) buy-dresses (d) none

23. The girl with short red hair has a pet hare.

(a) girl-short (b) with-pet (c) hair-hare (d) red-pet

24. Jack rode the bicycle on the busy road.

(a) rode-road (b) the-the (c) on-busy (d) none

25. Sit here and hear the soft music played on the radio.

(a) sit-soft (b) here-music (c) soft-radio (d) here-hear

26. Hi guys! See my new shoes with high heels.

(a) Hi-guys (b) see-new (c) Hi-high (d) see-heel

27. Apply brake to the car or you will hit the pole and break it.

(a) the-the (b) brake-break (c) you-and (d) hit-it

28. Harry has been growing vegetables in his garden and has sown a few bean seeds.

(a) has-his (b) growing-seeds (c) Harry-garden (d) been-bean

29. He must stop junk food and then wait to lose weight

(a) wait-weight (b) junk-lose (c) stop-wait (d) and-then

30. Whether or not the weather changes, we are going for a picnic.

(a) whether-we (b) weather-whether

(c) change-picnic (d) none

Directions (Qs. 31 to 35) : Read the questions and choose the correct option.

31. Which of the following is not a homograph?

(a) bow-bow (b) dual-duel (c) row-row (d) lead-lead

32. Which of the following is a homophone?

(a) ewe-you (b) ding-dong (c) rise-rise (d) does-does

33. Which of the following is a homonym?

(a) band (b) dough (c) same (d) none

34. Choose the odd one out.

(a) ill-hill (b) tick-tack (c) grass-class (d) dear-deer

35. Sea : See :: main

(a) mane (b) male (c) made (d) main

RESPONSE GRID

LEVEL 1

1. a b c d	2. a b c d	3. a b c d	4. a b c d	5. a b c d
6. a b c d	7. a b c d	8. a b c d	9. a b c d	10. a b c d
11. a b c d	12. a b c d	13. a b c d	14. a b c d	

LEVEL 2

1. a b c d	2. a b c d	3. a b c d	4. a b c d	5. a b c d
6. a b c d	7. a b c d	8. a b c d	9. a b c d	10. a b c d
11. a b c d	12. a b c d	13. a b c d	14. a b c d	15. a b c d
16. a b c d	17. a b c d	18. a b c d	19. a b c d	20. a b c d
21. a b c d	22. a b c d	23. a b c d	24. a b c d	25. a b c d
26. a b c d	27. a b c d	28. a b c d	29. a b c d	30. a b c d
31. a b c d	32. a b c d	33. a b c d	34. a b c d	35. a b c d

Solutions with Explanation

LEVEL-1

1.	(a)	2.	(c)	3.	(b)	4.	(c)	5.	(d)	6.	(c)	7.	(d)	8.	(a)
9.	(c)	10.	(b)	11.	(c)	12.	(c)	13.	(a)	14.	(b)				

LEVEL-2

1.	(c)	2.	(b)	3.	(a)	4.	(c)	5.	(c)	6.	(a)	7.	(b)	8.	(c)
9.	(d)	10.	(a)	11.	(c)	12.	(a)	13.	(b)	14.	(d)	15.	(a)	16.	(b)
17.	(c)	18.	(d)	19.	(c)	20.	(b)	21.	(a)	22.	(b)	23.	(c)	24.	(a)
25.	(d)	26.	(c)	27.	(b)	28.	(d)	29.	(a)	30.	(b)	31.	(b)	32.	(a)
33.	(a)	34.	(d)	35.	(a)										

16 CHAPTER FOREWORD

Vocabulary is like the backbone of every language. The knowledge of words and their usage help us speak and write lucidly.

Let's solve the given word search.

Find the names of different types of apes and monkeys in the following word search.

I	M	Y	R	M	I	S	U	A	J	U	C	N	S	M
M	D	Q	F	W	S	S	P	E	R	O	E	C	D	A
R	N	N	T	H	K	O	P	H	H	Q	P	U	N	N
A	H	H	K	N	R	A	A	J	E	O	P	O	H	D
N	Y	C	C	U	G	Z	D	T	E	X	Q	Y	Z	R
O	T	U	E	C	H	I	M	P	A	N	Z	E	E	I
B	I	U	C	T	W	S	G	B	A	K	H	D	P	L
O	R	A	N	G	U	T	A	N	A	D	A	F	X	L
A	F	H	W	P	R	I	V	W	C	B	P	Z	V	Z
S	I	V	M	U	E	J	P	M	I	V	O	T	R	C
T	S	Z	G	U	A	I	F	D	D	O	V	O	R	K
I	G	N	J	V	X	D	F	A	E	A	Q	S	N	M
I	A	O	W	L	H	D	Y	I	Q	K	J	I	Y	R
L	J	L	S	M	X	F	K	L	A	E	Y	Y	H	B
G	I	Q	T	D	B	I	A	O	N	G	V	V	Q	H

Words to look for

BABOON

CHIMPANZEE

LANGUR

MANDRILL

ORANGUTAN

Chapter 16

Vocabulary

Real Life Examples

- Learning vocabulary words is part of basic education at any age. You may have to learn vocabulary words when learning a foreign language.
- Some people are visual learners - they learn best by seeing something over and over. When we speak to people of different culture we are exposed to an amazing range of cultural influences and occupations, all of which introduce us to new words.
- Activities like crossword puzzle become more interesting when we have a good vocabulary.

Historical preview

- In a famous cartoon by Walt Disney, Mickey Mouse is an apprentice to a wizard and makes errors that cause chaos!
- Can you find the meaning of apprentice?

LEARNING OBJECTIVES

This lesson will help you to:—

- improve your vocabulary.
- know about the ways to improve your vocabulary.
- learn the proper usage of vocabulary in sentences.

QUICK CONCEPT REVIEW

Vocabulary is commonly defined as "all the words known and used by a particular person". Knowing a word, however, is not as simple as being able to recognize or use it.

A vocabulary usually develops with age, and serves as a useful and fundamental tool for communication and acquiring knowledge. Acquiring an extensive vocabulary is one of the largest challenges in learning a second language.

Once the reading and writing vocabularies start to develop, through questions and education, the child starts to discover the anomalies and irregularities of language.

Vocabulary is the study of:

- The meanings of words

Many words have several different meanings.

- How the words are used

Study the words in context; apply what you learn by writing sentences with your words.

- Root words, prefixes, suffixes

Root words - help to understand words. The base of the word that can be used to construct other words.

For example - running; reader; teacher (the base of the word is underlined.)

Prefixes and suffixes are letters that are added to the beginning or end of a word.

For example : un + happy — unhappy (prefix)

pre + assessment — preassessment (prefix)

great + ly — greatly (suffix)

act + tion — action (suffix)

Studying these will aid in the study of vocabulary.

❖ Analogies

This is comparing two pairs of words and choosing the pairs that go together.

For example: gas: car:: electricity : toaster

cow: mammal:: snake: reptile

pencil: write:: scissors: cut

The importance of a vocabulary

❖ An extensive vocabulary aids expression and communication.

❖ Vocabulary size has been directly linked to reading comprehension.

❖ A person may be judged by others based on his or her vocabulary.

PLAY TIME

The vocabulary-centered game of Scrabble was originally conceived long back. It now sells in more than 120 countries, making it one of the most successful board games ever. You can play Scrabble using 100 lettered tiles, each with its own number value, that you must use to form words on the board. Each word must at least crisscross on another word already created. Scrabble makes a good vocabulary-building game because it places the highest value on less frequently used letters, such as "X" and "Q," leading players to come up with obscure words.

Multiple Choice Questions

LEVEL-1

Directions (Qs. 1 to 10): Given below is vocabulary related to food habits. Choose the correct options to fill up the blanks.

1. **The tea was very hot so she had to ________ at it very slowly.**

   (a) slice (b) stir (c) starve (d) sip

2. **This medicine is very ________ tasting.**

   (a) flavours (b) bitter (c) fried (d) chew

3. **Many people believe that taking lots of ________ C can help prevent colds.**

   (a) mineral (b) fats (c) vitamin (d) roughage

4. **No food can grow in the area because there is no rain, so many people are beginning to ________.**

   (a) starve (b) bland (c) taste (d) ripe

5. **Would you like another ________ of pizza?**

   (a) bite (b) grind (c) chew (d) slice

6. **We ________ a chicken for supper on the last night we were camping.**

   (a) flavours (b) raw (c) roasted (d) sauce

7. **She made a ________ drink using a banana, orange juice, milk, and frozen blueberries.**

   (a) delicious (b) fried (c) pretty (d) bland

8. **These bananas are getting pretty ________; we'd better eat them soon.**

   (a) sip (b) frozen (c) bitter (d) ripe

9. **Be sure you ________ the sauce regularly so that it doesn't burn.**

   (a) pour (b) stir (c) chop (d) slice

10. **Tofu has a fairly ________ taste, but it's not bad when mixed into a vegetable sauté.**

    (a) salty (b) sour (c) bland (d) tangy

Directions (Qs. 11 to 15) : Complete the analogies by choosing the correct option.

11. **Orange : juice :: chocolate :**

    (a) milkshake (b) roll (c) cake (d) none of these

12. **cherry : tomato :: baby :**

    (a) chocolate (b) corn (c) salad (d) peas

13. **young : baby :: old :**

(a) kid (b) table (c) man (d) friend

14. **magic : tricks :: comedy :**

(a) singing (b) acting (c) dancing (d) jokes

15. **bird : feather :: dog :**

(a) fur (b) skin (c) cover (d) coat

Directions (Qs. 16 to 21) : Choose the correct prefix/suffix from the options given below.

16. **school**

(a) un (b) mis (c) pre (d) re

17. **match**

(a) mis (b) pre (c) re (d) dis

18. **turn**

(a) post (b) re (c) hood (d) tion

19. **mother**

(a) hood (b) mid (c) ly (d) All a, b and c

20. **purple**

(a) ish (b) ed (c) er (d) ward

21. **large**

(a) er (b) est (c) ly (d) all above

Directions (Qs. 22 to 25) : Identify the root word and choose the correct option.

22. **movement**

(a) move (b) ment (c) vement (d) none

23. **aquarium**

(a) quar (b) aqua (c) rium (d) none

24. **contradict**

(a) con (b) trad (c) dict (d) contra

25. **vocalize**

(a) voca (b) vocal (c) vocali (d) lize

DIRECTION (For Qs. 26 & 29): Choose the correct option.

26. How do you spell the word for a machine that allows you to travel up and down in buildings? [2018]

(a) Elevator (b) Elavator (c) Elavetor (d) Ellevetor

27. How do you spell the word that means to assess something? [2018]

(a) Apprisal (b) Apreysel (c) Appaysal (d) Appraisal

28. In modern society the very young and old are considered to be the most ______ to illness. [2019]

(a) espouse (b) creative (c) vulnerable (d) convoluted

29. There was a ________ mistake made by the referee, which meant that we lost. [2019]

(a) substitute (b) colossal (c) carrier (d) reconciliation

LEVEL-2

Directions (Qs. 1 to 3): Choose the correct options to match the following sentences.

1.

	List I		List II
A.	Pelé is perhaps the most famous	1.	as well as clowns and games to entertain the children.
B.	I know the tune to that song,	2.	when the band appeared on stage.
C.	The festival featured a number of musical performances,	3.	but I don't know the words.
D.	The audience applauded wildly	4.	soccer player in the history of the sport.

	A	B	C	D
(a)	1	2	3	4
(b)	2	3	4	1
(c)	3	4	1	2
(d)	4	3	1	2

2.

	List I		List II
A.	Sue's daughter is very talented	1.	It sounds real, but it is purely from the writer's imagination.
B.	My daughter did a wonderful sketch	2.	I'm sure she will become a professional actress some day.
C.	The band rehearsed for weeks	3.	of a dragon in only a few minutes.
D.	This story is fiction.	4.	before finally beginning to record.

	A	B	C	D
(a)	1	2	3	4
(b)	2	3	4	1
(c)	3	4	1	2
(d)	4	3	1	2

3.

	List I		List II
A.	The students were sharing folk tales	1.	performs tricks for spectators.
B.	The children assembled on stage	2.	half the audience fell asleep.
C.	They have a whale in the aquarium that	3.	from their countries in class today.
D.	The play we saw was really boring	4.	to sing the national anthem.

	A	B	C	D					
(a)	1	2	3	4	(b)	2	3	4	1
(c)	3	4	1	2	(d)	4	3	1	2

Directions (Qs. 4 to 6): Given below are sentences related to vocabulary of different habitats. Choose the correct statements from those given below.

4. A. The Eiffel ___tower___ is probably the most famous landmark in Paris.

B. I don't like to keep birds in a ___shed___; it seems cruel to prevent them from flying around.

C. We've just rented a ___studio___ for my mother to do her painting.

D. The prisoners dug a ___stairs___ under the fence in order to escape from the jail.

(a) A and B are correct (b) B and D are correct

(c) C and D are correct (d) A and C are correct

5. A. The police finally had to put up a ___bench___ in the middle of the street in order to stop a teenager who had been speeding through the downtown core.

B. He and his neighbour worked together to build a nice ___fence___ between their two yards.

C. The old woman was gasping for breath by the time she reached the top of the ___port___.

D. My children love to erect___ towers ___out of blocks and then knock them over.

(a) A and B are correct (b) B and D are correct

(c) C and D are correct (d) A and C are correct

6. A. The fishing boats were gathered in the ___bench___ to wait out the storm.

B. The old man fell asleep on the ___booth___ in the park.

C. The train finally came into the ___station___, over an hour behind schedule.

D. He grew up in a house with a dirt floor and no running water in a ___slum___in the city.

(a) A and B are correct (b) B and D are correct

(c) C and D are correct (d) A and C are correct

Directions (Qs. 7 to 21): Given below is vocabulary related to nouns, verbs and adjectives. Choose the correct options to use them in the sentences.

7. **She's not really a friend; she's just an ________.**

   (a) acquaintance (b) apology (c) companion (d) relative

8. **Many people believe that our ________ is becoming more violent.**

   (a) family (b) office (c) stadium (d) society

9. **I will never babysit my neighbour's little boy again. The kid is a real ________.**

   (a) naughty (b) brat (c) obedient (d) novice

10. **You should ________ this with your parents before you make any decision.**

    (a) fight (b) chat (c) discuss (d) quarrel

11. **It is going to be difficult to find a ________ between the two groups because their needs are so different.**

    (a) compromise (b) agreement (c) solution (d) satisfaction

12. **Its good to know more than one language if you plan on doing business with ________ countries.**

    (a) domestic (b) member (c) native (d) foreign

13. **She had a terrible ________with her best friend when they misunderstood each other.**

    (a) row (b) chat (c) fall (d) patch

14. **The people remained ________ to the king, and refused to fight against him.**

    (a) brave (b) honest (c) loyal (d) stubborn

15. **He has been an important ________ of the team ever since he joined.**

    (a) party (b) customer (c) person (d) member

16. **My daughter ________ to both the chess and badminton clubs at her school.**

    (a) comes (b) belongs (c) joins (d) plays

17. **I really owe you an ________ for behaving badly last Friday. I was totally upset, and didn't know what I was doing.**

    (a) astrology (b) obedience (c) apology (d) eagerness

18. **Her ________ for others led her into a life of volunteer work.**

    (a) honesty (b) compassion (c) value (d) courage

19. **My little sister always tries to ________ me when she gets in trouble.**

    (a) cheat (b) clap (c) blame (d) party

20. **In my culture, we ________ to our ancestors every day.**

    (a) pray (b) talk (c) think (d) see

21. **He ________ in the test; he kept looking at my paper every time the teacher turned her back.**

    (a) escaped (b) stole (c) cheated (d) clapped

Directions (Qs. 22 to 31): Find out the synonyms of the following words.

22. Polite

(a) coarse (b) rude (c) well mannered (d) honest

23. Temper

(a) heat (b) mood (c) calm (d) steel

24. Chorus

(a) refrain (b) order (c) dance (d) shout

25. Rude

(a) polite (b) impolite (c) tough (d) shallow

26. Selection

(a) choice (b) reality (c) rejection (d) belief

27. Foolish

(a) cunning (b) forward (c) silly (d) polite

28. Toxic

(a) poisonous (b) bitter (c) beneficial (d) action

29. Meeting

(a) function (b) programme (c) assembly (d) party

30. Childish

(a) infantile (b) fishy (c) solid (d) naughty

31. Domesticate

(a) foreign (b) cultivate (c) usable (d) wastage

Directions (Qs 32 to 35) : Read the following passage and write down the pairs of antonyms that you find in it. One has been done for you.

Once when King Alphanso was going on a horse, he saw a cart stuck in a loose mud. The mule-driver was trying hard to pull it out, but failed. The king got down from his horse and went to help the mule driver. Both of them pulled and pushed until they succeeded in removing it from the puddle and getting the mule on firm ground. It was no easy job and both of them were soiled with mud. A number of people collected by this time and they stood watching. As the king dusted himself and sat on his horse, the driver recognized the king and begged for forgiveness. The king told him that he had done his duty as a man. He may be a king but as a man he should help those who are in difficulty.

Example: LOOSE- hard

32. PULLED

(a) throw (b) escaped (c) catch (d) pushed

33. FAILED

(a) cheated (b) fought (c) succeeded (d) thought

34. SOILED

(a) dusted (b) cultivated (c) washed (d) dried

35. **STOOD**

(a) mat (b) fat (c) pat (d) sat

Directions (Qs 36 to 40) : Select the correct opposite from the following list.

36. **Wonderful**

(a) exciting (b) terrible (c) lazy (d) funny

37. **Tiny**

(a) huge (b) minute (c) small (d) tinge

38. **Ancient**

(a) public (b) age (c) fast (d) modern

39. **Humble**

(a) humility (b) proud (c) powerful (d) hopeless

40. **Common**

(a) active (b) rare (c) uncommon (d) discommend

Directions (Qs 41 to 46) : From the following pairs select the incorrect word.

41. **Disproper, disappear**

(a) 1st word (b) 2nd word (c) both (d) none

42. **Inefficient, ineven**

(a) 1st word (b) 2nd word (c) both (d) none

43. **Misfortune, mismake**

(a) 1st word (b) 2nd word (c) both (d) none

44. **Disfertile, dishonest**

(a) 1st word (b) 2nd word (c) both (d) none

45. **Unequal, uncool**

(a) 1st word (b) 2nd word (c) both (d) none

46. **Hopeless, boldless**

(a) 1st word (b) 2nd word (c) both (d) none

Directions (Qs 47 to 51) : Give antonyms of the following words.

47. **Nervous**

(a) relaxed (b) anxious (c) worried (d) tense

48. **Grim**

(a) horrible (b) dismal (c) gloomy (d) cheerful

49. **Gratitude**

(a) disregard (b) appreciate (c) thankful (d) pleased

50. **Vigilant**

(a) attentive (b) cautious (c) heedful (d) oblivious

51. **Triumph**

(a) failure (b) victory (c) success (d) conquest

Directions (Qs. 52 to 62) : Choose the correct option from those given below.

52. **That which cannot be seen**

(a) insoluble (b) inaudible (c) invisible (d) incredible

53. **That which cannot be heard**
(a) incredible (b) invisible (c) insoluble (d) inaudible

54. **That which cannot be believed**
(a) indelible (b) incredible (c) invincible (d) ineligible

55. **That which cannot be solved**
(a) insoluble (b) invisible (c) ineligible (d) indivisible

56. **That which cannot be conquered**
(a) invincible (b) inexplicable (c) indelible (d) incredible

57. **One who is all powerful**
(a) omniscient (b) omnipotent (c) omnipresent (d) omnivorous

58. **One who is unable to pay off debts**
(a) amateur (b) fatalist (c) stoic (d) bankrupt

59. **The want of government in a country**
(a) autocracy (b) anarchy (c) democracy (d) bureaucracy

60. **One who abstains from alcoholic drink**
(a) philatelist (b) tourist (c) teetotaller (d) astrologer

61. **One who writes the life story of another person**
(a) curator (b) astronaut (c) author (d) biographer

62. **The girl was very young to suffer from such a/an __________ .** **[2020]**
(a) policy (b) vehemence (c) infirmity (d) agency

RESPONSE GRID

LEVEL 1

1. a b c d	2. a b c d	3. a b c d	4. a b c d	5. a b c d
6. a b c d	7. a b c d	8. a b c d	9. a b c d	10. a b c d
11. a b c d	12. a b c d	13. a b c d	14. a b c d	15. a b c d
16. a b c d	17. a b c d	18. a b c d	19. a b c d	20. a b c d
21. a b c d	22. a b c d	23. a b c d	24. a b c d	25. a b c d
26. a b c d	27. a b c d	28. a b c d	29. a b c d	

LEVEL 2

1. a b c d	2. a b c d	3. a b c d	4. a b c d	5. a b c d
6. a b c d	7. a b c d	8. a b c d	9. a b c d	10. a b c d
11. a b c d	12. a b c d	13. a b c d	14. a b c d	15. a b c d

16. a b c d	17. a b c d	18. a b c d	19. a b c d	20. a b c d
21. a b c d	22. a b c d	23. a b c d	24. a b c d	25. a b c d
26. a b c d	27. a b c d	28. a b c d	29. a b c d	30. a b c d
31. a b c d	32. a b c d	33. a b c d	34. a b c d	35. a b c d
36. a b c d	37. a b c d	38. a b c d	39. a b c d	40. a b c d
41. a b c d	42. a b c d	43. a b c d	44. a b c d	45. a b c d
46. a b c d	47. a b c d	48. a b c d	49. a b c d	50. a b c d
51. a b c d	52. a b c d	53. a b c d	54. a b c d	55. a b c d
56. a b c d	57. a b c d	58. a b c d	59. a b c d	60. a b c d
61. a b c d	62. a b c d			

Solutions with Explanation

LEVEL-1

1. (d)	2. (b)	3. (c)	4. (a)
5. (d)	6. (c)	7. (a)	8. (d)
9. (b)	10. (c)	11. (a)	12. (b)
13. (c)	14. (d)	15. (a)	16. (c)
17. (a)	18. (b)	19. (d)	20. (a)
21. (d)	22. (a)	23. (b)	24. (d)
25. (b)	26. (a)	27. (d)	28. (c)
29. (b)			

LEVEL-2

1. (d)	2. (b)	3. (c)	4. (d)
5. (b)	6. (c)	7. (a)	8. (d)
9. (b)	10. (c)	11. (c)	12. (d)
13. (a)	14. (c)	15. (d)	16. (b)
17. (c)	18. (b)	19. (c)	20. (a)
21. (c)	22. (c)	23. (b)	24. (a)
25. (b)	26. (a)	27. (c)	28. (a)
29. (c)	30. (a)	31. (b)	32. (d)

33. (c)	34. (c)	35. (d)	36. (b)
37. (a)	38. (d)	39. (d)	40. (b)
41. (a)	42. (b)	43. (b)	44. (a)
45. (b)	46. (b)	47. (a)	48. (d)
49. (a)	50. (d)	51. (a)	52. (c)
53. (d)	54. (b)	55. (a)	56. (a)
57. (b)	58. (d)	59. (b)	60. (c)
61. (d)			

62. (c) infirmity

17 CHAPTER FOREWORD

After all these chapters, you are now one smart cookie! puzzled? It simply means that you are an intelligent person, having read all the topics. "Smart cookie" is an idiom. This chapter is all about idiom and phrases.

Directions: Complete each idiom on the left with the correct animal word. Then match the idioms to their definitions on the right.

1	to take the ________ by the horns	☐	a	to ignore a problem because trying to deal with it could cause an even more difficult situation
2	to do the ________ work	☐	b	to talk and think a lot about something
3	to flog a dead ________	☐	c	to do the hard boring part of a job or task
4	to keep the ________ from the door	☐	d	to have more important or more interesting things to do
5	to let sleeping ________ s lie	☐	e	to face a difficult or dangerous situation directly and with courage
6	to let the ________ out of the bag	☐	f	to do something badly; to make a mess of something
7	to smell a ________	☐	g	to have enough money to avoid going hungry
8	to have other/bigger ________ to fry	☐	h	to reveal a secret
9	to have a ________ in your bonnet	☐	i	to waste your effort by trying to do something that is no longer possible
10	to make a ________'s ear of something	☐	j	to sense that someting is wrong about a situation

17 Chapter — Idioms and Phrases

LEARNING OBJECTIVES

This lesson will help you to:—

- learn idioms and phrases.
- understand their meanings.
- understand their correct usage.

QUICK CONCEPT REVIEW

Idioms are words or phrases with an informal meaning that is different from the words' dictionary definitions. For example, "under the weather" is an idiom: it means "sick," not "beneath rain or sunshine." English speakers use idioms every day, often without even realizing it, and non-native speakers must learn at least the most common ones in order to understand conversational English.

For example:

- At home :- to be familiar with. He is equally at home in German and French.
- By virtue of:-on account of. He occupied the chair at the meeting by virtue of seniority.
- Fair play:-equal conditions for all. All political parties want fair play in the elections.
- In full swing:-working busily. The share market was in full swing.
- Well off:-rich. These people are very well off.

Real Life Example

Trying to figure out English idioms on your own can be frustrating. English idioms are an important component of natural English. English idioms are non-literal phrases that have a meaning that's different from the individual words. Phrases such as "saved by the bell," "it's raining cats and dogs" and countless others are a common part of the English vernacular. Whether you're learning English for the first time or just looking to add to your vocabulary, idioms are a great place to start.

Amazing Fact

To "shed crocodile tears."

Crocodiles have a reflex that causes their eyes to tear when they open their mouths. This makes it look as though they are crying while devouring their prey. In fact, neither crocodiles nor people who shed "crocodile" tears feel sorry for their actions.

Historical preview

"Bury the hatchet."

- Native Americans used to bury weapons to show that fighting had ended and enemies were now at peace. Today, the idiom means to make up with a friend after an argument or fight.

"Raining cats and dogs."

- In Norse mythology, the dog is associated with wind and the cat with storms. This expression means it's raining very heavily.

PHRASES

A phrase is a group of words that has a particular meaning when used together, or which someone uses on a particular occasion.

For example:

He disposed off his car for a small sum.

Here the phrase 'disposed off' can easily be replaced with "sold", so, that's how we use a phrase.

PROVERBS

A short well-known statement that gives advice or expresses something that is generally true. Take the famous proverb:

Slow and steady wins the race. 'A penny saved is a penny earned' is another example of a proverb.

Multiple Choice Questions

LEVEL-1

Directions (Qs. 1 to 20): Choose the correct option.

1. **A man of straw**
   (a) A man of no substance
   (b) A very active person
   (c) A worthy fellow
   (d) An unreasonable person
2. **A black sheep**
   (a) An unlucky person
   (b) A lucky person
   (c) A disgraced member of a group
   (d) A partner who takes no share of the profits
3. **To beg the question**
   (a) To refer to
   (b) To raise a particular question to ask
   (c) To raise objections
   (d) To be discussed
4. **To play second fiddle**
   (a) To be happy, cheerful and healthy
   (b) To reduce importance of one's senior
   (c) To support the role and view of another person
   (d) To do back seat driving
5. **To leave someone in the lurch** **[2015]**
   (a) To compromise with someone
   (b) To annoy someone
   (c) To put someone at ease
   (d) To desert someone in his difficulties
6. **To pick holes**
   (a) To find some reason to quarrel
   (b) To destroy something
   (c) To criticise someone
   (d) To cut some part of an item
7. **To put one's hand to plough**
   (a) To take up agricultural farming
   (b) To take a difficult task
   (c) To get into unnecessary things
   (d) Take interest in technical work
8. **To be above board** **[2013]**
   (a) To have a good height
   (b) To be honest in any business deal
   (c) To have no debts
   (d) To try to be beautiful
9. **To end in smoke**
   (a) To make completely understand
   (b) To ruin oneself
   (c) To excite great applause
   (d) To overcome someone

10. **To have an axe to grind**
(a) A private end to serve
(b) To fail to arouse interest
(c) To have no result
(d) To work for both sides

11. **To cry wolf**
(a) To listen eagerly
(b) To give false alarm
(c) To turn pale
(d) To keep off starvation

12. **To drive home** **[2014]**
(a) To find one's roots
(b) To return to place of rest
(c) Back to original position
(d) To emphasise

13. **To catch a tartar**
(a) To grapple with a formidable opponent
(b) To fight with a strong enemy
(c) To meet with disaster
(d) To deal with a person who is more than one's match

14. **To keep one's temper**
(a) To become hungry
(b) To preserve one's energy
(c) To remain calm
(d) To be aloof from

15. **To make clean breast of**
(a) To gain prominence
(b) To praise oneself
(c) To confess without reservation
(d) To destroy before it blooms

16. **To smell a rat**
(a) To see signs of plague epidemic
(b) To get bad smell of a dead rat
(c) To suspect foul dealings
(d) To be in a bad mood

17. **To hit the nail right on the head**
(a) To do the right thing
(b) To destroy one's reputation
(c) To announce one's fixed views
(d) To teach someone a lesson

18. **To set one's face against**
(a) To oppose with determination
(b) To judge by appearance
(c) To get out of difficulty
(d) To look at one steadily

19. **To bait a trap**
(a) To plan an idea
(b) To make conspiracy
(c) To get into problem
(d) To entire by trickery or deception

20. **Cold shoulder**
(a) a show of indifference
(b) discomfort
(c) disrespect
(d) discipline

21. **I can be round to help you at ______ because I live next door.** **[2018]**
(a) the drop of a hat
(b) a cold day in June
(c) up and down
(d) the last straw

22. **It was _______ last week. I had to wear a sun hat for most of it.** **[2018]**
(a) like the oven (b) the hot one (c) a scorcher (d) up in smoke

LEVEL-2

Directions (Qs. 1 to 5): In list I, idioms are given and in list II, the sentences are completed in a way so that the meaning of the idiom becomes clear. Match List I with List II.

(Critical Thinking)

1.

	List I		List II
A.	You should keep him at arm's length	1.	he obviously has much better skills.
B.	He is sitting on the fence, trying to	2.	so do not worry.
C.	He is willing to play second fiddle although	3.	see which side he should cheer for.
D.	I have the whole plan at my fingertips	4.	because he may have a bad influence on you.

	A	B	C	D					
(a)	1	2	3	4	(b)	2	3	4	1
(c)	3	4	1	2	(d)	4	3	1	2

2. [2013]

	List I		List II
A.	A bird in the hand is worth two in the bush so	1.	it will grow out of control.
B.	I paid through the nose for	2.	get the job at first.
C.	Janet broke the ice and started	3.	the over-priced video game.
D.	We have to nip the problem in the bud or	4.	a conversation with the shy boy.

	A	B	C	D					
(a)	1	2	3	4	(b)	2	3	4	1
(c)	3	4	1	2	(d)	4	3	1	2

3.

	List I		List II
A.	He held his tongue and managed	1.	he is the one who did it.
B.	She is a greenhorn and it takes time for her	2.	so you may like it but he may not.
C.	I am cocksure that	3.	to keep the secret to himself.
D.	One man's meat is another man's poison	4.	to learn all the skills needed for the job.

	A	B	C	D					
(a)	1	2	3	4	(b)	2	3	4	1
(c)	3	4	1	2	(d)	4	3	1	2

4.

	List I		List II
A.	By hook or by crook, we have to submit	1.	the assignment by the end of this month.
B.	You must not put all your eggs in one basket	2.	try to find some alternatives.
C.	His words carry weight	3.	because he is well respected.
D.	Half a loaf is better than none	4.	be grateful for what you get.

	A	B	C	D		A	B	C	D
(a)	1	2	3	4	(b)	2	3	4	1
(c)	3	4	1	2	(d)	4	3	1	2

5.

	List I		List II
A.	He took the law into his	1.	to impress his boss.
B.	He was like a dog with two tails	2.	my grandfather firmly believes in the saying.
C.	Colin put his best foot forward in the project	3.	own hands and killed the robber.
D.	"Spare the rod and spoil the child"	4.	when he won the final game.

	A	B	C	D		A	B	C	D
(a)	1	2	3	4	(b)	2	3	4	1
(c)	3	4	1	2	(d)	4	3	1	2

Directions (Qs. 6 and 7): There are four sentences given. They can be correct or incorrect. Based on it, choose the correct option.

6. **A. A rolling stone gathers no moss, so one should stick to what one is doing.**

   B. Birds of a feather fly together. So, it is not surprising to see the two hang around all the time.

   C. You do not need to argue because actions always speak louder than words.

   D. You must draw a parallel between what you can and cannot do. (Tricky)

   (a) A and B are correct. (b) B and D are correct.

   (c) C and D are correct. (d) A and C are correct.

7. **A. New brooms sweep clean, but I doubt if the new boss can sustain this pace.**

   B. Granny used to spin yarns about her experiences during the Japanese Occupation.

   C. She pulled connections in order to get the job.

   D. He stayed calm and did not turn a foot.

   (a) A and B are correct. (b) B and D are correct.

   (c) C and D are correct. (d) A and C are correct.

8. **Fill in the blanks in the table given below. Choose from the given options.**

There is no ________	and fast rule to do the job.
He let the ________	out of the bag and announced the new plan.
He pulled up his ________	and started all over again.
I know ________	was not built in a day.

(a) cat, socks, hard, Rome (b) Rome, hard, socks, cat
(c) hard, cat, socks, Rome (d) socks, hard, cat, Rome

Directions (Qs. 9 and 10): Read the sentences and choose the correct option.

9. **(A) Although he offers a lot of ideas, there is little substance. After all, empty vessels make the most noise.**

   (B) You should set a good example and practise what you preach.

   (a) TT (b) TF (c) FT (d) FF

10. **(A) Do not be so hard on him. To fail is human, to forgive is divine. [2015]**

    (B) It is better to ask for their help because many hands make more work.

    (a) TT (b) TF (c) FT (d) FF

Directions (Qs. 11 to 20): Fill in the blanks with the correct option.

11. **He kept beating around the ______ and did not get to the point.**
    (a) street (b) wood (c) bush (d) grass
12. **Let's be patient and continue to work at it. Every cloud has a silver _____. [2016]**
    (a) lining (b) spark (c) streak (d) line
13. **It's a trivial matter. Don't make a mountain out of a ______.**
    (a) hill (b) peak (c) molehill (d) hillock
14. **The news was like a bolt from the ______. I never expected it to happen to me.**
    (a) blue (b) shock (c) sky (d) cloud
15. **He arrived in the _____ of time to save her from a lot of embarrassment. [2013]**
    (a) crux (b) nick (c) tip (d) tick
16. **The cat disappeared in the dark in the twinkling of a/an ______.**
    (a) star (b) eye (c) light (d) lash
17. **Romeo takes up two jobs to make ends ______.**
    (a) meet (b) stay (c) float (d) burn
18. **He is a Jack of all ______ but master of none.**
    (a) sorts (b) trades (c) things (d) tricks
19. **He turned ______ and ran away immediately.**
    (a) head (b) feet (c) tail (d) back
20. **Let's bury the ______ and be friends again.**
    (a) hatchet (b) weapon (c) gun (d) knife

Directions (Qs. 21 to 25): Read the given situations. Choose the most appropriate idiom or proverb which matches with the situation.

21. I thought Aditya would be a good worker, but it turns out that he can't cut the mustard. [2014]
- (a) He is not good in cooking.
- (b) He does not know how to collect mustard.
- (c) He cannot deal with problems and difficulties.
- (d) None of the above.

22. Nishi decided that she would go out on a limb and ask Satyam to the Annual dance competition.
- (a) Nishi will take a risk.
- (b) Nishi will fight.
- (c) Nishi will take some vehicle.
- (d) Nishi will go out of the way to ask him.

23. Mukund thought his mom would let him go to the party, but no dice.
- (a) There was no vehicle to go.
- (b) There was no money.
- (c) Mom was not available.
- (d) Mom denied and there was no possibility.

24. Rohan was too tired to finish the assignment, so he decided to hit the hay.
- (a) He prepared to go for sleep.
- (b) He postponed his assignment for the next day.
- (c) He thought it was useless to do the work.
- (d) None of the above.

25. Abhijeet was excited when he found out that he would have his own flat given by his company. It was just the icing on the cake. [2016]
- (a) The flat was small but good.
- (b) The flat was beautiful.
- (c) The flat was an additional benefit to the salary he was getting.
- (d) Both (b) and (c)

RESPONSE GRID

LEVEL 1

1. a b c d	2. a b c d	3. a b c d	4. a b c d	5. a b c d
6. a b c d	7. a b c d	8. a b c d	9. a b c d	10. a b c d
11. a b c d	12. a b c d	13. a b c d	14. a b c d	15. a b c d
16. a b c d	17. a b c d	18. a b c d	19. a b c d	20. a b c d
21. a b c d	22. a b c d			

LEVEL 2

1. a b c d	2. a b c d	3. a b c d	4. a b c d	5. a b c d
6. a b c d	7. a b c d	8. a b c d	9. a b c d	10. a b c d

11. [a] [b] [c] [d] 12. [a] [b] [c] [d] 13. [a] [b] [c] [d] 14. [a] [b] [c] [d] 15. [a] [b] [c] [d]

16. [a] [b] [c] [d] 17. [a] [b] [c] [d] 18. [a] [b] [c] [d] 19. [a] [b] [c] [d] 20. [a] [b] [c] [d]

21. [a] [b] [c] [d] 22. [a] [b] [c] [d] 23. [a] [b] [c] [d] 24. [a] [b] [c] [d] 25. [a] [b] [c] [d]

Solutions with Explanation

LEVEL-1

1.	(a)	2.	(c)	3.	(b)	4.	(c)	5.	(d)
6.	(c)	7.	(b)	8.	(b)	9.	(b)	10.	(a)
11.	(b)	12.	(d)	13.	(b)	14.	(c)	15.	(c)
16.	(c)	17.	(a)	18.	(a)	19.	(d)	20.	(a)
21.	(a)	22.	(c)						

LEVEL-2

1. (d) 2. (b) 3. (c) 4. (a) 5. (c)

6. (d) B. Birds of a feather flock together. So, it is not surprising to see the two hang around all the time.
D. You must draw a line between what you can and cannot do.

7. (a) C. She pulled strings in order to get the job.
D. He stayed calm and did not turn a hair.

8. (c) 9. (a)

10. (d) A. Do not be so hard on him. To err is human, to forgive is divine.
B. It is better to ask for their help because many hands make work light.

11. (c) 12. (a) 13. (c) 14. (a) 15. (b)

16. (b) 17. (a) 18. (b) 19. (c) 20. (a)

21. (c) If you can't cut the mustard, you cannot deal with problems or difficulties.

22. (a) Go out on a limb means-to take a risk.

23. (d) No dice is used when something that you say in order to refuse a request or to make clear that something is not possible.

24. (a) Hit the hay means prepare for sleep.

25. (c) Icing on the cake means an additional benefit to something already good.

18 CHAPTER FOREWORD

Stories are interesting, whether they are fairy tales or comics or any other kind of story.

Let's learn to write a story.

Given below is a "story map" that will help you create your story. Fill in the details and you have the story ready!

Let's create a story map. Use your imagination and throw in the best vocabulary you know.

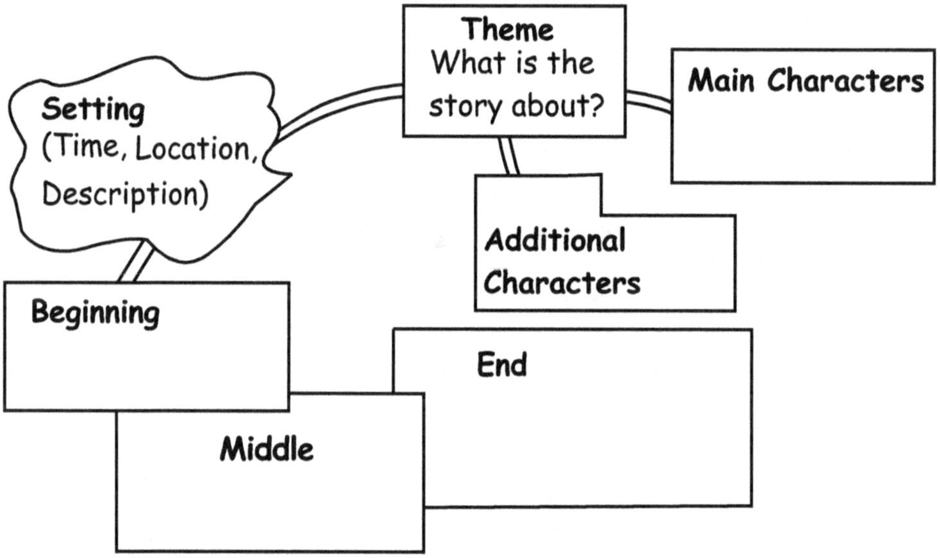

Theme
What is the story about?

Main Characters

Setting
(Time, Location, Description)

Additional Characters

Beginning

End

Middle

Chapter 18

Story Writing

LEARNING OBJECTIVES

This lesson will help you to:—

- write a story.
- understand how to use prompts to build a story.
- understand how to use pictures to build a story.

Real Life Examples

- You watch cartoons everyday. They all are stories. Chota Bheem, Doraemon, Shin Chan they all are characters which take you to the imaginary worlds. The movies we watch are also stories told.
- Caution: When you watch cartoons or movies you must keep this in mind that it is all imaginary. You must know that what is shown on TV is fantasy and not real. SO, DO NOT APPLY IT IN REAL LIFE AND DO NOT GET CARRIED AWAY.
- Smallest Story: Once I was travelling from Edinburgh London. A man came and sat on the opposite berth. He asked me-" Do you believe in ghost?" I said, " No". He vanished.

QUICK CONCEPT REVIEW

In class-4 you can learn to communicate in complete thoughts for different purposes. At the beginning of class-4, you may still write in short, literal, choppy sentences but as you progress through the year, you learn to write more detailed essays and stories to communicate what you are learning. To help yourself learn how to write events in a story for a more flowing account, you can think of the story as a recipe. Using story maps and plot planners, you can gain proficiency in using literary devices to spin tales that fascinate readers with interesting details.

The outline of a story is the basic framework of a story. It is often just a skeleton outline. It shows us some of the main facts of the story and tells in brief what the story is like. We have to fill in all the details relevant to the story and thus make up a readable story.

IMPORTANT HINTS

The following few hints will tell you how to build up a story from a given outline

1. Read the given outline carefully. Note all the points. Follow as strictly as possible the sketch provided.
2. Be careful to connect the points given in the outline naturally, so that the whole will read well as a connected piece of good composition.

3. You must use your imagination in filling the details of action, gesture and conversation that should connect one point with the next.
4. Where ever possible, introduce dialogue or conversation; but be careful to make it natural and interesting.
5. The conclusion or ending of a story should be striking and interesting.
6. If you are asked to give a title or heading to the story you may name it (i) after the main character, (ii) object or incident of the story.
7. Revise your writing and remove all mistakes in spelling, grammar, punctuation, etc.

Story Map

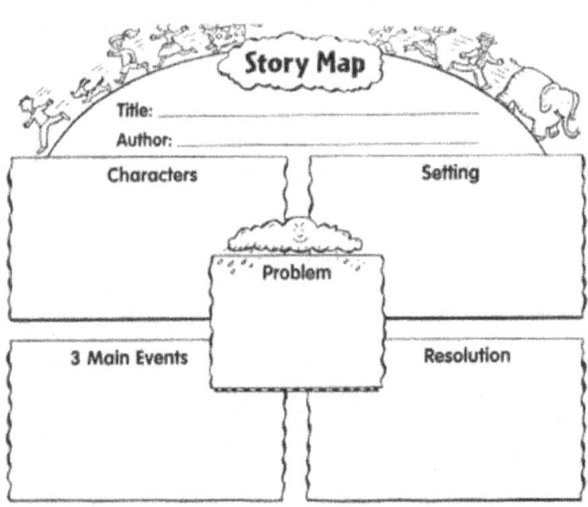

Plot Planner

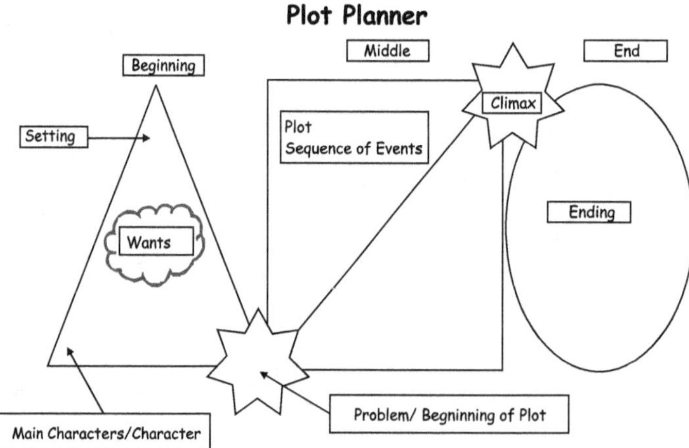

Examples

HINT BASED

(A) An old lady becomes blind _______ calls in a doctor _______ agrees to pay large fee if cured, but nothing if not _______ doctor calls daily _______ covets lady's furniture

_______ delays the cure _______ every day takes away some of her furniture _______ at last cures her _______ demands his fees _______ lady refuses to pay, saying cure not complete _______ doctor brings a court case _______ judge asks lady why she will not pay _______ she says sight not properly restored _______ she cannot see all her furniture _______ judge gives verdict in her favour _______ moral.

Complete story:-

PICTURE BASED

(B) Complete story: Title _______ " The goose that laid golden eggs"

One day a poor farmer while cutting wood in the forest found a goose. He brought it home and gave it some food and water and a place to live in. The next morning when the farmer woke up , he was surprised to see that the goose had laid a golden egg. He told about this to his wife and she suggested him to sell the egg in the market in exchange of food and fuel. Again on next morning when the farmer woke up he found the same goose had laid another golden egg. Both the farmer and his wife became very happy. Now every day the goose used to lay a golden egg. One day the farmer became greedy and thought of cutting the stomach of the goose and getting all the eggs at once and becoming a very rich person in the village. He took a sharp knife and killed the goose but in vain, he got none. He realised his mistake and again became a poor man.
Moral:_______ "Greediness is a curse."

Multiple Choice Questions

LEVEL-1

Directions (Qs. 1 to 5): Try and answer these general knowledge questions about stories.

1. **Who wrote the famous Panchtantra?**

   (a) Aryabhatta (b) Valmiki (c) Vishnu Sharma (d) Chanakya

2. **What are the stories, which are passed from one generation to another verbally, called?**

   (a) Fable (b) Tale (c) Parable (d) Short story

3. What are the stories, which have animal characters behaving like humans, called?

(a) Fable (b) Tale (c) Parable (d) Short story

4. Who is the writer of the famous Harry Potter Series?

(a) C.S. Lewis (b) R.L. Stevenson (c) J.K. Rowling (d) R.K. Narayan

5. Who is the writer of the famous "Malgudi Days"?

(a) C.S. Lewis (b) R.L. Stevenson (c) J.K. Rowling (d) R.K. Narayan

LEVEL-2

Directions (Qs. 1 and 2): Given below is a story, but its sequence has been jumbled, read carefully and choose the correct sequence from the options given below.

1.

1. On the other hand the tortoise was moving slowly in its own pace and left the hare back.
2. Now the hare and the tortoise decided to run a race, to prove who was the fastest runner.
3. Both of them started from a certain point with their own speed.
4. One day when it was boasting of its speed among its friends, the tortoise challenged it.
5. As the hare leaped and jumped it reached the midway beforehand and thought of taking a short nap and fell asleep.
6. There was a rabbit that was very proud of himself because he was the fastest runner.

7. When the hare woke up it found that the tortoise had won the race. This teaches us that 'slow and steady wins the race.'

(a) 2.4.6.3.5.7.1. (b) 6.4.2.3.5.1.7. (c) 4.6.2.1.7.5.3. (d) 1.3.5.7.2.4.6.

2.

1. Bears do not harm dead people.
2. The other one replied, "Don't trust a false friend."
3. But the other was not able to climb a tree, so he lay down motionless.
4. One day two friends were travelling in a forest, suddenly a bear appears.
5. The friend on tree climbed down and enquired from the other what the bear had whispered into his ears.
6. As the bear came near he sniffed and prowled off.
7. One of them hastily climbs up a tree.

(a) 6.3.1.2.4.5.7. (b) 3.4.5.7.6.2.1. (c) 4.7.3.6.1.5.2. (d) 7.5.3.1.2.4.6.

Directions (Qs.3 & 4): Suggest a suitable title and give the moral for the given stories.

Once upon a time a rich merchant was returning home through a forest with lots of money. On his way three dacoits robbed him. The dacoits were very hungry so they decided to celebrate their victory with food and wine. One of the robbers went to a nearby village to buy some food and wine. On the other hand the other two robbers decided to kill him on his return because they wanted to deprive him of his share of the booty. The robber who had gone to bring food was no less greedy than the other two. He too thought of killing his companions and keep the entire booty to himself. So he made his purchases and mixed some poison in the wine. When he returned back he was killed by the other two. Nonetheless when both of them took the poisoned wine they also died in the same way.

3. What can be the suitable title for this story?

(a) The three dacoits (b) The merchant

(c) The lost treasure (d) Three greedy dacoits

4. What is the moral of this story?

(a) You must be united

(b) You must not kill anyone

(c) If you try to kill others, you get killed yourself

(d) Greed kills everyone

Directions (Qs. 5 and 6) : Suggest a suitable title and give the moral for the given stories.

A slave in ancient Europe had a cruel master. He ran away into a forest and slept that night in a cave. He woke up by terrible roar, saw a lion coming into the cave. The lion was quite gentle and held up his wounded paw. Though terrified the slave takes out a big thorn from the lion's paw. The lion felt relieved, grateful and wagged his tail. Now the slave and the lion lived together as friends. But one day the slave was caught by his master. He was condemned to be thrown to lions. In the arena the lion rushes to attack him but when he saw the same slave, he recognised and licked his feet to the great astonishment of the slave. It was the same lion. The judge heard the whole story and freed the slave and gifted the lion to him.

5. **What can be the suitable title for this story?**
   (a) The Lion (b) The slave and the lion
   (c) The slave (d) The lion in pain
6. **What is the moral for this story?**
   (a) You must help others
   (b) You must not hurt animals
   (c) Gratitude should always be remembered
   (d) You must love animals

Directions (Qs. 7 to 17): Complete the story by filling in the blanks and also identify the moral of the story.

A ___(7)___ boy was given the work by the villagers to take their sheep out for ___(8)___ daily in the morning and return back in the ___(9)___ . The boy gets bored of his ___(10)___ work and thought of pricking a joke to entertain himself. He shouted,"wolf! Wolf! Save me", all the villagers leaving their work in the middle ___(11)___ to help the boy. But to their utter dismay there was no wolf. The boy ___(12)___ at them. Now he played the same joke again and again to ___(13)___. the villagers. After ___(14)___ day's the villagers got ___(15)___ with him and understood his silly pranks. One day a wolf came in ___(16)___ , the boy shouted for help but none of the villagers turned up to help him. The wolf came and destroyed the whole flock of sheep. The boy somehow saved himself and cried for his mistakes.

7.	(a) cobbler	(b) carpenter	(c) shepherd	(d) baker
8.	(a) grazing	(b) amazing	(c) playing	(d) working
9.	(a) night	(b) twilight	(c) evening	(d) dawn
10.	(a) interesting	(b) useful	(c) amazing	(d) monotonous
11.	(a) rushed	(b) slowed	(c) walked	(d) jumped
12.	(a) cried	(b) laughed	(c) threw	(d) played
13.	(a) entertain	(b) amuse	(c) harass	(d) joy
14.	(a) few	(b) much	(c) lot of	(d) little
15.	(a) happy	(b) entertained	(c) jovial	(d) angry
16.	(a) real	(b) imagination	(c) fantasy	(d) movie

17. **What is the moral of this story?**
   (a) Playing pranks on others can harm you a lot.
   (b) We must entertain others.

(c) We must help others.

(d) We must not make our elders angry.

Directions (Qs. 18 to 28): Complete the story by filling the blanks and also identify the moral of the story.

A jackal wanted to eat sugarcanes on the other side of the river. He could not ___(18)___ and wondered how to get ___(19)___. He thought of an idea to befool the camel. The jackal told the ___(20)___ that there is sugarcane on the other side. The camel agreed to carry the jackal across in return for the information. As they ___(21)___ . the river the jackal finished his meal and thought of playing ___(22)___ on the camel. It ___(23)___ round the field ___ (24)___. Hearing this, the villagers rushed out and saw the camel in the sugarcane field. They started beating the camel with sticks, somehow it saved itself and ran ___(25)___ the river. The jackal took no time to ___(26)___ on the back of the camel. The camel asked the jackal why he had played such a trick on him. Jackal replied that he always ___(27)___ after a good meal. The camel understood the trick of the jackal and in return said that he always takes a bath after a good meal. Saying this he rolled in the river, the jackal nearly got drowned and somehow managed to save itself and asked to forgive him.

18. (a) swim (b) jump (c) play (d) sing

19. (a) behind (b) beside (c) under (d) across

20. (a) lion (b) elephant (c) camel (d) deer

21. (a) jumped (b) hid in the (c) crossed (d) went

22. (a) music (b) trick (c) song (d) piano

23. (a) ran (b) swam (c) cuddled (d) cried

24. (a) howling (b) laughing (c) merrily (d) sadly

25. (a) under (b) below (c) till (d) towards

26. (a) crawl (b) wriggle (c) climb (d) tickle

27. (a) cries (b) howls (a) enjoys (d) entertains

28. **What is the moral of this story?**

(a) You must not irritate others
(b) Honesty is the best policy
(c) Tit for Tat
(d) You must not consider anyone weak.

Direction (Qs. 29 & 30): Identify the stories by the titles.

29.

(a) Captain hook the hero
(b) The little princess
(c) Peter Pan
(d) The Lion King

30.

(a) The lion king
(b) Simba and the animals
(c) The Jungle book
(d) The animal farm

RESPONSE GRID

LEVEL 1

1. a b c d 2. a b c d 3. a b c d 4. a b c d 5. a b c d

LEVEL 2

1. a b c d 2. a b c d 3. a b c d 4. a b c d 5. a b c d
6. a b c d 7. a b c d 8. a b c d 9. a b c d 10. a b c d
11. a b c d 12. a b c d 13. a b c d 14. a b c d 15. a b c d
16. a b c d 17. a b c d 18. a b c d 19. a b c d 20. a b c d
21. a b c d 22. a b c d 23. a b c d 24. a b c d 25. a b c d
26. a b c d 27. a b c d 28. a b c d 29. a b c d 30. a b c d

Solutions with Explanation

LEVEL-1

1. **(c)** **2.** **(b)** **3.** **(a)** **4.** **(c)**
5. **(d)**

LEVEL-2

1. **(b)** 1. There was a rabbit that was very proud of himself because he was the fastest runner.

2. One day when it was boasting of its speed among its friends, the tortoise challenged it.
3. Now the hare and the tortoise decided to run a race, to prove who was the fastest runner.
4. Both of them started from a certain point with their own speed.
5. As the hare leaped and jumped it reached the midway beforehand and thought of taking a short nap and fell asleep.
6. On the other hand the tortoise was moving slowly in its own pace and left the hare back.
7. When the hare woke up it found that the tortoise had won the race, which teach us that 'slow and steady wins the race.'

2. (c) 1. One day two friends were travelling in a forest, suddenly a bear appears.
2. One of them hastily climbs up a tree.
3. But the other was not able to climb a tree, so he lay down motionless.
4. As the bear came near he sniffed and prowled off.
5. Bears do not harm dead people.
6. The friend on tree climbed down and enquired from the other that what did the bear whisper into his ears.
7. The other one replied, "Don't trust a false friend."

3. (d)	**4.** (d)	**5.** (b)	**6.** (c)
7. (c)	**8.** (a)	**9.** (c)	**10.** (d)
11. (a)	**12.** (b)	**13.** (c)	**14.** (a)
15. (d)	**16.** (a)	**17.** (a)	**18.** (a)
19. (d)	**20.** (c)	**21.** (c)	**22.** (b)
23. (a)	**24.** (a)	**25.** (d)	**26.** (c)
27. (b)	**28.** (c)	**29.** (c)	**30.** (c)

19 CHAPTER FOREWORD

Wow! my grandma sent me a gift. I'd like to thank her by writing a letter. Do you know how to write a letter? This chapter will help you learn about letters.

Some things are better told formally, especially in formal letters.

For example :

FORMAL: I am disturbed about your lack of response on this issue.

INFORMAL: I am worried that you haven't answered me.

Directions: Match each of the informal words in the left column to its more appropriate formal word in the right column.

________	1.	hello	A.	an issue
________	2.	tell (somebody)	B.	disturbed
________	3.	a problem	C.	contact
________	4.	at a very last time	D.	discuss
________	5.	worried	E.	Dear Sir/Madam
________	6.	speak (to somebody)	F.	take actions (regarding)
________	7.	do not want to listen	G.	cause
________	8.	get in touch (with)	H.	ignore
________	9.	do something about	I.	during unsociable hours
________	10.	make	J.	yours faithfully
________	11.	bye	K.	inform (somebody)

19
Chapter

Letter Writing

LEARNING OBJECTIVES

This lesson will help you to:—

- ❖ learn about letter writing.
- ❖ learn how to write Informal Letter (personal).
- ❖ learn how to write Formal Letter (application).

QUICK CONCEPT REVIEW

All of us are required, every now and then, to write letters, either to our friends, relatives or teachers. So every educated person should know how to write a clear, precise and readable letter. There are various types of letters that we are usually required to write in our everyday life but the two most important forms which you should know in class-4 are ---personal letters and applications.

Real Life Examples

- ❖ People typically write letters either by hand or on the computer. Everyone should learn to write letters. This is a skill that people use throughout life in many personal and professional contexts.
- ❖ Encouraging yourself to write letters from an early age will improve your communication, social and handwriting skills.

FORM OF LETTERS

Letters are messages, and certain letter forms have been established by experience and custom as the most useful forms learned and used by every letter writer, for; neglect of them is a sign of ignorance and carelessness. There are several different kinds of letters (such as informal letters and formal letters) each of which has its own particular form; but there are certain matters of form which apply to all.

In all kinds of letters there are six points of form to be attended to:---

1. The Heading which consists of (a) the writer's address and (b) the date.
2. The courteous Greeting or Salutation.

Activity

- Have you ever written letter to God? Whenever you feel sad or dejected try writing an informal letter to God mentioning about your experience. What will happen next? You will feel much better and sadness will reduce.
- Write an informal letter to any fairy tale character whom you like to give suggestion or share how you feel about the experience which they had. Example- My dear little Red Riding hood, you should have listened to your mother.........

3. The Communication or Message ------ The Body of the letter.
4. The Subscription, or courteous Leave -taking, or Conclusion.
5. The Signature.
6. The Superscription on the envelope.

CLASSIFICATION OF LETTERS

1. **Informal Letters** (personal or friendly) ------ Informal letters are easy to write in terms of format, tone and language. These kinds of letters are written to friends, relatives and parents. Their style is chiefly conversational.

How to write Informal Letter

Start: The address and date should be on left hand corner of the letter.

Salutation: This would normally start with either "Dear..." or "Hi..."- with no comma afterwards.

Body: The first paragraph usually starts with greeting and asking about the health like "how are you dear"

In the second paragraph, you can ask questions or you can answer to the questions asked by the recipient - maybe asking for an opinion or advice.

You can also write something about yourself or what's new in your life, to make it conversational and interesting.

Closing: At the end do not close your letter directly with sincerely, you could use expressions such as "I look forward to hearing back from you soon" or simply "Hope to hear from you soon" and also "Keep in touch".

When ending a letter you could sign off with a variety of expressions... obviously keep in mind the person you are writing to.

Best Wishes," "Sincerely (yours)," "(Lots of) Love," "(Best) Regards," etc.

Example: Informal Letter.

Your friend has recently passed the final examination of class-4 securing the highest marks. Write a letter to him/her congratulating on his/her brilliant success.

A-6/9, Fort Villa

Pratap Road

Jaipur

9th March 2013

Dear ABC

I have just heard that you have passed your final exams with flying colours. May I offer you my heartiest congratulations? It is an achievement of which you ought to be proud. You really worked very hard and certainly deserved to be the topper. You are sure to win a scholarship.

Mother joins me in singing your praises. She says your parents ought to be proud of you. All my best wishes for your promotion to class-5 and I hope you enjoy your new class and studies.

Yours lovingly

PQR

2. **Formal Letters:** Formal letters are official letters written to communicate a request, complain or bring to notice an issue at hand. An application to your principal, headmistress or teacher can be in the form of Leave-application, Permission-letter or Complaint-letter. Formal tone of language, style and format should be adopted to write any sort of applications. The matter has to be precise and perfect.

How to write formal letter

Start: The address and date to the person you are writing should be on top left hand corner of the letter.

Salutation: This would normally start with either "Sir..." or "Madam..."- with comma afterwards.

Subject: reference to your leave, permission or complaint.

First Paragraph

You should write what is the issue or the reason for writing the complain letter. Be sure to write the following information if applicable to the situation date, time, name of the person.

Second Paragraph

What would you expect from the school, teacher, and principal to solve the issue.

Third Paragraph

End the letter by writing ,"Thanking you," or,"With Regards". In the next line "yours faithfully," or "yours sincerely".

In the end write your name, class, section and roll number.

Amazing facts:

❖ The record for the longest letter was established in 1952, during the Korean War. A lady in Brooklyn, New York, wrote to her boyfriend, a private detective in the U.S. Army, serving in Korea. Instead of using regular writing paper, this ingenious lady used the narrow tape that is found on adding machines, 3,200 feet of it! The letter took her one month to write.

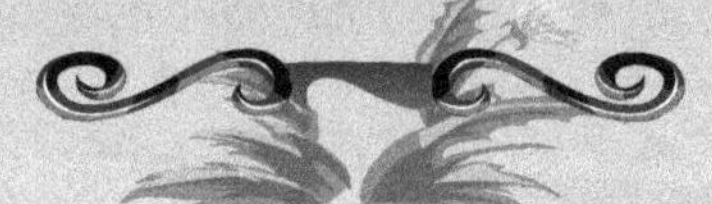

Example: Formal Letter.

Write a letter to your landlord to undertake the repairing work of the whole building.

To

Mr. Rajesh Kumar Singh

D-339, Indirapuram

Lucknow

12th March 2013

Sir

I shall be obliged if you please take the trouble of sending your man round as soon as possible to attend some of the repairs which are urgently needed in the house I am occupying. During the recent rains, the roofs of the drawing room and the kitchen leaked badly, disfiguring the walls and spoiling the whole furniture. The roofs should be repaired without a moment's delay, since the rainy season has set in.

Further, I should like to remind you of your promise to get the whole building whitewashed in October next.

Please treat these matters as urgent.

With Regards

Yours faithfully

A.K. Roy

Professor

R.N. Tagore college

Where all do we write letters?

(a) Within schools: Letter writing is part of the required curriculum. Visits to museums or farms prompt thank you letters, for example contacting schools in other countries and exchanging letters.

(b) At home: Within the home, letter writing has many uses. It encourages good manners, especially writing 'thank you' letters, you can write invitations, you can write letters to friends and relatives, Pen pals are always popular, giving insights into other's lives, especially overseas.

Multiple Choice Questions

LEVEL-1

Directions (Qs. 1 to 5): Choose the correct option.

1. If a sender wants to send any important message, then which of these methods should take the least time to reach the receiver?

(a) telegram (b) e-mail (c) postcard (d) inland letter

2. In which of these communications the sender sends a message without writing anything ?

(a) sms (b) postcard (c) telephone (d) e-mail

3. Which of the following does not come under the category of Formal letters ?

[2014]

(a) official letters (b) invitation letters

(c) business letters (d) friendly letters

4. **Which of the following does not come under the category of Informal letters ?**
   (a) letters to newspapers (b) letters to congratulate
   (c) letters of condolence (d) letters to parents

5. **If you want to write a letter about a general issue or matter of public awareness of your country or society you should write to--- [2015]**
   (a) the principal of your school (b) the chairman of your company
   (c) the editor of a newspaper (d) the landlord of your building

LEVEL-2

Directions (Qs. 1 to 20): Given below are two letters with so many mistakes. Mistakes are marked bold and underlined, re-write the letters correctly.

1. **You are living in a hostel in Dehradun. Write a letter to your father, who lives in Pune, to send you some money as you urgently require to buy some books and stationery.**

Modern School

Dehradun

20th March 2013

My dear Father

I am well here and wish to here the same from you. Today I got the result of my final (**<u>1. xams</u>**) in which I have secure 3rd rank in my (**<u>2. Sekson</u>**) with highest marks in English (**<u>3. Grammer</u>**), Spelling-(**<u>4. Diktason</u>**) and (**<u>5. Envirmental</u>**) studies. Now I am prompted to class-5 and very (**<u>6. Excit</u>**) to join the new class. Our classes will (**<u>7. Comense</u>**) from 10th April 2013. In the (**<u>8. Meenwhyle</u>**) I need to bring some books and stationery so please send me Rs 6000/- to enable me buys the (**<u>9. Nidful</u>**).

Hope mother and my little sister are do well. I miss you all very much and had think of joining you all after my term end but could not due to our extracurricular activities in school. Take care.

With Love!

Your loving son

Ayush.

1.	(a)	exams	(b)	mexas	(c)	emxa	(d)	no change
2.	(a)	secson	(b)	section	(c)	sekson	(d)	no change
3.	(a)	grrammer	(b)	grammar	(c)	grammer	(d)	no change
4.	(a)	dictasion	(b)	dictation	(c)	ditation	(d)	no change
5.	(a)	enveronmntl	(b)	enviranmentol	(c)	environmental	(d)	no change
6.	(a)	excited	(b)	exsite	(c)	axited	(d)	no change
7.	(a)	cummenc	(b)	commence	(c)	comense	(d)	no change

8.	(a)	minwhil	(b)	meanwhile	(c)	meenwlhile	(d)	no change
9.	(a)	needfull	(b)	neadful	(c)	needful	(d)	no change

2. **Write a letter to a publisher, ordering him some books you will require in your new class, as they are not available in the market.**

B-179, Defence colony

Canal East Road

Patna

To

The Publisher

Wisdom Books Pvt Ltd

Circus View Road

New Delhi

12th April 2013

Sir

I shall be ...**10.obilyzed**... if you will send me the...**11. folowing**.... books as ...**12.suun**... as possible. These books have gone out of ...**13.stok**.... in our market and I ...**14.neaed**... them soon.

1. ..**15.Basiks**... of English Grammar-part-iv
2. ...**16.Aksess**.. to English Activities-part-iv
3. ..**17. Envirmental**.... Studies for class-iv
4. Spell It Perfectly-part-iv
5. Radiant Reader for class-iv
6. Book on..**18. Fabels**.. for class-iv

You can send these ...**19.throu**... your reliable carrier service, to the above address and your bill will be paid on ...**20.receit**... through cash on delivery.

Thanking you!

Yours faithfully,

Arpan Dutta.

10.	(a)	obilyzed	(b)	obliged	(c)	oblize	(d)	olbiged
11.	(a)	following	(b)	flowong	(c)	folowing	(d)	flowing
12.	(a)	suun	(b)	soan	(c)	soon	(d)	seen
13.	(a)	stock	(b)	stok	(c)	stoock	(d)	stuk
14.	(a)	nead	(b)	need	(c)	nid	(d)	no change
15.	(a)	basics	(b)	basiks	(c)	bacics	(d)	baceeks
16.	(a)	aksess	(b)	access	(c)	axess	(d)	axcis

17.	(a)	enveronmntl	(b)	enviranmentol	(c)	environmental	(d)	no change
18.	(a)	fabels	(b)	flables	(c)	fables	(d)	faable
19.	(a)	through	(b)	throu	(c)	throo	(d)	thorough
20.	(a)	receit	(b)	receipt	(c)	receeet	(d)	recit

RESPONSE GRID

LEVEL 1

1. a b c d 2. a b c d 3. a b c d 4. a b c d 5. a b c d

LEVEL 2

1. a b c d 2. a b c d 3. a b c d 4. a b c d 5. a b c d
6. a b c d 7. a b c d 8. a b c d 9. a b c d 10. a b c d
11. a b c d 12. a b c d 13. a b c d 14. a b c d 15. a b c d
16. a b c d 17. a b c d 18. a b c d 19. a b c d 20. a b c d

Solutions with Explanation

LEVEL-1

1. **(b)** e-mail via internet which reaches the fastest.

2. **(c)** in telephone we talk to give our message.

3. **(d)** friendly letters are informal letters.

4. **(a)** letters to the editor of newspaper are formal letters.

5. **(c)** the editor will publish your letter in the newspapers to create awareness among the public.

LEVEL-2

1.	**(a)**	**2.**	**(b)**	**3.**	**(b)**	**4.**	**(b)**
5.	**(c)**	**6.**	**(a)**	**7.**	**(b)**	**8.**	**(b)**
9.	**(c)**	**10.**	**(b)**	**11.**	**(a)**	**12.**	**(c)**
13.	**(a)**	**14.**	**(b)**	**15.**	**(a)**	**16.**	**(b)**
17.	**(c)**	**18.**	**(c)**	**19.**	**(a)**	**20.**	**(b)**

20 CHAPTER FOREWORD

Did you know, comprehension is the reason for reading. If we can read the words but do not understand them, we are not really reading. This chapter will help you strengthen your comprehension skills.

Let's begin by solving the exercise given below.

Directions: Read the passage given below and answer the following questions.

Reema has a garden at her backyard. There are roses of all colours. She planted a lily, a marigold and a tulip yesterday. But the sunflower is dying due to the bad weather. Her favourite flower is Night Queen as it smells pleasant at night. She is also fond of vegetation. Her mother grows cabbages, potatoes and tomatoes in the garden. They take special care of cucumbers and carrots as they rot very quickly. I also want to have a fruit garden in my house. I will grow bananas, apples, lemons and papayas. But mango is the king of fruits and my favourite too.

Q1. Name four things Reema grows in her backyard.

____

Q2. Which is her favourite flower? Why?

____

Q3. What does Reema's mother grow?

____

Q4. Which plants need special care?

____

Q5. Do you like gardening? If so, what would you like to grow in your garden?

____

Chapter 20 Comprehension

LEARNING OBJECTIVES

This lesson will help you to:—

- learn what comprehension is.
- learn about reading comprehension passages.
- learn and understand about solving comprehension questions.

QUICK CONCEPT REVIEW

Comprehension

- Comprehension is the understanding and interpretation of what is read. This understanding comes from the interaction between the words that are written and how they trigger knowledge outside the text.
- It is the process of making meaning from a written text. Comprehensions fall under of variety of topics and are formulated in diverse ways.
- Comprehension is the fundamental purpose of reading.
- It includes making sense of words, connecting ideas between text and prior knowledge, constructing and negotiating meaning in discussions with others, and much more.
- Comprehension of the passage that is followed by questions has to be answered keeping only the passage in mind.

Real Life Example

In our day to day life, we read and comprehend various things from newspapers to books and magazines.

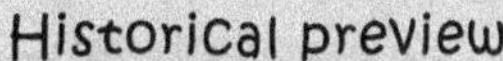

Historical preview

During the last century comprehension lessons usually consisted of students answering teachers' questions, writing responses to questions on their own, or both. The whole group version of this practice also often included "Round-robin reading", wherein teachers called on individual students to read a portion of the text. In the last quarter of the 20th century, evidence accumulated that the read-test methods assessed comprehension more than they taught it. The associated practice of "round robin" reading has also been questioned and eliminated by many educators.

Amazing Facts

- The biggest barrier to comprehension is lack of fluency.
- English is the most difficult major language to listen to comprehend and to read.

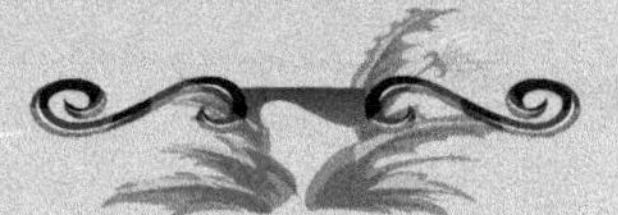

Misconcept/Concept

Misconcept: Real comprehension is a matter of finding the author's exact meaning.

Concept: Comprehension means to decode the meaning in between the lines. Even experienced reviewers interpret an author's work differently. This diversity of interpretation is usually a result of different backgrounds and experiences. Thus the real comprehension is a matter of understanding the meaning which may or may not be exact inference as the author's.

Steps for solving comprehension passage questions

1. Understand the passage.
2. Identify the type of question.
3. Simplify the question.
4. Construct the answer.

FOUNDATIONS FOR COMPREHENSION

- **Conceptual knowledge:** Children need familiarity with the topics they read and some understanding of the main concepts in narrative texts.
- **Language skills**
- **Text features:** You need to know how titles, pictures, captions, and headings relate to the meaning of text.
- **Strategies:** Comprehending text requires you to use a variety of strategies such as making and checking predictions, asking and answering questions, looking back in text to monitor understanding, and occasionally stopping to paraphrase or summarize the important information.
- **Fluent decoding:** Comprehension is difficult when you focus all the energy and cognitive resources on saying the words correctly. Comprehension is easier when decoding is automatic so you must learn to recognize words quickly and accurately.

Multiple Choice Questions

LEVEL-1

Directions (Qs. 1 to 4): Read the passage given below and answer the following questions.

In India, people celebrate the festival of Holi (pronounced "hoh-lee") in March. This festival occurs after the wheat harvest. Wheat is used to make many dishes in India. Holi celebrates the triumph of good over evil. Holi is a very bright celebration. People light bonfires, tell stories, and cover each other in a variety of coloured powders. These powders are called gulal (pronounced "goo-lahl"). People are then sprayed with water, and everyone becomes a beautiful, brightly coloured mess. This custom of colouring people comes from a legend about a trickster who loved to trick his friends by pouring coloured water on them.

1. **The festival of Holi occurs after**
   (a) the month of March.
   (b) the wheat harvest.
   (c) people are sprayed with water.
   (d) people are covered with colorful powders.
2. **The custom of colouring people during Holi comes from**
   (a) a legend about a trickster.
   (b) stories that are told around a bonfire .
   (c) the triumph of good over evil.
   (d) harvesting wheat in March.
3. **Which word best describes the festival of Holi?**
   (a) Colourful (b) Tricky (c) Flavourful (d) Wet
4. **As used in paragraph 2, which of the following best illustrates the actions of a trickster?**
   (a) For Tony's birthday, Mike brings him a soccer jersey signed by his favorite player.
   (b) Micah invites Delea to work with his group for a school project, and then he asks his mom to bake brownies when the group meets to work.
   (c) Jill excitedly convinces Mae to come to see a rabbit outside, but it turns out that the rabbit is a stone statue. Jill placed in the garden.
   (d) Robert refuses to let Travis play basketball at lunch, because Travis is just learning to play.

Directions (Qs. 5 to 11): Read the passage given below and answer the following questions.

Next week I am on vacation. While I am on vacation, I will work on two projects.

First, I will fix the washing machine. The washing machine has been broken for two weeks. To fix it, I will need three tools: a screwdriver, a wrench, and a clamp. It will take one day to fix the washing machine.

Next, I will fix our back porch. This is a bigger project. It will probably take about two days to fix the back porch, and will require a screwdriver, a hammer, nails, and a saw.

My vacation starts on Monday. I have a lot of work to do but hopefully I can relax after I finish my work.

5. **Which of these tools will the author use more than once?**
   (a) a screwdriver (b) a hammer (c) a clamp (d) a saw
6. **As used in paragraph 2, what does 'require' mean?**
   (a) need (b) use (c) find (d) buy
7. **Which of the following tools does the author not need to fix the back porch?**
   (a) a screwdriver (b) a wrench (c) nails (d) a saw
8. **What is the earliest day that the author can finish both projects?**
   (a) Monday (b) Wednesday (c) Thursday (d) Friday
9. **On which project will the author need to use the most tools?**
   (a) Fixing the washing machine
   (b) Fixing the back porch
   (c) Both projects need the same number of tools
   (d) Neither project needs any tools
10. **According to the passage, fixing the back porch will take longer because**
   (a) the author really doesn't want to do it (b) it has been broken longer
   (c) it needs more tools (d) it is a bigger project
11. **The author of this passage can best be described as**
   (a) interesting (b) lazy (c) constructive (d) intelligent

Directions (Qs. 12 to 16) : Read the passage and answer the questions by choosing the correct option.

NAVRATRI FESTIVAL

Navratri in Tamil Nadu, Dusshera fest in Karnataka, Durga Puja in West Bengal, Daandiya Raas in Gujarat - the festival of nine nights take a different name in the different regions of India. Households in South India celebrate Navratri as Kolu, wherein figurines of Gods and Goddessess are displayed in odd numbered steps.

Dolls are an important ingredient for Navratri. Doll making is one of the ancient crafts of India.

Down South, dolls are sourced from all over the country for the festive season. It is said that in olden times, artisans used to be brought home to make these dolls. However, this practice has faded into oblivion as people started to prefer readymade toys to enrich their Kolu Padi.

Kolu dolls from Puducherry (Pondicherry) are special. The clay obtained from the banks of river Sankarabarani is fine and strong enough to make even big dolls. The clay is kneaded with hands and feet to make it supple and then cast into plaster of paris moulds. Then they are sundried and fired in a kiln after which they are brightly painted.

12. **In South India, Navratri is celebrated as**
    (a) Kolu
    (b) Dusshera
    (c) Durga Puja
    (d) Daandiyaa Raas
13. **Navratri is important as a**
    (a) way of strengthening unity in diversity
    (b) celebration of different festivals
    (c) doll festival
    (d) regional festival
14. **This practice in paragraph 4 refers to**
    (a) celebrating Navratri
    (b) displaying dolls
    (c) using readymade toys
    (d) bringing home artisans to make dolls
15. **The clay obtained from the banks of river Sankarabarani is most suitable for making dolls because**
    (a) it is fine and strong
    (b) it is supple
    (c) it is found in plenty
    (d) it can be easily kneaded
16. **The word 'oblivion' (Paragraph 3) means**
    (a) fading away (b) darkness (c) forgetfulness (d) shade

For Qs. 17-21 : Read the passage and answer the questions that follow :

For more than ten years, there has been agreements with countries such as Switzerland that have been keen to have "brain exchange" programmes with India. In the past, it was assumed that both or all countries that have signed agreements for cooperation in education management and science and technology could benefit from sharing their brightest and best minds. In general, these programmes have led to increased development for diversifying cooperation in economic and other sectors as well.

Of late there has been a move toward the supply of funding for international travel and engagement for younger and younger people. There are have been discussions about the ethics and coordination of the possibility of transplanting; not just moving the student but also their entire support network. People have put a whole range of ideas forward as to why being educationally mobile should be an option and an almost equal amount of negative reasons for students to stay in their home.

One thing that is definite is that even though there seems to be largescale competition throughout the world for resources, jobs and security. There is no doubt that the last decade has shown that there is a strong correlation between a country's success and its educational or knowledge based ties. This relationship is clearly beneficial but the issues concerning the answers to a range of questions that are now just being asked about the permissibility of allowing "brain exchanges" earlier and earlier are yet to be answered fully. **[2018]**

17. **Choose the best title or heading for the passage.**
    (a) More brains more work
    (b) Exchange and trust
    (c) Easy school swap
    (d) Best brains borrowed

18. Everyone agrees, __________.

(a) there are benefits of this type of programme

(b) it is a lot more than just education at stake

(c) we can all make children work harder

(d) to lend more money to develop countries who need better jobs

19. What does 'their' underline in the second paragraph refer to?

(a) Funders (b) Families (c) Students (d) Programmes

20. How are the agreements about children studying abroad weighted?

(a) They are weighted equally for both sides

(b) People think kids should stay at home

(c) Researchers say everyone should be able to travel

(d) They don't know enough yet.

21. What does the word 'correlation' mean in final paragraph?

(a) Escape (b) Relationship (c) Most recent (d) Last

For Qs. 22-26 : Read the passage and answer the questions that follow :

In 2014, the islanders of the Isle of Head chose altogether to stop government interference on their small island. They decided to purchase the whole island as a consortium now known as 'The Isle of Head Organisation' or TIHO for short. They now, like many other islands off the west coast, can set their own standard of living using a village tribunal system. In fact, this was what they were after originally. This way of living is not unfamiliar, but what they have decided to do on their island is somewhat quirky.

Head currently has limited access to the mainland and as the population shrank as too did the number of visitors; consequently, there is no need for frequent ferries. Althought, it's not unknown for there to be multiple sailings at the weekend which people like greatly for the ease of access. That combined with a journey time of just over 25 minutes on calm seas and sometimes over 1 hour per sailing on other days has meant that the service operates on a 'need to' basis and sails only once there are enough passengers waiting to make the crossing worthwhile.

The village has several highly skilled citizens which has proved useful as they have decided that they will, in the most part, be self-sufficient. Central to this philosophy is the principle that they will educate their own primary and secondary school pupils and that the three 20-year olds will study together communicating through the web colleges and universities elsewhere. It has been raised as a potential issue and there is an inquiry ongoing to check that the education the islanders get is of a suitable standard. **[2018]**

22. Choose the best title or heading for the passage.

(a) School's Out

(b) The Way Ahead

(c) Mainland Headache

(d) Tihotastic

23. What was the reason they wanted to buy the island?

(a) Rules (b) Money

(c) Schools (d) Transport

24. How often does the ferry sail these days?

(a) When it needs to (b) At least twice a day

(c) On a seasonal schedule (d) At the weekends only

25. The Islanders don't __________.

(a) happen to need any books

(b) want any help from the mainland

(c) desire to usage of mobile connections

(d) think they need any more ferries

26. What is the meaning of the word 'quirky' in the first paragraph?

(a) Sure footed (b) Educational (c) Underdeveloped (d) Strange

DIRECTION (For Qs. 27-31): Read the passage and answer the questions that follow:

(1) Recently Elon Musk, founder of SpaceX made a giant step towards being the first moon tour provider by signing up his first passenger; the Japanese billionaire and entrepreneur Yusaku Maezawa. If all goes according to plan, in 2023, Maezawa will become the first passenger and private astronaut to travel to the Moon. He will also join the elite group of just 2 dozen humans who have been fortunate enough to see Earth's satellite up close.

(2) Maezawa does not plan to take family or friends on this historic excursion. Instead, the former drummer from the punk rock band Switch Style, says, "I would like to invite six to eight artists from around the world to join me on this mission to the Moon. These artists will be asked to create something after they return to Earth, and these masterpieces will inspire the dreamer within all of us." Through the guest list has not been determined, he indicated they would be of the same caliber as genuises, such as Pablo Picasso, Andy Warhol, Michael Jackson, Coco Chanel and John Lennon. "These are all artists that I adore, but sadly are no longer with us."

(3) The mission, entitled #dearMoon, will be conducted in a Big Falcon Rocket (BFR). First announced by Musk in 2016, the reusable spacecraft, which is still in the early stages of development, is being designed such that it can be refueled both on Earth and in space. Standing 387 feet tall, its 31 main engines, fueled by liquid oxygen and methane, will provide 5,400 tons of thrust and be capable of carrying a payload of over 100 metric tons to low-Earth orbit.

(4) Though the details of the week-long mission have not been finalised, Musk expects the spacecraft to skim past the lunar surface, fly beyond it, and then pass close to the Moon again before heading back to the Earth. **[2019]**

27. Choose the best title or heading for the passage.

(a) Space Open for Hosts (b) Rich Men Go

(c) Artists in Space (d) A Dozen Less on the Moon

28. Maezawa wants to be the first to ________.

(a) fly around the moon (b) paint the moon

(c) walk on the moon (d) leave a footprint on the moon

29. What did Maezawa do before he was a billionaire businessman?

(a) He was an astronaut (b) He was a musician

(c) He flew planes (d) He was an entrepreneur

30. Which paragraph explains the specifications of the ship?

(a) 1 (b) 2 (c) 3 (d) 4

31. What does the word 'skim' mean in final paragraph?

(a) Hike (b) Rest (c) Haunt (d) Graze

For Qs. 32-36 : Read the passage and answer the questions that follow :

(1) With over 64 million monthly active players, up to 1 million of whome are logged on simultaneously during peak times, chances are you have heard of the online game creation platform. Fans are probably also aware that all the games in the Lego-like virtual world are created by users, typically teens and young adults.

(2) What is not as widely known is that the California-based company gives 30 percent of any revenues earned from the games to the creators. In 2017, they paid out $30 million, $3 million of which went to one developer while two others received $2 million apiece. In 2018, the company has distributed an astounding $70 million to the most popular games created by members of its four-million-strong developer base. Although the percentage of player/developers is tiny, those lucky few, around 1 percent get substantial payouts.

(3) Among the biggest beneficiaries of the revenue-sharing policy is Alex Jafanz, the publisher of a role-playing game where inmates escape from prison and run from the police. While the 19 year old and his business partner have created several other games on the platform, none have been as popular. Just three days after its release on April 21, 2017, the game boasted 75,000 concurrent players, the highest ever on the development platform game. Within three weeks, Jafanz's games reached 44 million place visits, making it the fastest-growing game ever in the company's 14 year history!

(4) As to what inspired these young entrepreneurs to develop or design games? They are all former game players and just wanted something different. Many just thought it would be fun to make a game that they wanted to play themselves, with little thought about the potential acclaim and remuneration they could receive for developing the highest grossing games. So, if you are a fan, you may be on the path to prosperity - provided you use your imagination and work hard, of course! **[2019]**

32. Choose the best title or heading for the passage.

(a) Most Popular Game in the World

(b) Happy Games Prove Games Work

(c) Bad Luck for Late Comers in Game World

(d) Young Developers Make Millions

33. How much profit goes to the developers?

(a) 2% (b) 3% (c) 30% (d) 1%

34. Jafanz and his partner created the _________.

(a) most popular game on the platform
(b) most expensive game in the world
(c) biggest surprise the game community has seen
(d) game that people want removed because it is violent

35. Which paragraph explains why kids have been making games?

(a) 1 (b) 2 (c) 3 (d) 4

36. What does the word 'remuneration' mean in final paragraph?

(a) Fee (b) Award (c) Fame (d) Contact

Directions (Q. No. 37 and 41): Read the passage and answer the questions that follow.

1. Fiona walked across the kitchen to the far end where she saw a door leading to the backyard of the house. When she tried to open the door to the back she struggled because it was locked. She thought that this was strange because it had never been locked before and she had no idea where the key was. There was music playing in the background and she noticed that it was her father's favourite song about a cowboy or something; it wasn't a tune that she particularly favoured.
2. She chose to go and find her mother who she thought might be at the front of the house on the veranda with her uncle and aunty. It turned out that her mother was with them and that she had left the key on the table in the kitchen. Fiona went back and checked but couldn't find it. She looked around and eventually found it on the sideboard next to the fruit bowl.
3. When Fiona eventually got outside into the back garden, it had started to rain lightly and it made the garden look like a movie set. She set up her table and got her tea and book and sat down to relax. As she did, she heard a loud banging noise coming from over the wall. This was not good, and it was really vexing her and ruining her quiet time. Fiona decided to text her neighbour who was in the same year as her at school. She asked what all the noise was about and how long it would last. There was no reply to her text, so she packed up and went inside again.

37. Where was Fiona? **[2020]**

(a) At school (b) At her neighbour's backyard
(c) At her house (d) At her uncle's house

38. Fiona _______ her dad's favourite song. **[2020]**

(a) hadn't noticed (b) didn't like
(c) wanted to listen to (d) loved

39. What was Fiona looking for? **[2020]**

(a) Keys (b) Toys
(c) Books (d) Fruit bowl

40. Fiona decided to text her ________ who was in the same year as her at school. [2020]

(a) neighbour (b) cousin

(c) friend (d) sister

41. What is the meaning of the word 'ruin' in the third paragraph? [2020]

(a) Growth (b) Ascent

(c) Devastate (d) Advantage

Directions (Q. No. 42 to 46): Read the passage and answer the questions that follow.

Most people would shudder at the idea of getting caught up in a 73.5-feet wave. But for Brazilian pro-surfer Maya, it presented the perfect opportunity to break her 2018 world record for the largest wave surfed by a female. The athlete skillfully conquered the massive wave earlier this year, at the inaugural World Surf League (WSL) Nazaré Tow Surfing Challenge in Praia do Norte, Portugal. It was the same site where she made her first world record by riding an equally intimidating 68-feet wave.

"I was in the zone and braver than I usually am on that day," said Gabeira. "I was risking more than I usually like to do. When I let go of the rope, I had a feeling it could be the one but wasn't sure. The speed was very high, but the noise that the wave made when it broke made me realize that this was probably the biggest wave I'd ever ridden."

Though Gabeira completed the incredible feat on February 11, 2020, her record was not announced by the Guinness World Records until September 10, 2020. That's because the WSL officials had to first determine whether it was the Brazilian surfer or her competitor, Justine Dupont, who had ridden the largest wave. The wave's height from trough to crest is usually estimated with the help of photos and videos. However, the proximity of the large swells ridden by the two pro-surfers. and the possibility of a new world record being established, warranted a more rigorous analysis.

42. The first record was made by Gabeira on/in _____. [2021]

(a) a 73.5 feet wave (b) 2018

(c) 2020 (d) 2010

43. What made the surfer realise, "it was probably the biggest wave"? [2021]

(a) The water (b) The speed

(c) The noise (d) The time

44. Who made sure the record was made by Gabeira? [2021]

(a) Nazaré Tow Surfing Challenge (b) Guinness World Records

(c) World Surf League (d) Brazil government

45. The height of the wave is from __________ . [2021]

(a) trough only (b) trough to crest

(c) crest only (d) sea

46. The word 'intimidating' means _______. **[2021]**

(a) terrifying (b) possible

(c) enjoyable (d) fruitful

Directions (Q. No. 47 to 51): Read the passage and answer the questions that follow.

A tiny mouse was born between two bags of corn kernels in a cargo ship's hold. Her mother had been chased away and had disappeared out-of-view. Frightened, the baby mouse snuggled between the bags and waited. The waves rocked the vessel gently and she soon fell asleep.

A loud horn startled her out of her dreams. The ship stopped, and many voices were heard, along with the footsteps going back and forth.

The baby mouse stood still, her heart pounding like a drum roll, until someone lifted up one of the bags and yelled, "Marcos, hand me the broom. I have found another mouse!"

As he turned to look at the mouse again, she had disappeared. She was already making her way out of the ship, scurrying between people's legs, down the ramp and onto the dock. Sameone stepped on her tail, but she managed to escape.

The baby mouse stopped running and looked around. The warm sand felt good under her paws. The salty wind blew gently between her ears, carrying dolphins' conversations and seagulls' cries.

The baby mouse could see the ship from far away. She watched as sailors, appearing to be the size of corn kernels, went up and down the ramp, carrying wooden cases and other supplies.

The baby mouse realized how hungry she was. She nibbled on a seaweed and spat it back out. She was lucky enough to find a plump, juicy berry to fill up her minuscule stomach. She lingered a bit longer to watch the sunset, reflecting on the sea in a million colours, and then yawned.

Using a piece of sea sponge as a pillow, the little mouse snuggled in an empty seashell and drifted off to sleep. That was the beginning of her new life as a sea mouse.

47. What is the passage about? **[2022]**

(a) The sea (b) The baby mouse

(c) Corn kernels (d) Cargo ship

48. Where was the baby mouse born? **[2022]**

(a) On ramp (b) In a bag

(c) On a cargo ship (d) In sea

49. What felt good under the baby mouse's paws? **[2022]**

(a) Warm sand (b) Salty wind

(c) Sea waves (d) Sea sponge

50. The baby mouse lingered a bit longer to watch the _________ . **[2022]**

(a) seagulls (b) sunrise

(c) seashell (d) sunset.

51. In the passage, the word 'minuscule' means _________ . **[2022]**

(a) tiny (b) large (c) happy (d) serene

Direction for Q. No. 52 to 55: Read the passage carefully and answer the questions that follow:

When was the last time you saw someone wearing a hat? A head cover of some sort probably, but not a hat. No one knows for sure when the use of hats originate(d) But we do know why people wore them and still do. Hats are worn for two primary reasons. One, for protection, and two, for decoration. In parts of the world where the weather is hot and sunny, people cover their heads from the sun with wide-brimmed hats. Maxicans wear one such hat called the sombrero. Indian wear a topi, pagdee or a cloth roughly tied around the hea(d) One kind of pagdee or the turban is worn by Sikhs for religious reasons. Farmers in Rajasthan and some other states wear a pagdee for traditional reasons as well as for protection from the sun. In other parts of the world where the climate is cold, people often wear fur or wool hats and some of them even have aerflapls. Then there are decorative hats worn as an accessory to a person's clothing like a harlequin hat. A South American cowboy wears hat, which is the part of his traditional costume, while a North American cowboy wears a wide-brimmed hat, which protects him from the sun. A hat can also tell us about the occupation of its wearer. Fire-fighters, coal-miners, nurses and policemen wear special hats which look very common and amusing.

52. When did the use of hats originate? [2022]
(a) Long, long ago (b) No one knows for sure
(c) 10 years ago (d) All of these

53. A sombrero is a: [2022]
(a) Hat with ear flaps (b) Cloth tied round the head
(c) Wide-brimmed hat (d) Fire-fighters hat

54. Farmers in Rajasthan wear a pagdee: [2022]
(a) For religious reasons (b) As a part of their tradition
(c) To protect themselves from the sun (d) Both (B) and (C)

55. Fire-fighters, nurses and coal-miners and policemen wear: [2022]
(a) The same kind of hat (b) Colourful hats
(c) Common to their profession (d) Both (A) and (B)

56. Arrange P, Q, R and S to make a meaningful sentence. [2022]
P : made our Q : lives very R : technology has S: easy and comfortable
(a) RSQP (b) RPQS (c) PQRS (d) PRSQ

57. Identify predicate in the following sentence:
Every student wants to pass the exam. [2022]
(a) Every student (b) Exam
(c) Wants (d) Wants to pass the exam

58. Identify the kind of sentence.
Knowledge makes us powerful. [2022]
(a) Interrogative (b) Exclamatory (c) Assertive (d) Imperative

LEVEL-2

Directions (Qs. 1 to 8): Read the passage given below and answer the following questions.

Lilly loves her new town. She loves the mall. She loves the parks. She also loves her school. Most of all, though, Lilly loves the seasons. In her old town, it was hot all the time.

Sometimes it is cold in Lilly's new town. The cold season is in winter. Once in a while it snows. Lilly has never seen snow before. So for her, the snow is exciting as well as very beautiful. Lilly has to wear gloves to keep her hands warm. She also wears a scarf around her neck.

In spring, flowers bloom and the trees turn green with new leaves. Pollen falls on the cars and windowsills and makes Lilly sneeze. People work in their yards and mow their grass.

In summer, Lilly wears her old shorts and sandals— the same ones she used to wear in her old town. It's hot outside, and dogs lie in the shade. Lilly and her friends go to a pool or play in the water sprinkler. Her father cooks hamburgers on the grill for dinner.

Lilly's favorite season is autumn. In autumn, the leaves on the trees turn yellow, gold, red, and orange. Halloween comes in autumn, and this is Lilly's favourite holiday. Every Halloween, Lilly wears a costume. Last year she wore a mouse costume. This year she will wear a fish costume.

One evening in autumn, Lilly and her mom were sitting together on the porch. Mom tells Lilly that autumn is also called "fall". This is a good idea, Lilly thinks, because in fall all of the leaves fall down from the trees.

1. **Which of the following words best describe the way Lilly feels about living in her new town?**
   (a) Skeptical, meaning questioning or showing doubt
   (b) Apprehensive, meaning anxious or worried
   (c) Overjoyed, meaning extremely happy
   (d) Content, meaning satisfied with what one is or has
2. **This passage is mainly about**
   (a) Lilly's favourite season (b) Lilly and the four seasons
   (c) Lilly's favourite activities during winter (d) Lilly's favourite Halloween costumes
3. **What is Lilly's favorite thing about her new town?**
   (a) Her school (b) Going to the pool
   (c) The food (d) The seasons
4. **In paragraph 2 the author writes, "She also wears a scarf around her neck." What is the best way to rewrite this sentence while keeping its original meaning?**
   (a) In addition, she wears a scarf around her neck.
   (b) However, she wears a scarf around her neck.
   (c) Nevertheless, she wears a scarf around her neck.
   (d) As a result, she wears a scarf around her neck.
5. **Which of the following best describes the structure of this passage?**
   (a) The author talks about Lily's new town, and then talks about how the seasons are changing.
   (b) The author introduces Lilly, and then describes her in relation to the four seasons.
   (c) The author introduces Lilly, and then explains why autumn is her favourite season.
   (d) The author discusses the four seasons, and then describes which one Lilly likes best.
6. **How is Lilly's new town different from her old town?**
   A. It snows in her new town.
   B. Lilly wears different summer clothes in her new town.
   C. Lilly wears a Halloween costume in her new town.
   (a) A only (b) A and B only (c) B and C only (d) A, B, and C

7. **Based on information in paragraph 5, which of the following costumes is Lilly most likely to wear next year? (Tricky)**
   (a) a princess costume (b) a fairy costume
   (c) a ghost costume (d) a bird costume
8. **Based on information in the passage, we can understand, which season has two names?**
   (a) spring (b) summer (c) fall (d) winter

Directions (Qs. 9 to 15): Read the passage given below and answer the following questions.

The living room does not look good. It looks bad without a carpet. Mary and Dan want to buy a carpet for their living room.

They go to the store. They look at the carpets. There are many colours. There are many sizes. Some have patterns. Some are plain.

Mary likes a pink and purple carpet. It has dots. Dan says no! He does not like the colours. He does not like the pattern. He does not like the size. The pink and purple carpet is too big.

Dan likes a green and red carpet. It has stripes. Mary says no! She does not like the colours. She does not like the pattern. She does not like the size. The green and red carpet is too small.

Mary and Dan see a tan carpet. It does not have dots. It does not have stripes. It is tan and plain. They like the tan carpet. They both like the colour. They both like the size. They both say yes!

Mary and Dan buy the tan carpet. They put the carpet in the living room. The living room looks wonderful with the new carpet.

9. **According to the passage, Mary and Dan want to put the new carpet in their**
   (a) bedroom (b) dining room (c) living room (d) bathroom
10. **According to the passage, the pink and purple carpet**
    (a) has dots (b) has stripes (c) is too small (d) is too plain
11. **According to the passage, the green and red carpet**
    (a) is plain (b) has dots (c) is too big (d) is too small
12. **According to the passage, both Mary and Dan like the**
    (a) pink and purple carpet (b) green and red carpet
    (c) tan carpet (d) blue carpet
13. **Mary and Dan do not see a**
    (a) black and blue carpet (b) pink and purple carpet
    (c) tan carpet (d) green and red carpet
14. **According to the passage, Mary and Dan see a**
    A. dotted carpet B. striped carpet
    C. plain carpet
    (a) A only (b) A and B only (c) B and C only (d) A, B, and C
15. **Based on information in the passage, it can be understood that both Mary and Dan would like which of the following carpets best?**
    (a) a grey carpet with no dots or stripes
    (b) a pink and yellow carpet with dots
    (c) a blue and green carpet with stripes
    (d) a black and white carpet with both dots and stripes

Directions (Qs. 16 to 24): Read the passage given below and answer the following questions.

Many people like to eat pizza, but not everyone knows how to make it. Making the perfect pizza can be complicated, but there are lots of ways for you to make a more basic version at home.

When you make pizza, you must begin with the crust. The crust can be hard to make. If you want to make the crust yourself, you will have to make dough using flour, water, and yeast. You will have to knead the dough with your hands. If you do not have enough time to do this, you can use a prepared crust that you buy from the store.

After you have chosen your crust, you must then add the sauce. Making your own sauce from scratch can take a long time. You have to buy tomatoes, peel them, and then cook them with spices. If this sounds like too much work, you can also purchase jarred sauce from the store. Many jarred sauces taste almost as good as the kind you make at home.

Now that you have your crust and your sauce, you need to add the cheese. Cheese comes from milk, which comes from cows. Do you have a cow in your backyard? Do you know how to milk the cow? Do you know how to turn that milk into cheese? If not, you might want to buy cheese from the grocery store instead of making it yourself.

When you have the crust, sauce, and cheese ready, you can add other toppings. Some people like to put meat on their pizza, while other people like to add vegetables. Some people even like to add pineapple! The best part of making a pizza at home is that you can customize it by adding your own favourite ingredients.

16. The author's main purpose in writing this passage is to

(a) describe the history of pizza

(b) teach a healthier way to make pizza

(c) outline steps to make a basic pizza at home

(d) provide tips about how to make your pizza especially delicious

17. As used in paragraph 1, which word means the opposite of complicated?

(a) difficult (b) simple (c) easy (d) manageable

18. As used in paragraph 3, which is the best synonym for purchase?

(a) forget (b) buy (c) ask (d) cook

19. In paragraph 3, the author writes, "Many jarred sauces taste almost as good as the kind you make at home." The purpose of this statement is to

(a) clarify a later statement (b) provide an example

(c) clarify an earlier statement (d) support the previous paragraph

20. In paragraph 4, the author asks a series of questions in order to

(a) support the idea that most people cannot make homemade cheese

(b) reinforce the idea that most people probably live on farms

(c) prove that store-bought cheese tastes better than homemade cheese

(d) emphasize the superiority of homemade cheese over store bought cheese

21. As used in paragraph 5, which is the best definition for customize?

(a) to make personal (b) to prepare for more than one

(c) to eat while hot (d) to desire

22. According to the author, which of the following ingredients do you need to have ready before you can add the toppings?

A. crust B. sauce C. cheese

(a) A only (b) A and B only

(c) B and C only (d) A, B, and C

23. Which of the following words best describe how the author feels about making a pizza from scratch?

(a) helpful (b) understanding (c) enthusiastic (d) negative

24. Which of the following conclusions would work best at the end of this passage.

(a) Although the crust, sauce, and toppings are all important ingredients in pizza, it is clear that the cheese is most important. Therefore, be sure your cheese is homemade.

(b) It can be understood that making your pizza from scratch should be avoided at all costs. Use store bought ingredients and save yourself a heap of trouble.

(c) As you can see, cooking a pizza can be fun, but it can also be very expensive. But, as you can see, the best things are worth paying for.

(d) Once you have prepared the crust, sauce, cheese, and toppings, you are ready to bake your pizza. I think you will see that making pizza at home can be a good alternative to purchasing it from the store.

Directions (Q. No. 25 to 29): Read the passage and answer the questions that follow.

1. Anna didn't care about Christmas gifts or decorating Christmas trees. She did not wish for Santa or a new toy. For 6 year old Anna eating marshmallows without her mother breathing down her neck was more important than the holiday season. She had been counting days on her little fingers when Halloween will come and when she will be the official owner of her own sweets with various choices.

2. Anna was busy counting her Halloween harvest. This year she had gone one block extra because she was no longer a baby who cried when the street light flickers at night. Yes, there were times when she thought she might drop her candy basket and run home to her mother crying but this year Anna decided to become a big girl and earn extra sweets for herself without her big sister or mother accompanying her.

3. Proud of herself for not letting the street lights scare her, Anna opened a caramel candy and popped it in her mouth as a reward. "Ann...I've to rush to the supermarket to get some groceries, it will take me a while okay...you hear me dear?" Anna instantly replied "Yes, mom!" Anna went back to counting her candies from Halloween when suddenly she remembered her mother saying, "it will take me a while". Anna staring at her marshmallow collection started wondering what if she finished it all before her mother comes back?

4. Usually when she eats more than 3 pieces her mother gives her the look, first the look, than the full name and lastly the "no more candies for ten days as a punishment". A sudden impulse took over her and she started filling her mouth with marshmallows. First went the pink ones, then the yellow then the white. She was giggling internally thinking there's no one to give her the disapproving look. Anna thought to chew them at once and relish it all. The only problem was she couldn't move her jaw! She tried a few movements but she had stuffed too many of them. Her mouth hurt.

5. After 5 brave seconds Anna broke into tears in pain and frustration. But no one was in the house. Thinking about this made Anna's tears roll faster. Now she missed her mother's

glare. It was not until an hour later her mother came home, by the time Anna had enough time to count the numbers of marshmallows she stuffed in her mouth. "8!" she thought to herself. It took her only eight of them to make her hate marshmallows for life.

25. The reason Anna was excited for the holiday season was because ________. [2020]

(a) she could decorate the Christmas tree
(b) she wanted a new toy
(c) she would get various sweets on Halloween
(d) her mother would buy her a new dress

26. Anna was proud of herself this year because she ________. [2020]

(a) had made new friends
(b) was no longer scared of the flickering street light
(c) got many sweets for Halloween
(d) got to eat many candies

27. When she was filling her mouth with marshmallows. Anna was ________. [2020]

(a) already crying (b) angry at herself
(c) giggling internally (d) feeling frustrated

28. After realizing she couldn't move her mouth, Anna lasted for _______ seconds before breaking down into tears. [2020]

(a) 3 (b) 5 (c) 10 (d) 20

29. The word 'impulse' in the 4th paragraph means ________. [2020]

(a) pressure (b) anger (c) whim (d) calm

Directions (Q. No. 30 and 34): Read the passage and answer the questions that follow.

One day a man stopped to help an old lady who was stranded on the side of the road.

He decided to help her, so he stopped his old Jazz next to her Mercedes and got out. The old lady seemed a bit frightened and nervous because of his shabby appearance. The man, sensing this, approached carefully and tried to calm her.

He said to her, "Don't worry. I'm here to help you. My name is John William." He proceeded to fix her flat tire and became dirty and slightly injured in the process.

When he was finished, the lady asked him how much she owed him. He responded by telling her that if she really wanted to repay him, she could pass on the kindness to someone else in their time of need.

Later that evening the lady stopped at a small, dingy cafe. The waitress who served her was pregnant and tired. Despite her apparent exhaustion, the waitress was very sweet and friendly.

The lady wondered how someone who was so tired from a long day of work could still be so friendly and kind to her.

The lady wondered how someone who was so tired from a long day of work could still be so friendly and kind to her.

Then she remembered John. When the lady finished her meal, she paid with a hundred dollar bill. The waitress went to get change and when she came back, the lady was gone.

She left a note on the napkin... "You don't owe me anything. Somebody once helped me, just like I'm helping you now. If you really want to pay me back, do not let this chain of love end with you."

The waitress found five one hundred dollar bills under the napkin.

That night, the waitress went home early. She thought about the lady and the money she left. She wondered how the lady could possibly know how much they needed it.

She knew her husband was worried and she was worried about him. She couldn't wait to tell him the good news.

Then she hugged him and whispered...Now everything will be okay. I love you, John William.

30. The old woman was driving ________. **[2021]**

(a) Jazz (b) Mercedes (c) bike (d) van

31. What was wrong the old lady's vehicle? **[2021]**

(a) No fuel (b) Low battery

(c) Flat tire (d) No key

32. How did the man ask the old lady to pay him? **[2021]**

(a) With money (b) By giving him her car

(c) By passing on the kindness (d) By giving him a job

33. The old lady left _______ for the waitress. **[2021]**

(a) five hundred dollars (b) one hundred dollar

(c) only change (d) just a handwritten note

34. The word 'dingy' means ________. **[2021]**

(a) dirty (b) closed (c) clean (d) bright

Directions (Q. No. 35 to 39): Read the passage given below and answer the following questions.

The first woman to travel in space was Soviet cosmonaut, Valentina Tereshkova. She was born on 6 March 1937, in the village of Bolshoye Maslennikovo in central Russia. Her mother was a textile worker, and her father was a tractor driver who was later recognised as a war hero during the Second World War. At the time of his death on the Finnish front, Tereshkova was only two years old.

After leaving school, Tereshkova followed her mother into work at a textile factory. Her first adventure of flying was when she joined a local skydiving and parachutist club. It was her hobby of jumping out of planes that appealed to the Soviets' space programme committee. On applying to the cosmonaut corps, Tereshkova was eventually chosen from more than 400 other candidates.

Tereshkova received 18 months of severe training with the Soviet Air Force after her selection. These tests studied her abilities to cope physically under the extremes of gravity, as well as handle challenges such as emergency management and the isolation of being in space alone. At the age of 24; she was honourably inducted into the Soviet Air Force. On 16 June 1963, Tereshkova was launched on a solo mission aboard the spacecraft, Vostok 6. She spent more than 70 hours orbiting the Earth, two years after Yuri Gagarin's first human-crewed flight in space. Tereshkova still holds the title of the youngest and the only woman to have been on a solo space mission.

Today, she holds the position of Deputy Chair for the Committee for International Affairs in Russia. She also remains active within the space community and is quoted as suggesting that she would like to fly to Mars - even if it were a one-way trip.

- Royal Museums Greenwich

35. What is the passage about? **[2022]**

(a) Vostok 6 (b) Bolshoye

(c) Valentina Tereshkova (d) Yuri Gagarin

36. Which hobby of Tereshkova impressed the Soviets' space programme commity? **[2022]**

(a) Jumping out of spacecrafts (b) Jumping out of planes

(c) Jumping out of parashutes (d) Jumping out of rockets

37. Tereshkova still holds the title of the youngest and the only woman to have been on a __________. **[2022]**

(a) solo space mission (b) crew space mission

(c) double space mission (d) human-crewed flight

38. How many hours did Tereshkova spend orbiting the Earth on her mission? **[2022]**

(a) 75 hours (b) 72 hours

(c) 78 hours (d) 70 hours

39. In the third paragraph, the word 'inducted' means __________. **[2022]**

(a) rampant (b) rescued

(c) admitted (d) expelled

RESPONSE GRID

LEVEL 1

1. a b c d	2. a b c d	3. a b c d	4. a b c d	5. a b c d
6. a b c d	7. a b c d	8. a b c d	9. a b c d	10. a b c d
11. a b c d	12. a b c d	13. a b c d	14. a b c d	15. a b c d
16. a b c d	17. a b c d	18. a b c d	19. a b c d	20. a b c d
21. a b c d	22. a b c d	23. a b c d	24. a b c d	25. a b c d
26. a b c d	27. a b c d	28. a b c d	29. a b c d	30. a b c d
31. a b c d	32. a b c d	33. a b c d	34. a b c d	35. a b c d
36. a b c d	37. a b c d	38. a b c d	39. a b c d	40. a b c d
41. a b c d	42. a b c d	43. a b c d	44. a b c d	45. a b c d
46. a b c d	47. a b c d	48. a b c d	49. a b c d	50. a b c d
51. a b c d	52. a b c d	53. a b c d	54. a b c d	55. a b c d
56. a b c d	57. a b c d	58. a b c d		

LEVEL 2

1. a b c d	2. a b c d	3. a b c d	4. a b c d	5. a b c d
6. a b c d	7. a b c d	8. a b c d	9. a b c d	10. a b c d
11. a b c d	12. a b c d	13. a b c d	14. a b c d	15. a b c d
16. a b c d	17. a b c d	18. a b c d	19. a b c d	20. a b c d
21. a b c d	22. a b c d	23. a b c d	24. a b c d	25. a b c d
26. a b c d	27. a b c d	28. a b c d	29. a b c d	30. a b c d
31. a b c d	32. a b c d	33. a b c d	34. a b c d	35. a b c d
36. a b c d	37. a b c d	38. a b c d	39. a b c d	

Solutions with Explanation

LEVEL-1

1.	(b)	2.	(a)	3.	(a)	4.	(c)	5.	(a)	6.	(a)	7.	(b)	8.	(b)
9.	(b)	10.	(d)	11.	(c)	12.	(a)	13.	(c)	14.	(d)	15.	(a)	16.	(a)
17.	(d)	18.	(a)	19.	(c)	20.	(a)	21.	(b)	22.	(b)	23.	(a)	24.	(a)
25.	(b)	26.	(d)	27.	(c)	28.	(a)	29.	(d)	30.	(c)	31.	(d)	32.	(d)
33.	(c)	34.	(a)	35.	(d)	36.	(a)								

37. (c) At her house
38. (b) didn't like
39. (a) Keys
40. (a) neighbour
41. (c) Devastate
42. (b) 2018
43. (c) The noise
44. (c) World Surf League
45. (b) trough to crest
46. (a) terrifying
47. (b) The baby mouse
48. (c) On a cargo ship
49. (a) Warm sand
50. (d) sunset
51. (a) tiny
52. (b)

53. (c)
54. (d)
55. (c)
56. (b)
57. (d)
58. (c)

LEVEL-2

1.	(c)	2.	(b)	3.	(d)	4.	(a)	5.	(b)	6.	(a)	7.	(d)	8.	(c)
9.	(c)	10.	(a)	11.	(d)	12.	(c)	13.	(a)	14.	(d)	15.	(a)	16.	(c)
17.	(b)	18.	(b)	19.	(c)	20.	(a)	21.	(a)	22.	(d)	23.	(c)	24.	(d)

25. (c) she would get various sweets on Halloween
26. (b) was no longer scared of the flickering street light
27. (c) giggling internally
28. (b) 5
29. (c) whim
30. (b) Mercedes
31. (c) Flat tire
32. (c) By passing on the kindness
33. (a) five hundred dollars
34. (a) dirty
35. (c) Valentina Tereshkova
36. (b) Jumping out of planes
37. (a) solo space mission
38. (d) 70 hours
39. (c) admitted

21 Chapter

Spell-Bee

It is necessary and also interesting to learn spellings as they form the base of any language. To be a high achiever in this section, students need to increase their vocabulary with correctly spelt words.

The best way to improve your spellings is to practise reading and writing with their correct spellings. If a student reads incorrect spellings, he gets exposure to these misspelt words and his mind learns the incorrect spellings. In this way whenever he writes in future, he makes mistakes in spelling. The learning process of an individual requires the involvement of several senses to learn quickly and in a better way. The individual should be familiar with his weak areas of spellings so as to work on those. The individual should be well aware about the affixes so that he can organize the words and is able to form relevant associations. The next way to improve one's spellings and vocabulary is to bring the words in daily use so that one becomes familiar with the particular words. In case an individual is facing difficulty in learning some words, he can make a list of such words, learn these spellings and frequently use them while speaking and writing.

Group learning is better than solo learning. Individuals in a group ask one another various questions concerning different things, persons and other ideas and practise using new words in such interaction. Thus, they acquire many words without putting much effort in learning them. Group discussion is the most appropriate way to learn one word substitution quickly.

This chapter will help you to:

- Find the correctly spelt word out of incorrectly spelled words.
- Use one word replacing a sentence.
- Fill the letters which are left out to complete the word.

Based on spelling, there are three sets of question in the Olympiad question paper. The first set contains 4 different words having one of them spelled correctly, and the rest of them are incorrectly spelled.

For example:

(a) litning (b) thursti (c) cauliflower (d) envalop

(a) knife (b) carrett (c) applicason (d) wizdum

If one is aware of the correct spelling of all these words, one can easily make out that '(c) cauliflower' and '(a) knife' are the only words which have been spelled correctly in this set. Hence '(c) cauliflower' and '(a) knife' should be marked as the answer.

The second set contains the same word spelled in 4 various ways; one out of them is the correct spelling of the said word.

For example:

(a) protein (b) preutin (c) prautine (d) proutin

(a) bravary (b) brevary (c) bravery (d) baravary

For the student who is familiar with the correct spelling of these words, there would be no hitch in choosing '(a) protein' and '(c) bravery' as the right answer.

And the third set contains only one word in which some blank spaces are provided to insert the right letter(s) taken from the options given.

For example:

1. p — ati — um

   (a) l,m (b) m,l (c) n,l (d) l,n

2. ba — hel — r

   (a) c,e (b) h,o (c) c,o (d) o,c

One who is acquainted with the spelling of the given word would not hesitate to state that '(d) l,n' is the right option because missing places in the first word given requires 'l,n' to make the word 'platinum' while in the second, option '(c) c,o' is required to make the word 'bachelor'

Multiple Choice Questions

(Directions for questions 1-20): Choose the correctly spelt word.

1. (a) fabulous (b) soulve (c) convence (d) pice

2. (a) awesom (b) flavour (c) queston (d) tomoro

3. (a) pomegrenets (b) degire (c) curse (d) pazzel

4. (a) ternip (b) defferent (c) qoschan (d) vegetable

5. (a) important (b) shaede (c) dakness (d) celeberate

6. (a) fastivel (b) friend (c) aple (d) haarmless

7. (a) breth (b) tith (c) unfortunate (d) docter

8. (a) gless (b) televgion (c) carret (d) envelope

9.	(a)	cauliflower	(b)	patato	(c)	lihgt	(d)	spich
10.	(a)	onnion	(b)	computer	(c)	breenjal	(d)	kniphe
11.	(a)	shert	(b)	wijdom	(c)	cotton	(d)	protin
12.	(a)	groth	(b)	matal	(c)	bouttle	(d)	plastic
13.	(a)	mason	(b)	paetriot	(c)	enfaint	(d)	feild
14.	(a)	athiest	(b)	robber	(c)	stoone	(d)	bulleats
15.	(a)	spinister	(b)	leavs	(c)	beggar	(d)	slaeve
16.	(a)	problam	(b)	narvous	(c)	cumpetison	(d)	traitor
17.	(a)	cattle	(b)	oustrich	(c)	solger	(d)	cuntrie
18.	(a)	fruts	(b)	kerosene	(c)	engene	(d)	staer
19.	(a)	douckyard	(b)	flieght	(c)	orchard	(d)	crocdile
20.	(a)	reasort	(b)	thiater	(c)	paetrol	(d)	tannery

(Directions for question 21–40): Select the word which is not misspelt.

21.	(a)	nursery	(b)	nersary	(c)	nursury	(d)	narsury
22.	(a)	garmants	(b)	garments	(c)	garmints	(d)	gaarmaents
23.	(a)	orinamants	(b)	orenaments	(c)	ornaments	(d)	ornamaents
24.	(a)	matireal	(b)	matearial	(c)	metarail	(d)	material
25.	(a)	leather	(b)	laether	(c)	lathar	(d)	lather
26.	(a)	moovei	(b)	movie	(c)	muvie	(d)	mouvie
27.	(a)	tarrifi	(b)	taryfy	(c)	terrify	(d)	tairify
28.	(a)	mamorise	(b)	maemurise	(c)	mimorise	(d)	memorise
29.	(a)	believe	(b)	beleve	(c)	beleave	(d)	beleive
30.	(a)	hight	(b)	height	(c)	hieght	(d)	haihgt
31.	(a)	justefy	(b)	jastifi	(c)	justify	(d)	jastefi
32.	(a)	ansure	(b)	aensure	(c)	eansore	(d)	ensure
33.	(a)	classify	(b)	classefy	(c)	clasifi	(d)	clasifie
34.	(a)	civel	(b)	civil	(c)	cevil	(d)	civill
35.	(a)	firtaile	(b)	fartile	(c)	fertile	(d)	faretile
36.	(a)	bello	(b)	belloe	(c)	beloe	(d)	bellow

37. (a) scream (b) screem (c) skream (d) skrim

38. (a) laggage (b) luggage (c) leggage (d) laggege

39. (a) vacason (b) vacsion (c) vacation (d) vacetion

40. (a) friquant (b) freaqant (c) friequent (d) frequent

(Directions for Questions 41-50): Select the word which can be replaced for the given sentence.

41. A person bound to serve his master ----------

(a) slave (b) maid (c) servant (d) waiter

42. A person who deals in selling and purchasing business ------------

(a) Washerman (b) merchant (c) mason (d) labourer

43. A person who runs a shop ---------------

(a) farmer (b) runner (c) shopkeeper (d) athlete

44. One who is suffering from some ailments and requires medical help -------

(a) doctor (b) nurse (c) spot boy (d) patient

45. The heavenly body that gives us light and warmth ----------------

(a) sun (b) moon (c) star (d) earth

46. A tool with which a nail is inserted into a wall --------------------

(a) pliers (b) hammer (c) screwdriver (d) spade

47. The family pertaining to a king --------------

(a) common (b) extraordinary (c) royal (d) venerated

48. Animals which feed on other animals ------------------

(a) herbivorous (b) omnivorous (c) none (d) carnivorous

49. The person who manages the library ----------------

(a) peon (b) headmaster (c) librarian (d) teacher

50. A faithful animal that is usually kept as a pet -------------

(a) whale (b) crocodile (c) lion (d) dog

(Directions for questions 51-60) Fill in the blanks with the suitable alphabet provided as the option to make a meaningful word:

51. Fre __ __ ent

(a) k,u (b) c,u (c) q,u (d) e,q

52. ama ___ ___ ng

(a) i,z (b) z,o (c) e,z (d) z,i

53. ski ___ l ___ ul

(a) f,i (b) l,f (c) i,v (d) b,i

54. fa ___ o ___ s

(a) o,n (b) o,n (c) m,u (d) o,m

55. ent ___ ___ e

(a) r,e (b) e,r (c) r,i (d) i,r

56. achi ___ vem ___ nts

(a) a,e (b) e,a (c) e,e (d) e,o

57. di ___ ___ erent

(a) e,f (b) e,e (c) f,f (d) f,e

58. sta ___ ___ ment

(a) d,e (b) t,u (c) e,t (d) t,e

59. mater ___ ___ l

(a) i,e (b) a,i (c) i,a (d) i,e

60. extr ___ ___ ely

(a) t,m (b) m,t (c) e,m (d) m,e

Directions (Q. No. 61 to 62): Choose the option with correct spelling.

61. **[2021]**

(a) Trensperent (b) Transparent (c) Trunsperunt (d) Transperant

62. **[2021]**

(a) Philosophy (b) Phylosophy (c) Philosphy (d) Phyilosophy

63. **[2022]**

(a) Coleague (b) College (c) Callague (d) Collegue

Directions (Q. No. 64 and 65): Choose the option with correct spelling.

64. What is the correct spelling of the word which describes the work of a person whose job is to treat sick animals? **[2020]**

(a) Vaterninary (b) Vetrinary (c) Veterenary (d) Veterinary

65. What is the correct spelling of a fruit? **[2020]**

(a) Loquat (b) Locquat (c) Lokwat (d) Looquet

66. Find the word that has been correct spent. **[2022]**

(a) Strategic (b) Stretagick (c) Strategic (d) Strategic

67. Find the word that has been misspelt. **[2022]**

(a) Abbreviate (b) Accalerate (c) Stimulate (d) Dissuade

RESPONSE GRID

1. a b c d	2. a b c d	3. a b c d	4. a b c d	5. a b c d
6. a b c d	7. a b c d	8. a b c d	9. a b c d	10. a b c d
11. a b c d	12. a b c d	13. a b c d	14. a b c d	15. a b c d
16. a b c d	17. a b c d	18. a b c d	19. a b c d	20. a b c d
21. a b c d	22. a b c d	23. a b c d	24. a b c d	25. a b c d
26. a b c d	27. a b c d	28. a b c d	29. a b c d	30. a b c d
31. a b c d	32. a b c d	33. a b c d	34. a b c d	35. a b c d
36. a b c d	37. a b c d	38. a b c d	39. a b c d	40. a b c d
41. a b c d	42. a b c d	43. a b c d	44. a b c d	45. a b c d
46. a b c d	47. a b c d	48. a b c d	49. a b c d	50. a b c d
51. a b c d	52. a b c d	53. a b c d	54 a b c d	55. a b c d
56. a b c d	57. a b c d	58. a b c d	59. a b c d	60. a b c d
61. a b c d	62. a b c d	63. a b c d	64. a b c d	65. a b c d
66. a b c d	67. a b c d			

Solutions with Explanation

1. (a)	**2. (b)**	**3. (c)**	**4. (d)**
5. (a)	**6. (b)**	**7. (c)**	**8. (d)**
9. (a)	**10. (b)**	**11. (c)**	**12. (d)**
13. (a)	**14. (b)**	**15. (c)**	**16. (d)**
17. (a)	**18. (b)**	**19. (c)**	**20. (d)**
21. (a)	**22. (b)**	**23. (c)**	**24. (d)**
25. (a)	**26. (b)**	**27. (c)**	**28. (d)**
29. (a)	**30. (b)**	**31. (c)**	**32. (d)**
33. (a)	**34. (b)**	**35. (c)**	**36. (d)**
37. (a)	**38. (b)**	**39. (c)**	**40. (d)**
41. (a)	**42. (b)**	**43. (c)**	**44. (d)**
45. (a)	**46. (b)**	**47. (c)**	**48. (d)**

49. (c) 50. (d) 51. (c) 52. (d)
53. (b) 54. (c) 55. (d) 56. (c)
57. (c) 58. (d) 59. (c) 60. (c)
61. (b) Transparent
62. (a) Philosophy
63. (b) Colleague
64. (d) Veterinary
65. (a) Loquat
66. (a) Strategic
67. (b)

www.ingramcontent.com/pod-product-compliance
Lightning Source LLC
LaVergne TN
LVHW080723170726
843469LV00082B/1899

* 9 7 8 9 3 5 5 6 4 4 2 8 2 *